The Eclipse of Christ in Eschatology

Toward a **Christ-Centered** Approach

by

Adrio König

WILLIAM B. EERDMANS PUBLISHING COMPANY
GRAND RAPIDS, MICHIGAN

 MARSHALL MORGAN & SCOTT
LONDON, ENGLAND

Adapted from *Jesus die Laaste, Gelowig Nagedink* Deel 2 (Pretoria: DRC Bookshop, 1980).

Copyright © 1989 by Wm. B. Eerdmans Publishing Co.
255 Jefferson Ave. S.E., Grand Rapids, Mich. 49503

First published in the UK in 1989 by Marshall Morgan and Scott Publications Ltd.
Part of the Marshall Pickering Holdings Group
34 - 42 Cleveland Street, London, WIP 5FB. U.K.

Library of Congress Cataloging-in-Publication Data

König, Adrio.
   The eclipse of Christ in eschatology: toward a Christ-centered
approach / by Adrio König.
      p.   cm.
  ISBN 0-8028-0356-3
   1. Eschatology. 2. Jesus Christ—Person and offices. I. Title.
BT821.2.K66 1989
236--dc19
                                    88-13933
                                       CIP

Eerdmans ISBN 0-8028-0356-3
Marshall Morgan & Scott ISBN 0 551 01922 0

Contents

Preface

This book presents a new approach to the "last things." It is so new that occasionally some readers might disbelieve their own eyes. For example, we affirm that not only will Jesus Christ come again in the last days, but that he was born in the last days, that the Holy Spirit was poured out in the last days, and that the first Christians even lived in the last hour.

What is offered here is utterly different from traditional battles between chiliasm and antichiliasm, premillennialism and postmillennialism. Here we discuss things of greater importance than disputes over whether Jesus will return once or twice, and whether there will be one or two resurrections and judgments. We make no attempt here to calculate the time of the second coming.

What, then, is presented here? Quite simply, we present the meaning of Jesus Christ for the doctrine of the "last things." But is it not rather strange to offer this as something new? Is Jesus' centrality to every aspect of the gospel not self-evident? It is, from the New Testament perspective. And yet, overall, little or no attention is paid to him in books on eschatology.

The point of departure in this book is that Jesus Christ is as important to eschatology as he is to every other part of the gospel. And the message of this book is that Jesus Christ himself is the last and the end, as he says of himself in Rev. 22:13, "I am the Alpha and the Omega, the first and the *last,* the beginning and the *end.*" This is of decisive importance for eschatology.

The fact that Christ himself is the last and the end means that God's creation goal is both revealed in him and attained by him. He fulfills the covenant—the complete harmony between God and humanity—by representing both God and humanity in his own person. Because he is the *last,* his entire history is the doctrine of the last things, or "eschatology."

This is why the apostles could proclaim that Christ was born in the last days, that the first Christians lived in the last hour, and that nevertheless we still await his return. In each phase of his history, he fulfills the covenant—God's creation goal—in some particular way: *for* us, especially during his earthly ministry; *in* us, in his work through the Holy Spirit; and *with* us, particularly at his second coming.

This structure also applies to the renewal of creation, because God has a purpose not only for individuals but for his whole creation. This is why the Bible begins with a perspective on heaven and earth—and ends with a message about the new heaven and new earth.

In this book we do not concentrate on polemics against other viewpoints. Here we attempt, rather, to combine into a useful perspective the biblical data about the meaning of Jesus for the end. Though most of the traditional problems come up for discussion, we discuss them in the light of him under whose Lordship the entire universe, everything in heaven and on earth, will be brought into unity (Eph. 1:10).

Abbreviations

BAGD	W. Bauer, W. F. Arndt, F. W. Gingrich, and F. W. Danker, *Greek-English Lexicon of the New Testament* (1979)
GN	Gute Nachricht
HNT	Handbuch zum Neuen Testament
ICC	International Critical Commentary
KEK	Kritisch-exegetischer Kommentar
KJV	King James Version
NAB	New American Bible
NEB	New English Bible
NICNT	New International Commentary on the New Testament
NIV	New International Version
NTD	Das Neue Testament Deutsch
RSV	Revised Standard Version
TDNT	G. Kittel and G. Friedrich, *Theological Dictionary of the New Testament* (1964-1976)
TEV	Today's English Version
TNTC	Tyndale New Testament Commentaries

Chapter 1
CHRIST AND THE END

WHAT THIS BOOK IS ABOUT

This book deals with the biblical message of the end, the end times, the way God achieves the goal he set for his creation. These days there is an intense interest in such matters, and one need not be a prophet to predict even greater interest in the "last things," as the final decade of our century runs its course. But it is remarkable—and disconcerting—that in many of the most popular expositions, Jesus plays practically no role at all. This is remarkable because, in the New Testament, Jesus is directly associated with the end, the end times, and God's purpose for creation.

But it is not only in popular, dramatic works that Jesus plays no role. In mainline churches and academic theological traditions, most treatments of eschatology relegate it to an appendix or last chapter on the "last things," and there the person and message of Jesus Christ play only an incidental role.

In this book, Jesus Christ occupies a central place.[1] *If the gospel is about him, so too is its message about the end. If he is the one around whom the whole New Testament revolves, then he is the one, too, around whom God's plans for the world revolve.* Indeed, the criterion for any book on eschatology should be: what place do the person and message of Jesus Christ have in it?

The eschatology offered here is not primarily concerned with the "last things"—though of course some "things" will be discussed. Instead, this book is first and foremost about the last One, he whom the New Testament calls the End and the Last One. Eschatology must be about him, because he himself is the realization of God's purpose in creating the world. One dare not overlook the fact that the New Testament forges a direct link between Jesus and the last days.

---

1. That this is not done at the expense of the Holy Spirit will become clear in Chapter 4.

THE LAST DAYS AND JESUS AS THE LAST ONE

We do not find the familiar phrase the "last things" in the Bible. What we do encounter there are other expressions which have also played an important role in eschatology, such as "the end of the age," "the last hour," and similar expressions having to do with the end. It is of the greatest importance that we carefully investigate the meaning of these phrases. They will help us to identify the end time, the time immediately before Christ's coming. Many may be surprised to discover that these terms are applied repeatedly to Christ's first coming and earthly ministry. According to Heb. 1:2, God has "in these last days" "spoken to us through his Son" (TEV).

According to 1 Peter, Christ was "revealed *in these last days* for your sake" (1:20 TEV). In his earthly activity, "the Kingdom of God has already come upon you" (Matt. 12:28) and the Kingdom is "among you" (Luke 17:21 TEV mg.).[2] Satan is bound by Jesus' exorcisms (Matt. 12:22-29; Luke 11:14-22), and it is during Jesus' earthly life that he "watches how Satan fell, like lightning, out of the sky" (Luke 10:18).[3] In Jesus, the "year of the Lord's favor" has dawned (Luke 4:17-22; Isa. 61:1ff.). It is important to note not only *that* Jesus exorcises demons, but also the way in which they react when they see him. They cry out in dread (Mark 1:23; 5:5-6, etc.), are completely powerless (1:34; 3:11; 5:12, etc.), and fear that Jesus will condemn them to torment and extermination (1:24; 5:7, etc.).

One cannot characterize these eschatological expressions as mere preliminary indications. The first coming and earthly ministry of Jesus are described in a *radical* and *absolute* way as the end and the last days. This is in precise agreement with Jesus' statements before his crucifixion that "*now* is the hour of judgment for this world; *now* shall the prince of this world be driven out" (John 12:31), that "the unbeliever has already been judged," and that "here lies the test: the light *has come* into the world, but people preferred darkness to light" (John 3:18-19). For believers, the following words have immediate currency: "anyone who gives heed to what I say and puts his

2. Most modern translations so render *entos humōn*. In fact, E. Stauffer has shown convincingly, in *New Testament Theology* (1955), 285-286, note 394, that "within you" is "an absurdity."

3. In *The Coming of the Kingdom* (1962), 63-64, H. Ridderbos declares, "The general meaning of this is clear: Satan himself has fallen with great force from his position of power. . . . The great moment of the breaking down of Satan's rule has come, and at the same time that of the coming of the kingdom of heaven."

trust in him who sent me has hold of eternal life, and does not come up for judgment, but has already passed from death to life" (John 5:24), because, during his ministry on earth, Jesus "broke the power of death" (2 Tim. 1:10).

Some would play the Synoptic Gospels (Matthew, Mark, and Luke) against Paul and especially against John. They insist that the Synoptics (which indeed announce an imminent end) all present this as being only in the future; first Paul, then (and especially) John, came to realize that the return would not be so soon as they had expected; then they began to speak of Jesus' earthly ministry and work through the Holy Spirit in terms of the end. But this is not correct. Each of the New Testament authors certainly has a different emphasis, but it is not true that their views oppose each other—much less irreconcilably so. In any case, that is not true of the eschatological character of Jesus', earthly ministry. To suggest that the Synoptics restrict eschatology to future events, opposing John's "realized eschatology" (i.e., that the end is already realized or present), is based on a faulty interpretation or oversimplification. To the contrary, we must state that John 12:31 is nothing less than an interpretation of Jesus' whole action against evil spirits during his earthly ministry—action which the Synoptics, no less than John, characterize as eschatological (Matt. 12:28.).

Nor are Jesus' incarnation and earthly ministry all that is spoken of in radically eschatological terms. The New Testament also views his crucifixion as an eschatological event. As we shall show further along, the words, "It is accomplished" (John 19:30) bear an exceptionally radical and comprehensive end meaning. Further, it is striking that each evangelist records Jesus' "eschatological discourse" shortly before his crucifixion, then shows how many of the events he presented as signs of an imminent *eschaton* occurred during his crucifixion. Since we shall discuss these extensively later on, we shall now simply mention them: the cooling of love and spread of lawlessness (Matt. 24:12; 26:33) find fulfillment in Matt. 26:56, 69ff.; the call to vigilance (24:42; 25:13) is fulfilled in 26:38; the exceptional natural phenomena viewed by Jesus and the Old Testament prophets as signs of the end occurred during the crucifixion (Isa. 13:10ff.; 13:13; Joel 2:10, 31; 3:15-16; Matt. 24:7, 29; 27:45, 51).

These parallels demonstrate the eschatological character of the cross. When Bultmann interpreted the cross eschatologically, this was entirely biblical. Why we must part company with him is simply because he does this at the cost of the rest of the history of Jesus, including his second advent.

To avoid vain repetition, we shall not now go into the eschatological interpretation of the resurrection. This will be dealt with extensively in due course. For the moment, let us briefly examine the New Testament to see if it also describes in end terms the Holy Spirit's coming and work and Christ's return.

In his Pentecost sermon, Peter affirms that the Holy Spirit has been poured out "in the last days" (Acts 2:17). Paul refers to the period in which the Church lives, after that outpouring, as the "time when the end is about to come" (1 Cor. 10:11 TEV), while James calls it "these last days" (Jas. 5:3 TEV) and the writer of 2 Peter "the last days" (2 Pet. 3:3). John goes further, and says, "this is the last *hour!*" (1 John 2:18; cf. 1 Tim. 4:1; 2 Tim. 3:1; Jude 18). Here we should also consider the "with" pronouncements of Paul, e.g., that we have been raised with Christ, and that together with him we have ascended into heaven (Eph. 2:6). Thus also is the interval between the Spirit's outpouring and Christ's return spoken of in radically eschatological terms.

References to the eschatological character of Christ's second advent are abundant. The New Testament speaks of "the salvation which is even now in readiness and will be revealed at the end of time" (1 Pet. 1:5). Indeed, there is—as one might expect—no really wide divergence of opinion on this point. *It is already clear from this brief survey of New Testament data that its authors all speak of Jesus' entire history in similar, radically eschatological terms.*

It is also remarkable that the New Testament authors cannot be so played against one another that, e.g., one describes Jesus' incarnation in eschatological terms but ignores future expectation, while another regards only future hope as eschatological and neglects the eschatological meaning of the incarnation, the resurrection, or the coming of the Spirit. The same author frequently stresses the eschatological character of more than one phase of Jesus' history. The author of Hebrews, e.g., discusses the incarnation in radically eschatological terms (9:26), then, a mere two verses later, states that Christ "will appear a second time" (TEV). Peter, too, writes of the incarnation in radically eschatological words (1 Pet. 1:20) after using almost identical terms in the same chapter about Christ's second coming (v. 5). In this case, the second advent is spoken of as that which will be revealed at the end of time, and Christ in his incarnation is described as he that "was revealed in these last days" (TEV). The same holds true of John, who within three verses (1 John 3:2, 5) refers to Christ's first and second comings by the same eschatological term, "appear" (TEV). Above all, the Synoptics describe both the past and the future in the same eschatological terms. Now we are in a position to draw some conclusions from this survey of eschatological terms in the New Testament.

First, the phrase "the last days" is never used in the New Testament for some future period. In every case, the author means either the time in which he himself is living (Acts 2:17; Jas. 5:3) or that in which Christ became man (Heb. 1:2). There are some who regard 2 Tim. 3:1 as an exception to this rule, but it is not. That Paul instructs Timothy to avoid the activities of those who behave in an evil manner in the last days establishes that Timothy himself lives in those days (v. 5). Even in 2 Pet. 3:3, "the last days" indicates a time in which the author and his readers live. This is why he can say precisely what the argument of scoffers at religion is (v. 4) and what willful errors they make (v. 5).

This means that the last days are those in which Jesus and the apostles act, and that there is no other, separate period called "the last days." The last days have already dawned. We no longer wait for them. Nor have they begun recently; they began almost two thousand years ago. We are still living in "the last days" in which Christ was born and worked.

Second, the entire history of Jesus Christ is described in such end (eschatological) terms as these. His birth, earthly life, crucifixion, resurrection, work through the Holy Spirit, and return are all described in the same radically eschatological terms. His return is no more eschatological than his earthly work or his resurrection. Some would attempt to distinguish between the period of the end—which they believe began with Christ's birth—and the "final" last days—a different time, immediately preceding his second advent. But there is no basis for this artificial distinction. The New Testament writers do not use separate terms for the time just before Christ's return. His entire history is described in the same eschatological terms. Indeed, by referring to the time in which he himself lived as "the last hour," John underscores the impossibility of treating Jesus' times—and the twenty centuries which followed—as a "non-final" end-time, while regarding the brief period just before his return as the final end-time (1 John 2:18).

This means that eschatology includes the entire history of Jesus Christ. Thus it is incorrect to confine one's attention to the second advent or "last things" when dealing with eschatology. If eschatology deals with the end, the last days, or the consummation, it must also involve the past (Jesus' earthly work) and the present (his work in the Holy Spirit).

Third, it will come as no surprise that the New Testament names Jesus himself the Last, the End, and the Omega. The apostles describe his history in eschatological terms because he himself is the end and the last. Observation of this fact produces a remarkable change in one's insight into eschatology. Naturally it is correct to say that every tick of the clock brings us nearer to the end (i.e., to Christ's return), but it is equally true to say that we now live in the end (i.e., in communion with Jesus, who is the end). In so saying, we state precisely what Paul implied by his famous expression "in Christ." Through faith we are "in Christ," united with him as members of his body. In the very same way we are through faith members of Christ, the end and the last. We live in the end as part of the end, Christ himself. In this sense it is not true that every tick of the clock brings us nearer the end, since the end is a person—and we are already in him and united with him. Before we go on to clarify what it means that Christ himself is the last and the end, it is necessary first to examine carefully a few of the texts just cited, which led us to conclude that the entire history of Jesus is eschatological.

DETAILED DISCUSSION OF SOME IMPORTANT TEXTS

In this section we intend to analyze in detail only a few of the most important texts, attempting to make quite certain that we grasp correctly the eschatological message of the New Testament on this point: that the whole history of Jesus Christ is eschatological. Four texts will be considered: Heb. 1:1-2 and 9:26, 1 Pet. 1:20, and Matt. 12:28. They have been chosen because they are representative of the type of text referred to in the preceding section.

Hebrews 1:1-2. "In the past God spoke to our ancestors many times and in many ways through the prophets, but in these last days he has spoken to us through his Son. . . " (TEV). Other translations read: "in these last days" (KJV, RSV, NIV), "in this final age" (NAB, cf. NEB), and "am Ende der Zeit" (GN).

What exactly does this expression mean? All these translations agree that Christ was born in the end, not at some midpoint or turning point in history. The New English Bible and New American Bible might be interpreted as referring to a period of time; the King James Version, Revised Standard Version, and New International Version use a technical term ("these last days") which was used in the Old Testament for the end of the world or of the present age (distinct from the age to come).

It is noteworthy that this text (like the others yet to be discussed) is seldom if ever explored or even mentioned in books dealing with the "last things." On the rare occasions when reference is made in passing to this text, it is usually dismissed blandly with a remark that "the last days" indicates no more than a new period of time. The assumption is allowed to remain that this specific period has no special eschatological meaning and that it will be succeeded by the actual or "final" last days—the last, brief period before Christ's return. It remains a striking fact, however, that this text knows nothing of such a time division. According to the text, Jesus Christ was born and worked on earth in the one and only "last days" period.

Moffatt explained that in the phrase translated "these last days" (*ep' eschatou tōn hēmerōn toutōn,* literally, "the end of these days"), we have a Hebraism—i.e., the writer's literal transposition of a Hebrew phrase into Greek.[4] We encounter the expression in such texts as Isa. 2:2. There "In the last days" (KJV; Heb. *b^e h^{a}rît hayyāmîm*) means neither the end of a specific period nor the end of time itself, but rather "in the end time," which is a well-known Old Testament expression.

Thus the meaning of the writer of Hebrews seems to be that Christ was born and did his work in the last days or end time, not that he would do so at the end of a certain period (after which some final "end time" would eventually come). Therefore Heb. 1:1-2 indicates decisively that the incarnation is an eschatological event. There is no talk here of the end of a certain period of time which would imply that, at a later stage, yet another and final end time would dawn.

Hebrews 9:26. "For then must he often have suffered since the foundation of the world: but now once in the end of the world *[epi synteleia tōn aiōnōn]* hath he appeared to put away sin by the sacrifice of himself" (KJV). Some other translations read: "at the end of the age" (RSV), "when all ages of time are nearing the end" (TEV), "at the climax of history" (NEB), and "at the end of the ages" (NAB and NIV).

Most commentaries do not support the New English Bible translation. Van Oyen's argument is decisive; he states that the two expres-

---

4. J. Moffatt, *Hebrews* (ICC; 1924), 4. O. Michel, *Der Brief an die Hebräer* (KEK 1975[13]), essentially agrees with this. His statement on this point is important, i.e., that these days are the last days, and that the time of the messiah is the end time. (See also note 10.)

sions, "since the foundation of the world" and "in the end of the world," represent two opposing extremes—the beginning and the end of the world. Christ's first coming is therefore the end![5] It is even to be disputed whether Westcott's distinction reflects the thought of the writer. Westcott states that we must distinguish between *telos,* which is not used here and refers to the "end" as a single, decisive act, and *synteleia,* which is used and means "end" in the sense of "consummation," implying an end of many parts and so occupying a period of time.[6] Although the author of Hebrews does indeed speak of Christ's return ". . . not to bear sin, but to bring salvation . . ." (v. 28), thus including more than one act (i.e., both first and second comings) in the end, his point is to characterize Christ's *first* coming as the absolute end—in opposition to the absolute beginning, the foundation of the world.

Just as in Heb. 1:1, so also here, the author of the letter sees Christ's first appearance as "the end"—and therefore as decisively eschatological. It is equally important, however, to note that he does not do this at the cost of future eschatology (Christ's return), but in the same breath (v. 28)!

1 Peter 1:20. "He [Christ] had been chosen by God before the creation of the world and was revealed in these last days *[ep' eschatou tōn chronōn]* for your sake" (TEV). Some other translations read: "in these last times" (KJV), "at the end of the times" (RSV), "in these last days" (NAB), "in these last times" (NIV), and "in this last period of time" (NEB).

F. W. Beare distinguishes between this verse and v. 5 in these terms: "The end of the times is thus the immediate prelude to the 'last time.'" Bigg has virtually the same idea in mind when he distinguishes between the last *day* as the day of judgment and the last *days, time,* or *hour,* which can mean either "the age of the Christian dispensation" or "that portion of it which lies nearest to the End."[7] Now, it is indeed true that there is a tendency to use the plural form of the expression ("the last *times* or *days*") to refer to the incarnation, earthly life, and work of Jesus, as do 1 Pet. 1:20 and Heb. 1:2 (cf. 9:26), while using either the singular or plural for the time after his resurrection (e.g., Jude 18;

5. H. van Oyen, *Christus de Hogepriester: De Brief aan die Hebreën (De Prediking van het Nieuwe Testament;* 1954), ad loc.

6. B. F. Westcott, *The Epistle to the Hebrews* (1950), 275.

7. F. W. Beare, *The First Epistle of Peter* (1970³); E. Bigg, *Peter and Jude* (ICC; 1956), both on 1:5.

1 Pet. 1:5, singular; 1 Tim. 4:1; 2 Tim. 3:1; 2 Pet. 3:3; Jas. 5:3; Acts 2:17, plural).[8]

Bigg's suggestion, however, that "the Last Days, Time, Hour are either the age of the Christian dispensation or that portion of it which lies nearest to the End, when the signs of the Parousia are beginning to show themselves" is unwarranted precisely because the plural is also applied to the time after the resurrection of Jesus—as we have demonstrated—and above all because the New Testament knows nothing of this distinction in the end time. The first Christians did not live in a period devoid of signs, expecting only much later "that portion of the Christian dispensation which lies nearest to the End." They simply accepted that they lived in the end time and knew of no further distinctions within it.[9]

The real contrast is not between 1 Pet. 1:5 and 1:20, but between the first and second halves of v. 20, i.e., "before the foundation of the world" and "this last period of time." This is the same contrast we have already encountered in Heb. 9:26 and which is also found in Paul (e.g., Col. 1:26-27; Rom. 16:25-26; Eph. 3:5). As in Heb. 9:26, the second member of the contrasted pair signifies the very *end* of this world or of the age, even as the first looks back to the very *beginning*.[10] Peter

8. Only in A. van Speyr's *Die Katholische Briefe* (1961), ad loc., do I find the astounding view that there is no difference between 1 Pet. 1:5 and 1:20, because 1:20 also looks to the return of Christ.

9. Bigg, ad loc. This proposition anticipates our later discussion of the "signs of the times."

10. In *Die Gedankeneinheit des Ersten Briefes Petri* (1902), 102, J. Kögel correctly points out that—as with Heb. 1:1, already considered—*ep' eschatou tōn chronōn* goes back to the Old Testament expression b^e $a\hbar^a r\hat{\imath}t$ $hayy\bar{a}m\hat{\imath}m$. In the Septuagint this is rendered just as it is in Heb. 1:1. That this expression really does look to the end (and not to the beginning of the period of the end) is evident from the fact that the rabbis expressed it by *qēṣ* (G. Kittel, *TDNT* II, 698).

Kögel confirms this by saying "for the Jews, the appearance of the Messiah was directly connected with the end of time, so that when the Messiah appears, the end will be there." But Kögel's further conclusion is unacceptable. In the first place, it is not true that all New Testament writings except 1 Peter and Hebrews shift the end to Jesus' return. John (1 John 2:18) also taught that his readers lived in the last hour. We shall demonstrate that the synoptists also took this position.

What is more, Kögel's view that 1 Peter and Hebrews make of the last days a period which is merely inaugurated by Christ's appearance and concluded by his return (102-103), is open to misunderstanding (cf. A. M. Stibbs and A. F. Walls, *1 Peter* [TNTC; 1959], ad loc.). Kögel is overanxious to systematize 1 Pet.

also teaches that Jesus actually appeared in "the end of time," and not merely in "the last period" in the sense of an indefinite span at the start of which he was manifested. Christ was not revealed at the *inception* of such a period (nowhere in the New Testament is such a thought expressed) but at the *end of time*. Christ's first appearance was an entirely eschatological event.

Matthew 12:28. "But if it is by the Spirit of God that I drive out the devils, then be sure the kingdom of God has already come upon you" (NEB). Luke 11:20 is also important here: "But if it is by the finger of God that I drive out the devils, then be sure the kingdom of God has already come upon you" (NEB). Other translations of Matt. 12:28 have: "that the Kingdom of God has already come upon you" (TEV), "then the kingdom of God is come unto you" (KJV), "then the kingdom of God has come upon you" (RSV), "then the reign of God has overtaken you" (NAB), and "then the kingdom of God has come upon you" (NIV). Translations of Luke 11:20 show no significant differences.

Let us consider first the meaning of "has come upon" *(ephthasen)*. There is near unanimity that this word (unlike *engiken*) means "has come." Consequently, here is a clear pronouncement that the kingdom of God has already arrived during the earthly ministry of Jesus.

The context of this statement gives us an indication of what Jesus understood by "the kingdom of God." What led up to this statement was his healing of one who had been demon-possessed. The Pharisees tried to offset the impact of this miracle on the crowd by ascribing Jesus' power to Satan. But Jesus exposed the senselessness of their argument by saying: "if it is by the Spirit of God that I drive out devils, then be sure the kingdom of God has already come upon you."[11] Thus

---

1:5 and 1:20 and not to leave them "unrelated" *(unverbunden nebeneinander)*. There is a very strong possibility that these statements in 1 Peter and Hebrews actually are "unrelated" and that some special significance is to be attached to this. Apart from this, Kögel suggests a valuable connection between Peter's concept of the end of time (1 Pet. 1:2) and the refugees *(parepidēmoi, 2:11ff.).*

11. The problem with Jesus' "proof" that the kingdom has come cannot be minimized. If indeed his exorcism of demons is proof that the kingdom of God has come in him (Luke 11:20), why are not the "your sons " exorcisms of 11:19 equal proof that the kingdom has come in them?

However, two elements in Luke 11:20 must be noted. First, Jesus adds "by the finger of God," which makes his work "distinct from the charms and incantations used by Jewish exorcists, who did not rely simply upon the power of God" (A. Plummer, *Luke* [ICC; 1960], ad loc.). So if Jesus relies entirely upon God

he indicated that his power over demons (which he showed repeatedly—see Matt. 8:28ff.; Mark 1:21ff.; 9:14ff.) was a sign that the kingdom of God had come.[12] In fact, it is not only his power over demons but all his miracles which are placed in intimate connection with the kingdom of God by such verses as Matt. 4:23, 9:35, 10:7-8, etc.

These signs of the kingdom fulfill the Old Testament's expectation that at the end of days, the Lord would rule over all people and powers. Ridderbos is correct in viewing the divine kingship as the kernel of the kingdom of God—a concept which, as elsewhere he rightly affirmed, received a complex meaning in Jesus' preaching. It is during the rule of God that his royal majesty, power, and might will be revealed. That rule is a twofold lordship which involves both redemption and judgment—disclosed so as to make it plain that God will not abandon the world to perdition, but rather act as his people's savior and lead them to even greater promises.[13]

Whenever Jesus expels the adversary and his cohorts, whenever he breaks their hold over people, whenever he heals suffering, it is clear that what the Old Testament expected as the "kingdom of God" has become a reality in Jesus. This is not merely provisional. Ridderbos demonstrates convincingly that the coming of this kingdom was an end-time expectation of the Old Testament, which regarded it as inaugurating the "day of the Lord," the day of judgment which also would be the day of redemption.[14]

This well-known expression, "the day of the Lord," is equally important in connection with the eschatological significance of the earthly ministry of Jesus. We must therefore devote some of our discussion to it.

The day of the Lord. This expression must have found its way into the faith of Israel at a very early period. When it first appeared

---

without calling on other aids, this is proof that his exorcism is the work of God—and that the kingdom of God has come.

Further, it is *Jesus* who expels the demons. His exorcisms cannot be viewed as isolated from his other works, his values, and his self-awareness. Should someone else do what *he* does, that is not at all the same thing; it is his person which makes the difference.

12. With reference to Luke 17:21, Stauffer (p. 123) declares of the kingdom of God that, "It is already there, in his person and in his work."

13. Ridderbos, 18-22. We will go into the meaning of "kingdom of God" (including its Old Testament meaning) at a later stage.

14. Ridderbos, 5ff.

in the Old Testament writings (Amos 5:20), Amos was already criticizing the meaning it had acquired among the people. This implies that the concept was generally held even before Amos's time (ca. 750 B.C.).

G. von Rad traces the concept of the day of the Lord back to the holy wars, those early wars in which the Lord intervened supernaturally on his people's behalf.[15] In the light of the content of the concept (war together with supernatural phenomena) and Isaiah's linking of it with the early wars (see Isa. 9:4; 28:21 in connection with Judges 7 and 2 Sam. 5:20, 25) this is an acceptable explanation.

The meaning of this day is firmly fixed on the future. Even when it was fulfilled by a specific historical event such as the fall of Jerusalem in 586 B.C., as is asserted by Ezekiel (13:5) and Jeremiah (Lam. 1:12; 2:1, 22), it retained characteristics typical of Old Testament promises which, though fulfilled, still directed people's hopes to further fulfillments in the future.[16] Increasingly it became an eschatological concept connected with the end.

It is, therefore, striking that the New Testament authors consistently presented the day of the Lord as fulfilled in Jesus' first advent, in his earthly ministry, and in his work in the Holy Spirit—as well as in the day of judgment. That is to say, the day of the Lord came already with the birth and life of Jesus. Jesus affirmed this in his sermon at Nazareth (Luke 4:16ff.). After reading from Isaiah 61, he declared, "Today, in your very hearing, this text has come true." This meant that he himself ushered in the "year of the Lord's favor" and that he performed those works which Isaiah 61 associated with it—as may also be seen in Matthew 11:5. Likewise, Mark (1:2) sees the day of the Lord (depicted in Mal. 3:1-2) as fulfilled by the coming of John the Baptist as the messenger and Jesus as Angel of the covenant.[17]

The resurrection of Jesus, too, may be regarded as fulfilling the

---

15. G. von Rad, *Old Testament Theology* (1962, 1965) II, 123ff. Cf. H. W. Robinson, *Inspiration and Revelation in the Old Testament* (1946), 138ff.

16. The way in which prophecies and promises are fulfilled is discussed extensively in Chapter 5.

17. In light of the connection between the day of the Lord and his coming and lordship, it is highly probable that Mark's second quotation (from Isa. 40:3) also implies that the day of the Lord is realized in the appearance of John the Baptist and Jesus, though Isaiah does not use the term "day of the Lord." His words in 40:10 ("Here is the Lord God coming in might, coming to rule with his right arm") agree with what is said elsewhere in the Old Testament about this day.

day of the Lord. Berkhof states that after the messianic passion on Golgotha, the resurrection was the dawning of the great day of the Lord. In doing so, he links Matt. 28:20 with Dan. 7:14.[18] Yet a further fulfillment of the day of the Lord is to be seen in the outpouring of the Holy Spirit. Peter said of the Pentecost event, "this is what the prophet spoke of." Then he quoted Joel 2:28-32, which deals with the signs of the coming of the day of the Lord.[19]

Notwithstanding these fulfillments, the day of the Lord retained its character of promise and so pointed the New Testament writers ahead to judgment day as the "last day" (e.g., 2 Pet. 3:12; Rev. 16:14). Berkhof maintains that in terms of this future meaning the day of the Lord is fulfilled by at least three of Jesus' deeds: his ascension to his Father, his sitting at God's right hand, and his return to reveal his power over the world.[20]

The cardinal point is that no matter which phase of his history we consider, it is *in Christ* that all these promises are fulfilled. To be specific, there is a remarkable link between the day of Yahweh and the coming and kingdom of the Lord. H. W. Robinson points to this link by beginning his chapter on the day of the Lord with the declaration that one of the important themes of the prophets' preaching was that human history will end in a full and final manifestation of Yahweh inaugurating his royal rule on earth. The day of the Lord is the central concept in all expectations of this consummation.[21] G. von Rad referred to this as well, saying that there was something noteworthy in these expectations of the day of the Lord: no matter where that day was discussed in the prophets, it led to a reference to Yahweh's personal appearance.[22]

H. H. Rowley draws attention to a more extended link, that between the day of the Lord, the kingdom of God, the Davidic leader, and the Son of man. To this may be added the connection between the day, the appearance, and the kingship of the Lord, which P. A. Verhoef

---

18. H. Berkhof, *Christ, the Meaning of History* (1966), 64-65.

19. At this point Acts 2:17 does not follow the Masoretic text ("and thereafter") but rather substitutes the expression "and in the last days." This agrees with the eschatological character assumed by the day of the Lord in such Old Testament passages as Isa. 2:2; Jer. 23:28; 30:24; 48:47; 49:39, Ezek. 38:16; Dan. 10:14; Hos. 3:5; and Mic. 4:1. Von Rad basically supports this position (*TDNT* II, 945-946).

20. Berkhof, 69.

21. Robinson, 135, 144.

22. G. von Rad, *Old Testament Theology* II, 119.

has highlighted.[23] That the New Testament speaks of the fulfillment of the day of the Lord in such unmistakable terms is further indication that in Jesus the kingdom has come. The connection between the appearance of the Lord (John 14:9) and the coming of the kingdom (Matt. 12:28) is clear in the New Testament.

When by Christ's appearing this kingdom comes, this is no mere conclusion of one period of world history and introduction to another. It is, in the fullest sense of the word, an *eschatological* event. For this reason Ridderbos speaks of the eschatological character of Jesus' appearance, describing his miracles as messianic deeds of salvation which bore an eschatological character. He even declares that the idea of the kingdom of God, which has arrived in Jesus, summarizes all that had been the object of Old Testament prophecy and of Israel's expectations since the earliest times.[24]

This is why Jesus himself related his coming and activity to various eschatological expectations of the Old Testament. He saw himself as the Son of man, for example—a figure which in Daniel bears a clearly eschatological character, since it is he who is to usher in the end time. One must also accept that, speaking in Matt. 12:28 ("the Kingdom of God has already come upon you"), Jesus had Dan. 7:22 in mind (Theodotion's Greek version can be translated, "the time has arrived and the saints have received the kingdom").[25]

W. G. Kümmel has also referred to Matt. 11:2-6. When in this passage Jesus replies to the question of John the Baptist, he undoubtedly uses a traditional description of the blessed end time,

23. H. H. Rowley, *The Faith of Israel* (1956), 199; P. A. Verhoef, *Die Dag van die Here* (1956), 89.

24. Ridderbos, 13, 52, 66. W. Grundmann declares (*TDNT* II, 302), "Like the whole history of Jesus, His miracles are an eschatological event." In this connection, H. van der Loos, *The Miracles of Jesus* (1965), 246ff., makes a number of important statements. He calls attention to a statement of Sevenster that "The healings and miracles must be 'evaluated' as signs of redemption by God. We are concerned with God's redeeming eschatological action" and declares: "We may regard the miracles of Jesus as deeds in which *Urzeit* and *Endzeit* meet one another," so that the miracles are "eschatological in nature." Approvingly he quotes Betz that in the acts of Jesus the *eschaton* is virtually present, and proceeds to show that, as early as Justin and Irenaeus, Jesus' miracles were seen as eschatological.

25. *Ho kairos ephthasen kai tēn basileian kateschon hoi hagioi;* cf. C. H. Dodd, *The Parables of the Kingdom* (1961) 28, note 1 (= 36, note 15 in the Fontana edition). Cf. also J. N. Geldenhuys *Luke* (NICNT; 1951), 332-333, note 10; Berkhof, 61.

namely, that that is the time in which the eschatological message of peace will be proclaimed to the poor. Similarly, the entry into Jerusalem, the cleansing of the temple, and the institution of the Eucharist are seen by Kümmel as eschatological fulfillments. In this way the presence of Jesus becomes a unique and final moment of decision and therefore changes a mere time of expectation of eschatological consummation into his actual "eschatological" presence.[26]

With this we conclude our treatment of a few important pronouncements in the New Testament concerning the eschatological character of the first coming and earthly activity of Jesus. It confirms the arguments of our previous section that the New Testament writers interpret the *entire* history of Jesus eschatologically. It reinforces the idea that Jesus himself—and for that reason, his entire history—is the Last, the End, the decisive factor in eschatology.

Eschatology is therefore not restricted to future expectation, and emphatically not to the last decade or two before the return of Christ. Eschatology includes Christ's past work, his earthly activity, crucifixion, and resurrection, as well as his present work through the Holy Spirit (which will receive fuller attention at a later stage of our study).

We are not yet ready to address ourselves to a discussion of the biblical concept that Jesus is himself the Last and the End. There yet remains an important phenomenon to be investigated. This investigation will lead us again to the insight that the New Testament views the entire history of Jesus as the end, the consummation, and the one, indivisible end time.

THE SAME CONCEPTS APPLIED TO THE ENTIRE HISTORY OF JESUS

In the preceding sections, we have shown that New Testament writers use eschatological terms for the entire history of Jesus. Concepts such as the last days, the end of the age, and the fulfillment are not reserved for some future time. Without distinction, these eschatological terms are used for any part of the history of Jesus. According to John, who wrote his letter in the first century, his audience was already living in the last hour!

But another remarkable phenomenon also occurs in the New

26. W. G. Kümmel, *Promise and Fulfilment* (1961²), 110, 153-154.

Testament: *the same terms* are used repeatedly for each phase of Jesus' history. Not all these terms are eschatological; but the very fact that they are applied to the various episodes of Jesus' history indicates that the New Testament does not distinguish between each of Jesus' comings so systematically as was done later. The New Testament views the whole history of Jesus much more as a unity.

Theology usually distinguishes between the first coming of Jesus, the second coming, and the interim between the two comings. But the New Testament knows nothing of these expressions. The Greek word most commonly used for his comings *(erchomai)* is used indiscriminately for all three. It is applied to his first advent or incarnation with marked frequency in the Synoptic Gospels (e.g., Matt. 5:17; 9:13; 10:34-35; 11:3, etc.). It appears also in John (1:11; 3:19; 5:43; 7:28, etc.) and in 1 Tim. 1:15. But this same word is used for the second advent just as frequently—extremely often in the Synoptics (Matt. 24:30, 44, 46; 25:13, 31, etc.; Mark 13:26; 14:62, etc.) and in Acts 1:11; 2 Cor. 4:5; 11:26; 2 Thess. 1:10; and Rev. 1:4, 7, 8, 11, etc. Further, it is striking that the same term refers to the coming of the Holy Spirit (e.g., John 15:26; 16:7, 8, 13). Yet more remarkable, Jesus himself uses this term about his future coming in such ways that it is often impossible to tell whether he means his resurrection, the outpouring of the Holy Spirit, or his second advent (cf. John 14:18 with vv. 16-17 and v. 28 with vv. 26-27; see also 16:16).[27]

27. W. Hendriksen, *An Exposition of the Gospel of John* (1961), sees this pronouncement as a reference to the coming of Jesus in the outpouring of the Holy Spirit, but declares (330-331): "Crucifixion, resurrection and the outpouring of the Holy Spirit must never be separated . . . Hence the question . . . 'Is he thinking of his bodily resurrection or of his return in the Holy Spirit?' is not entirely proper. In the thinking (and speaking) of Jesus these two are not so sharply separated."

F. Godet, *Commentary on the Gospel of John* (1914, 1916, 1921), ad loc., also believes that 14:18 is a reference to Pentecost, but mentions Chrysostom, Erasmus, Grotius, Hilgenfield, and Weiss among those who see it as a reference to the resurrection of Jesus. Godet's argument that these post-resurrection appearances lasted only a while and were no real return of Jesus, is unacceptable when it is recalled that Jesus' resurrection is indeed his first parousia.

Karl Barth's comment is apropos: "As is well known, the Fourth Gospel takes its own particular line in this matter. In fulfilment of the promise: 'I will not leave you comfortless; I will come to you'(Jn. 14:18), Easter, Ascension, Pentecost and *parousia* are here seen as a single event, with much the same foreshortening of perspective as when we view the whole range of the Alps from the Jura. This perspective is legitimate and necessary side by side with the other. The

From this it is clear that, without distinction, the New Testament authors refer to the various phases of Jesus' history quite simply as his "coming." They do not distinguish systematically between his first coming, the interim, and his second coming. In fact, a number of other terms are applied with similar lack of differentiation. These include "reveal" and "revelation," "appear" and "appearance," "time" and "opportunity," "eternal life," "hour," "day," and "the fullness of time."[28] The contexts of all these word-groups confirm Kittel's remark that the New Testament use of *eschatos* "reflects the fluidity of early Christian eschatology."[29] All the phases of Jesus' history are subject to the same lack of distinction in the choice of terms.

In consequence, we conclude that every part of Jesus' history is couched in characteristically eschatological or "end" terms; that these terms are used without system or distinction throughout; and that the New Testament regards as eschatological his incarnation, earthly work, crucifixion, resurrection, and ascension, the outpouring of the Holy Spirit, and Christ's future return. This data provides no justification for viewing any one phase of Jesus' history by itself (e.g., his return) as eschatological; rather, the whole of it together comprises the subject of eschatology.

THE CENTRAL FOCUS
OF THE OLD TESTAMENT PROMISES

Our conclusion that the New Testament describes all phases of Jesus' history in the same radically eschatological terms is supported by

---

Fourth Gospel shows us that it is necessary to understand the event of Easter and that of the *parousia,* with the intervening history of the community under the present power of the Holy Spirit, as different moments of one and the same act" (*Church Dogmatics* [1955-1969] III/2 497).

28. There is much to commend in Berkhof's interpretation (*Well-founded Hope* [1969] 20) of *parousia* in 2 Pet. 1:16 as the appearance (or first coming) of Christ. In fact Greijdanus's argument, *De eerste brief van den Apostel Petrus* (Korte Verklaring; 1950), ad loc., has already been demolished by the argument of preceding pages that, since *parousia* means "return" elsewhere in 2 Peter and the rest of the New Testament, it should mean that here, too. What is more, he does not answer arguments (noted in passing) which support the first coming, "making known," and glorification of Christ as the meaning of *parousia.*

29. Kittel; *TDNT* II, 697.

the sharp focus of the Old Testament prophets on a single, central point.

It is true that the promises (prophecies) and future expectations of the Old Testament present difficult problems, not least because of their great variety. This diversity must be attributed to the long period and widely differing circumstances in which they developed. But it has a deeper significance, one which is of a piece with progressive revelation.[30]

It was only gradually, for instance, that the prophets saw ever more clearly the relationship between the Lord and Israel; that this was not to be taken for granted but rather made specific demands on Israel; and that, in a real sense, the Israelites would be treated like the neighboring Gentiles when they refused to obey him. Consider Amos 9, especially v. 7. Amos had to prophesy against people who eagerly awaited the day of the Lord, expecting it to be a day of light for them. But he had to declare that it would be a day of darkness as well (e.g., Amos 5:18-20). Vriezen shows that similar calamities befell other expectations (e.g., that of the future Davidic kingdom).[31]

These richly varied ideas about the future fit in with the Israelite spirit, never prone to systematizing. As a result, not even modern theological science is able to form a closed image of their abundance and diversity.[32] On the other hand, it must be emphasized that the variety

---

30. C. Steuernagel, "Die Strukturlinien der Entwicklung der jüdischen Eschatologie," *Festschrift für Alfred Bertholet* (1950), 479. O. Weber, *Foundations of Dogmatics* II (1983), 664, expresses himself vehemently against the possibility of construing a consistent doctrine (*einheitliche Lehre* in the German original) out of biblical data. Although van Ruler adopted a firm stand against the idea of progressive revelation (because, according to him, it assumes an intellectualistic concept of revelation and a linear view of time, whereas the Bible teaches a *personal* revelation and assumes a cyclical view of time), Berkouwer and others show convincingly that van Ruler wrestles with a caricature, never seeing the true picture of progressive revelation. For one thing, progressive revelation need not take an intellectualistic view of revelation (seeing revelation rather as the history of God with his people). For another, the idea of linear time has once again grown important, through the influence of O. Cullmann's *Christ and Time* (1964), confirmed by H.D. Preuss, *Jahweglaube und Zukunftserwartung* (1968) 94.

31. T. C. Vriezen: *An Outline of Old Testament Theology* (1958), 356ff.

32. Steuernagel, 478. This does not conflict with the unity of the Old Testament promises to which subsequent pages refer and which rests, among other considerations, on Hebrew vocabulary—a single word sufficing for "later" and "last" as for "continuous" and "eternity"—and view of time (T. C. Vriezen, "Prophecy and Eschatology," *Supplements to Vetus Testamentum,* 1 (1953), 223-224.

of Israel's expectations for the future does not prevent them from being studied with profit. It is clear that certain expectations develop gradually in the Old Testament and run through to the end (e.g., the day of the Lord, the rule of the Lord, and the Davidic kingship). It is also clear that in the New Testament all these central expectations come together and find their fulfillment in Christ. This unity in Israel's vision of the future is assumed by such New Testament statements as Acts 13:27, 32, where it should be noted that both the "words of the prophets" (fulfilled in the sentencing of Jesus) and the "promise to the fathers" (doubtless a whole series of Old Testament prophecies which God fulfills by raising Jesus from the dead) are spoken of in an inclusive manner.

However, this central focus of the Old Testament promises is not demonstrated in the New Testament alone; it exists already in the Old. This is particularly so since the diversity of Old Testament eschatology must be seen to stem from both the unique character of prophetic promises and the indistinctness of the prophetic vision.

The promises of the Bible are not predictions which serve as prescriptions for future history so that the future can be described in advance and calculated in detail.[33] If this were so, a promise would become impotent immediately upon its fulfillment and thereafter be of no more than historical interest. Berkouwer draws attention to the significant fact that even after the coming of Christ, the Church retained the Old Testament as a real part of sacred Scripture, as a message still to be preached.[34] It had also already become apparent in the Old Testament that the fulfillment of certain promises (e.g., the land of Canaan, the day of the Lord, and the Davidic kingship) did not mean that they had evaporated in the fulfilled reality and so become of no further effect.[35] Rather they

---

33. We will go into this extensively later. However, it is an insight shared by leading Old Testament and New Testament scholars and systematic theologians.

34. Berkouwer, 135. Stauffer, 95, does not make sufficient allowance for this particular aspect of Old Testament promises when he states that in the coming of Christ, the Old Testament, "to speak theologically, outmoded itself."

35. G. von Rad, *Old Testament Theology* II, 117ff. The "Day of Yahweh" furnishes a good example; it was fulfilled at the fall of Jerusalem in 586 B.C. (cf. Ezek. 13:5; Lam. 1:12; 2:1, 22) and yet remains a promise for the future (Robinson, 136). Yet another example is 2 Cor. 6:2, in which Isa. 49:8 is quoted: a promise that was fulfilled in the return from Babylon; yet Paul sees it as fulfilled afresh in the "now" effected by Jesus' coming. There are many examples, of which the best known is doubtless Matthew's (1:23) citation of Isa. 7:14.

retained their character as promises and repeatedly drew the eyes of faith toward the future.[36]

One result of this repeated fulfillment of a given promise was that while prophets in differing circumstances did view the same fu-

---

36. It is generally agreed by Old Testament scholars and systematic theologians that certain promises are repeated throughout Old Testament history and often provisionally fulfilled, but that the promises are never replaced by these fulfillments. Often a promise retains its force and opens even wider vistas, so that "repeated" or "more extensive" fulfillments of a promise are spoken of. Cf. Barth, I/2, 94-101; III/2, 497ff.; J. Moltmann, *Theology of Hope* (1976), 106-117; R. Rendtorff, *God's History* (1969), 62ff.; Vriezen, 100ff.; G. von Rad, *Old Testament Theology* II, 363-374, 383ff.; F. Baumgärtel, *Verheissung. Zur Frage des evangelischen Verständnis des Alten Testaments* (1952), 86-128.

This insight is of cardinal importance to understanding Bible promises and their fulfillment. If promises were "predictions" of "things" to happen, they would "come to rest" by occurring as historical events. That they (e.g., the promised land and kingship) do not come to rest but retain the character of promises despite fulfillment (e.g., Canaan and David), pointing to the future, contradicts notions that they predict history in the sense of reporting it in advance. (See Berkouwer, 132-137.)

It is important to note that these repeated fulfillments are not terminated in the coming of Christ. Though on the whole the New Testament sees the promises of the Old fulfilled in Christ, Christ at once directs our view to the future (Von Rad, 383). Two questions now arise.

First, why don't the promises terminate in historical fulfillments? Moltmann (106) finds a reason in the "inexhaustibility of God's promise, who never exhausts himself in any historic reality but comes 'to rest' only in a reality that wholly corresponds to him." In so saying he has also answered in principle the next question to arise.

Second, will the promise ever come to rest? Yes, when God has reached his goal, when the covenant (Barth's "inner ground of creation") is fully realized (Vriezen, *Outline,* 337) and when God dwells with the new humanity on the new earth (Rev. 21). Only then will the reality in which the promises are realized be so transformed that it could bear the entire fulfillment of God's promises. It is therefore in complete harmony with the structure of Bible promises that Christ (the end) did not terminate his work at the incarnation. He was the fulfillment of the whole Old Testament complex of promises—but in an unrenewed reality which was incapable of containing the totality of final *(Endgültige)* fulfillment. So there remains of necessity a plus (an *Überschuss* or *Mehrwert* [Moltmann]), which also could not come to complete fulfillment in what Barth calls the second form of the parousia—and for the very same reason.

In consequence, the Church and world must still look for a third and future form of the parousia, when final fulfillment will be possible because it will take place on a new earth. Only then will the promises be fulfilled completely. (See also Moltmann, 120.)

ture reality (e.g., the day of the Lord), they referred to it by a variety of formulae. The indistinct, even sketchy character of Old Testament prophecies (the more appreciable in light of current emphasis on the "human element" in Holy Scripture) results from the prophets' groping for words to express promises without being able to say precisely what the fulfilled reality would look like. Thus, e.g., actual details of how the Holy Spirit was to be poured out could never be deduced from Joel 2. It is only in Acts 2 that it becomes clear how Joel 2 was indeed fulfilled at Pentecost, even though there was no literal fulfillment of such particulars as the moon turning to blood (v. 31).

Old Testament prophecies are also indistinct because their underlying unity, Jesus Christ, cannot be deduced directly from the Old Testament—only from its fulfillment in the New. G. von Rad states the matter convincingly. He declares that no extraordinary hermeneutical method is needed to demonstrate that the entire many-pronged thrust of Old Testament salvation events points beyond itself, toward its fulfillment in Christ. He continues, "This can be said quite categorically: *The coming of Jesus Christ as a historical reality* leaves the exegete no choice at all."[37] The italicized words are particularly important. They mean that final insight into the unity which underlies all Old Testament promises can be gained only from the historical reality of their fulfillment in Christ. As we shall see, this principle is of paramount importance for prophecies which have not yet been fulfilled—those, for example, which involve the return of Christ. They mean also that the Old Testament cannot be fully or finally expounded without the New.

Von Rad repeats this idea in another connection. Discussing the new typological exegesis of the Old Testament (not to be confused with that of the last century), he shows how there is a "remainder" or opening toward the future in such figures as Joseph and Moses. This cannot be determined simply by approaching the Old Testament as did Israel of old; only when we address ourselves to Old Testament history from a New Testament perspective can we understand these figures as prefigurations of Christ's coming.[38]

When von Rad points out that the fulfillment often exceeds all that could be expected from a promise itself,[39] it again becomes clear that justice can be done to the central focus of Old Testament prom-

---

37. G. von Rad, *Old Testament Theology* II, 374; italics added.
38. *Ibid.*, 371.
39. *Ibid.*, 373.

ises only as they are viewed in the light of Jesus, who is their central unity. But this unity truly is the core of Old Testament promises; we do not simply read it into them.

As Old Testament promises were given to provide us, not with advance history, but with full assurance of this unity (which is Jesus), it is impossible to deduce from them that Christ will come more than once. Only the historic reality of Jesus' coming makes this possible, suggests von Rad. The central thrust of the Old Testament promises is a reality to be fulfilled in Christ, not a number of random events described before their occurrence. To put it another way, the whole historic reality of Jesus—not any one part of it or any specific advent—is the fulfillment of Old Testament prophecy.[40]

It is significant that New Testament authors frequently see an Old Testament promise fulfilled in more than one phase of Jesus' history, be it his first coming, his coming in the Holy Spirit, or his second advent. According to John 19:37, for example, Zech. 12:10 is fulfilled in the crucifixion of Jesus; Matt. 24:30 and Rev. 1:7 see it fulfilled in the second advent. In the same way, according to Mark 1:2, Mal. 3:1-2 was fulfilled in John the Baptist; according to Rev. 6:17, it will be fulfilled in the final judgment. Further (see Acts 2:17-21), Peter sees Pentecost

40. W. Barclay, referring to Matt. 11:4-5 and Luke 7:22 in *Jesus as They Saw Him* (1962), 372ff., sees "a whole series of Messianic prophecies" fulfilled in Jesus. In *TDNT* IV, 295, G. Delling says, "The NT concept of fulfilment is summed up in the person of Jesus." R. H. Gundry, *The Use of the Old Testament in St. Matthew's Gospel* (1967), 205ff., lists important data for which he relies heavily on C. H. Dodd, *According to the Scriptures* (1952), 107ff., and which demonstrate that a majority of New Testament quotations of and allusions to the Old come from certain areas of the Old Testament and are not fragments chosen capriciously from any part of the Old Testament but represent "whole contexts selected as the varying expression of certain fundamental and permanent elements in the biblical tradition" (Dodd, 132). By quotations from Jesus himself and from the Evangelists, Gundry enlarges these areas somewhat to show that the following Old Testament figures of promise are applied *directly* to Jesus: the kingly Messiah, the Servant of the Lord (Isaiah), the Son of Man (Daniel), the Shepherd of Israel, and the Lord (Yahweh) himself. In addition, the following figures are applied *typologically* to Jesus: Moses, the Son of David, the representative prophet (of Jonah, Isaiah, Asaph, Elisha, and others), the representative Israelite, and the representative righteous leader.

When we contemplate the enormous number of quotations which Matthew gives in this regard, we get some inkling of how comprehensive was the Evangelists' vision of the fullness of the promises fulfilled in Christ. This is possible only because there is a central focus in the Old Testament promises.

as the fulfillment of Joel 2:28-32, while the author of Rev. 9:1ff. quotes extensively from Joel 2 when depicting the final judgment. Finally, we mention again the day of the Lord, which is fulfilled in the incarnation, in the interim, and in the second coming. Thus it is clear that the prophecies of the Old Testament view the history of Christ as a unity and that they describe his entire history in eschatological terms.

JESUS, THE GOAL OF CREATION

We have already dealt with a considerable amount of biblical data. We have established that, according to the New Testament, the last days began with the birth of Jesus, the outpouring of the Holy Spirit occurred in the last days, and early Christians referred to their own time as the last days—even as the last hour. For them, the last days were present already—not off in the future. Each and every section of Jesus' history, from his birth to his second coming, is described in eschatological terms; there is no segmentation of the last days—as if Jesus' ministry merely initiated them and there remained some "final end time" for the remote future. Jesus' entire history is "the end."

This same perspective was found in the Old Testament promises and prophecies. The prophets do not distinguish between specific parts of their messianic expectation. Rather is there an impressive unity of vision in their rich diversity of promises. Above all it was possible, once Christ had appeared, to proclaim comprehensively that all the promises were fulfilled in him. This is why certain promises are linked with more than one part of his history. For example, a given promise might be fulfilled both in his crucifixion and in the judgment at his return.

Because of what we have thus seen in both Testaments, it comes as no surprise that the New Testament calls Jesus "the last," "the end," and "the omega." Since his whole history is the end time, it is only natural that he himself is called *the End*.

It is certainly an unusual choice of words to call a *person* "the last" or "the end." These are phrases which normally refer to time. What then is intended by the biblical statements which call Jesus the alpha and omega (Rev. 1:8; 21:6; 22:13), the beginning and the end (22:13), and the first and the last (1:17; 2:8; 22:13)? We shall investigate these questions now, and it is important that we examine the meanings of "beginning," "first," and "alpha" before attending to "end," "last," and "omega."

The Beginning. Of what is Christ the beginning? In the texts just listed this expression always occurs in an absolute and comprehensive sense. Forthrightly and without qualification, Christ is called "the beginning and the end, the first and the last." Where these designations are used elsewhere in the Bible as designations for Christ, we are given clearer pictures of their meaning. In Rev. 3:14, for example, the concept of "beginning" *(archē)* is used to characterize Christ as the beginning of creation. The concept of "alpha and omega" plays an important role, too, and we know that it is related to the rabbinic expression "from aleph to taw." Aleph is the first letter of the Hebrew alphabet; taw is the last. Therefore, to observe the Law (Torah) "from aleph to taw" means to keep the entire Law. That Jesus is the alpha and omega does not limit his significance to the beginning and the end of history; it involves him in the whole of it. This is supported by Paul's assertion "that the universe . . . [will] be brought into a unity in Christ" (Eph. 1:10 NEB).

This verse highlights the special relationship which exists between Christ and all creation, which is more fully described in Col. 1:18, where Christ is designated without qualification as "the beginning." But our translation of *archē* as "beginning" is not adequate. In the New Testament this word frequently also implies power, lordship, or exaltation. Moreover, were *archē* taken here to mean no more than temporal beginning, it would merely repeat the thought of the previous verse which states: "He is before all things." Lohmeyer draws attention to the connection between all four concepts used in Col. 1:18 for Christ: head, origin, first, and supreme (NEB). Dibelius sees in "first born," "firstfruits," and "preeminent one" (1 Cor. 15:20, 23; Acts 3:15; 26:23; Heb. 2:10; 12:2) indications of *archē*'s true meaning in Col. 1:18.[41] These interrelated concepts show that Christ is not merely the beginning of creation in a temporal sense, but that as pilot and ruler he accompanies creation—or rather takes it along with him. He is not the deists' "beginning" who left creation to its own devices; he is rather the helmsman of creation, which is why everything can be brought together in him (Eph. 1:10).

The First. As is "beginning," "first" *(protos)* is used *without*

---

41. E. Lohmeyer, *Die Briefe an die Philipper, Kolosser und an Philemon* (KEK; 1964[13]), ad loc. points out that "beginning" and "firstborn" are closely related in the Old Testament: the firstborn is the beginning and head of his generation (e.g., Gen. 49:3; Deut. 21:17). M. Dibelius, H. Greeven, *An die Kolosser, Epheser, Philemon* (HNT; 1953[3]), ad loc.

qualification of Christ in Revelation. There, without further explanation, he is spoken of as the first and the last. Though Michaelis relates this concept only to Christ's preexistence, seeing the earliest time and the end time alone in "the first and the last,"[42] there is abundant evidence in the New Testament that it refers to Christ's position of power.

The term "first" is used frequently to indicate the *most important* person or ruler. Cullmann, a Protestant scholar, points to Matt. 10:2, where Peter—whose name always heads lists of the apostles—is designated "first." Not merely a matter of numerical sequence, this derives from the fact that Peter was the spokesman or leader of the disciples.[43] Matt. 20:27 and Mark 9:35 and 10:44 are further examples of "first" in the sense of rank (see also Matt. 19:30; 20:16; Mark 10:31; Luke 13:30; Acts 25:2; 28:17, where the plural is thus used). In Acts 28:7 the word for "first" is translated as "chief" (NEB). Further, the verb "to be first" *(proteuō)* is used of Christ in a context in which he is already referred to as the head, the beginning, and the first born in Col. 1:18. We have already mentioned Lohmeyer's statement that these terms are related to one another. Also important is that here Christ is said to be "in all things alone supreme" (NEB). The phrase "all things" occurs frequently in this passage and basically means "the universe." That Christ is the first, "alone supreme," means that he is Lord over the universe.

If we add to this that in Revelation Christ is often in a single breath referred to as the beginning and the first, it seems reasonable to suggest that more is indicated by "first" than mere time. As *first,* Christ is also *Lord* of creation.

We summarize by affirming that Christ, the beginning, the first, and the alpha, is he who is responsible both for creation's origin and for its continuous guidance and governance.

The End. Three facts are decisive to the meaning of Christ as the end *(ho telos).* First is the statement of Rev. 22:13, where "the end" is used in the closest possible connection with created reality and its final purpose (v. 12). Although "end" is used prominently here in the absolute sense for the termination of the present order, the context shows clearly that it has implications for the relationship of Jesus to *created reality:* Jesus is the end of reality in its present form. This view is supported by the use of "the end" in combination with "the beginning," and, as noted, "the beginning" involves Christ's relationship to cre-

42. W. Michaelis, TDNT VI, 867.
43. O. Cullmann, *Peter: Disciple—Apostle—Martyr* (1953), 24, 26; BAGD, s.v. 1.c.β.

ation (Rev. 3:14, etc.). As he is the beginning of creation, so he is its end.

It is not yet clear, however, exactly what "end" *(telos)* means in this connection. Analysis of its New Testament use reveals two primary meanings: "end" in the temporal sense (1 Cor. 15:24; Heb. 3:6, 14; 6:11; 1 Pet. 4:7; Rev. 2:26) and in the sense of "goal" (1 Tim. 1:5; Jas. 5:11; 1 Pet. 1:9).[44] Often it is difficult to determine which of these meanings the word conveys in a given statement. For example, opinions differ markedly over just what Paul meant when he said that "Christ is the *telos* of the Law" (Rom. 10:4).

We need to examine further the connection between the concepts of "end" and "goal." When an end is achieved, a goal is reached. So when Christ is called "the end" of created reality, he is not only its temporal end but also its accomplished goal. From what we have discovered about the meaning of "beginning" (that the Lord guides his creation as its pilot) we deduce that should creation reach its end, Christ would play the decisive role. For that reason the end would not be abortive but would accomplish creation's goal. That Christ is the *telos* as both the end and the goal of creation is supported by New Testament statements which teach that the whole creation is directed toward him, exists and continues in him (Col. 1:16-20), that it is reconciled by him (cf. Col. 1:20 with 2 Cor. 5:18-19), and that it is united in him (Eph. 1:10). But we must examine these statements more closely.

"For through him [Christ] God created everything. . . . God created the whole universe through him and for him. Christ existed before all things, and in union with him all things have their proper place" (Col. 1:16f. TEV). The NEB is similar to the TEV in v. 17: ". . . all things are held together in him." Both disagree with the KJV and the NAB, which state that all things continue to exist in Christ. Beyond mere continued existence, the TEV and the NEB see *ordered* existence—or existence *as it was intended to be*—spoken of in the word *sunestēken*. Is this broader translation justified by the context?

Most exegetes accept the wider reading. H. Ridderbos says that this expression elaborates on what precedes it by affirming not only individual existence but also existence together, the mutual bond of all things sustained by Christ.[45] A. S. Peake says that Christ "keeps all

44. Compare, for instance, P.J. du Plessis: *Teleios: The Idea of Perfection in the New Testament* (1959), 122-68, with BAGD, s.v.

45. H. Ridderbos, *Aan de Kolossenzen* (Commentaar op het Nieuwe Testament; 1960), ad hoc.

parts [of the universe] in their proper place and due relations and combines them into an ordered whole."[46]

Moreover, it is of great importance to appreciate with Ridderbos the distinction between *de facto* and *de jure* statements. Col. 1:17b does not say that all things have always retained their appropriate places in Christ or that they have already discovered their cohesion and coexistence in him. It asserts rather that only in Christ *can* things have this mutual bond and that, if they withdraw from this bond and from their relatedness to him, they lose the meaning of their existence and go astray.

Only by so expounding Col. 1:17 can v. 20 have meaning. For there we read that Christ has "reconciled all things." If v. 17 were a *de facto* pronouncement (saying, i.e., that all things already exist harmoniously in Christ), it could not have been placed before v. 20.

In Heb. 1:3 there is yet another nuance: "[Christ] sustains the universe by his word of power." The *de facto* fall of the creature is not under consideration here. Rather it is Christ's providence that is the theme. Just as he created all things, so he also bears and cares for them.[47] This carrying is not passive endurance of a burden. Christ is no Atlas shouldering the dead weight of the globe. His bearing of creation includes movement and progress toward a goal.[48] Despite this difference in nuance, it is correct to relate Heb. 1:3 to Col. 1:17. It is of great significance that the goal of creation is referred to in discussion of Col. 1:17 and Heb. 1:3, since this goal is indeed clearly referred to in Col. 1:16.

In Col. 1:16 Paul says that all things are created *for Christ*. Here we have the goal of creation. Creation is aimed toward Christ as its target; it moves toward him, and in him it will reach its goal. There is no contradiction between this and such statements as Rom. 11:36 and Heb. 2:10 where we read that God (the Father) is the purpose of creation, for there is no disunity between Father and Son. Neither is there any contradiction between Heb. 2:10 (which says that all things exist through God) and Col. 1:16 (where the same Greek construction is used to say that all things are created through Christ). Paul again re-

46. A. S. Peake: Colossians, *The Expositor's Greek Testament* (1903). Also J. B. Lightfoot, *Saint Paul's Epistles to the Colossians and to Philemon* (1961) and F. F. Bruce, *Colossians, Philemon, and Ephesians* (NICNT; 1984).

47. *Pherōn* in this statement is a Hebraism with *sābal* as its root and ultimately means "behüten," to protect (Michel, 100). It expresses motherly care for the creature of God in need.

48. Westcott, ad loc.

lates Father and Son as the goal of creation when in 1 Cor. 15:28 he says: "when all things are thus subject to him [the Son], then the Son himself will also be made subordinate to God who made all things subject to him, and thus God will be all in all."

The goal of creation, which is directed toward Christ, cannot fail. It is significant that Paul uses the aorist tense when asserting that all things are created *in* Christ, but then changes to the perfect tense when stating that all things are created *for* him. Thus there is a sense of finality in his statement. All things are indeed directed toward and en route to Christ, and in him they will reach their goal.[49] The fall has not rendered this goal unattainable. How this can be, we shall see presently; for now, suffice it to state that this possibility does *not* derive from the creatures!

It is sometimes claimed that the idea of Christ as creation's goal is only found at this point in Paul's writings, in Colossians 1. But the same thought, in modified form, occurs often in Pauline literature (e.g., Rom. 8:19ff.; 1 Cor. 15:28; Eph. 1:10). In this connection Schlier's exegesis of Eph. 4:15b merits attention. If he is correct, the translation ought to read: "we shall cause all things to grow up toward him who is the Head, namely Christ."[50]

A similar understanding of Christ—especially if we accept Westcott's exegesis of "made" *(ethēken)*—is found in Heb. 1:2. There we read of "the Son whom he [God] has made heir to the whole universe." Westcott maintains that since there is no indication of just *when* Christ was made heir, this appointment belongs to God's eternity. Further on, Westcott correctly notes that the word "heir" reflects the original purpose of creation.[51] It seems we are safe, therefore, in concluding that the idea of Christ as the *goal* of creation is not foreign to the New Testament.

The connection between Col. 1:17 ("all things are held together in him") and v. 16 ("the whole universe has been created through him and for him") is now clear. It is possible for all things to be held together in their proper order in him, *because* he is the goal of creation. To put it another way, it is *because* creation is aimed at him and

---

49. H. Ridderbos, op. cit., points out essentially the same thing in connection with "made by him," i.e., that "by him" is not the indication of a single, past relationship but rather of an enduring one. If this holds for "by him," then it must also apply to "to him."

50. H. Schlier, *Der Brief an die Epheser,* (1971[7]), ad loc.

51. Westcott, ad loc.

reaches its goal in him that he is able to hold all things in their proper places.

In this light, the connection of Col. 1:20 with 2 Cor. 5:18-19 and Eph. 1:10 also becomes clear. Far from being alien to Paul's doctrine of the atonement, Col. 1:20 harmonizes with Paul's entire soteriology. If Christ is the goal of creation (1:16), only in him can things exist harmoniously (v. 17) and only through him can they be reconciled (v. 20). They become discordant when through sin they abandon their alignment with him; only through him are they restored to a correct relationship with God and each other (Eph. 2:14, 16). The entire hymn to Christ of Col. 1:15-20 must be seen as summed up in Eph. 1:10, which declares that it is God's purpose to bring "all in heaven and on earth" into "a unity in Christ."

At this point, it is of the greatest importance that we have a clear understanding of the bond between Christ and the whole of creation. From the nature of Christ, from the nature of creation, and, therefore, from the relationship between Christ and creation proceeds *his ability to sum up the universe in his person and to subject it to his lordship.* It is therefore not only a matter of power which renders subjugation possible that is at issue here, but also of the purpose and aim of creation in Christ. This is precisely what we found in Col. 1:16-17.

We are able to conclude from the New Testament data that when Christ is named "the end" in Revelation, both possibilities of meaning—termination and goal—are included. In and through Christ—and him alone—can creation reach its end and goal—that which is conceived and willed for it by God. Without or apart from Christ creation's end would be aborted, for Christ *is* its purpose.

The Last. We can deduce but one thing from the use of this term in Rev. 1:17; 2:8; and 22:13: that it points to precisely the same relationship of Jesus to creation as "beginning" and "first." From three other sources we can deduce more about this concept, however, and so we shall examine them.

First, we note that "the first and the last" is derived from similar expressions in Isa. 41:4; 43:10; 44:6; and 48:12.[52] The arresting feature of these is that they do not have temporal meanings. This is at once evident from what follows: "and besides me there is no God" (44:6; cf. 43:11). Since Hebrew poetry often repeats an idea in slightly dif-

---

52. Although the Septuagint does not use *eschatos* in these texts in Isaiah and is, indeed, circumlocutious, the writer of Revelation does use it and thus looks to the Masoretic text rather than the Septuagint (G. Kittel, *TDNT* I, 2).

ferent words (a device called parallelism), God himself is being more fully described. To speak of the Lord as "the last" does not mean simply that he outlasts everyone else, but that he is unique, for example that he is of incomparable power (Isa. 41:4). This expression is not so much concerned with *time,* then, as with affirming that the Lord *alone* is God and that he is unique.

Second, widespread New Testament use of "the last" demonstrates that this phrase is not only a temporal term but also a numerical term (Matt. 5:26; Luke 12:59) and a spatial term (Acts 1:8; 13:47). Even when it indicates time—i.e., the time of Christ's coming—it does not signify just the isolated time just before his second coming (the so-called "last days"), but also his incarnation and the period between his first and second comings.

An important third point is the contrast between Adam and Christ. Paul discusses at least four points of contrast in 1 Cor. 15:45-48:

the *first* Adam	the *last* Adam
an animate being	a life-giving Spirit
the first man	the second Man
"of the dust of the earth"	from heaven

Here, too, we are concerned with more than time. What is at issue is the decisive meaning of Christ in contrast with the "first" Adam, Christ's value and exaltation as the "second" man or "last" Adam. Just as calling Christ "the firstborn of every creature" (Col. 1:15 KJV) does not indicate time by implying that he was the first creature, but is rather an affirmation of his rank and the lordship which he exerts over the entire creation, the application of the term "the last" to Jesus testifies to his decisive meaning for creation. Although the temporal aspect cannot be eliminated (Jesus did in fact become man after Adam, and stands in a specific relationship to the "last days") it is in fact only *Jesus* who can be the last because he is what he is, and no other need come after him since in him creation reaches its goal. He is therefore the last both in the temporal sense and in the sense that he is decisive for creation.

We may sum up this section by saying that the beginning and end of creation come together in Jesus. The beginning and end of creation is a *person.* Beginning and end are not in the first instance indications of *time.* And the same applies to first and last, alpha and omega. The meaning of these concepts amounts to the following: That Christ is the alpha and the omega means that there is a special relationship between Christ and the *entire history* of the world. That Christ is called "the beginning" is not a reference only to a temporal relationship between Jesus and creation, but also includes the idea that Jesus is *Lord* of creation. As Lord he takes his creation along with him and sustains it. The same meaning is contained in the concept "first" which indicates rank rather than sequence. Christ as the "end" *(telos)* involves the ideas of both *terminus* and *goal* and amounts to the same thing as pronouncements (particularly of Paul) which depict Christ as the *goal* of creation. Christ as the "last" emphasizes his decisive meaning for creation. There is no one whose significance can in any way be compared with his decisive meaning for creation. *In brief then Christ is both the Lord of the whole of the history of created reality and the destination toward which all creation is moving—the destination which will be reached through him, the decisive One.*

It is clear why the New Testament does not describe limited *sections* of the history of Jesus as the last days, as the consummation (of the ages), or even as the last hour. Why would the last days be thought of by the apostles as lying somewhere in the future when the Last was among them as a person? For this reason, though the Old Testament could still speak of the last days as lying in the dim and distant future, the New Testament knows of the last days only in the past and present tense. *At that time, in the first century A.D., it was already the last days since they were the days (i.e. the history) of the Last One, Jesus Christ.*

Chapter 2

CHRIST AND ESCHATOLOGY

OTHER VIEWPOINTS

The insights in Chapter 1 are of decisive importance for one's view of eschatology. If eschatology has to do with the last days, the consummation, the goal of creation, and similar concepts, then the entire history of Jesus Christ must be included in eschatology. Indeed, he is himself the last One, the end, and even the goal of creation. It is consequently not correct to restrict eschatology to some fragment of his history—or worse, to a number of "things" which are still to come.

Surely no one will dispute the fact that certain things which happen today are part of eschatology. What is unacceptable, however, is restricting eschatology to these specific things, such as alleging that the end time or last days could not begin before the Jews had begun returning to Israel, or before the Antichrist appeared as a person, or before certain power groups were formed in the Near East. In this way a "real" end time is constructed—in opposition to the biblical message that the last days arrived with the birth of Christ because he, in his own person, is the end. In the light of this biblical message it is simply impossible to pretend that the past nineteen centuries are devoid of eschatology and that only now, for the first time, are we entering the last days. It is impossible, even arbitrary, to confine prophecies concerning the end time to, for instance, the final seven years before the return of Christ. This is often done, and it is characteristic of such views that Christ himself and his unique significance play only minor roles.[1]

But it is not just by the most conservative theologians that such limitations have been imposed on eschatology. According to *Bultmann,* history was actually terminated by the first coming and crucifixion of Christ. Everything has, in Bultmann's view, become "eschatological" except the actual history which Jesus Christ is still making

1. As in a book such as Hal Lindsey's *The Late Great Planet Earth* (1970).

and will continue to make. This history has vanished in favor of the decision to which the proclamation summons us, a decision which is limited to the personal sphere and which offers no perspectives on the renewal of history. One might have welcomed Bultmann's view of Jesus' earthly activity as being thoroughly eschatological were it not that he does so at the cost of Jesus' resurrection, his renewal of history through the Holy Spirit, his return, and his renewal of the earth. In fact Bultmann remains one of the few important theologians who take the eschatological character of the past (Jesus' earthly ministry) really seriously, but unfortunately he does so at the cost of the future.

Barth adopted a position which contrasted sharply with Bultmann's and, indeed, accorded full weight to Christ's resurrection as his first return, his coming in the Holy Spirit as his second return, and his second coming as the third or last return. But Barth did this at the cost of the earthly work of Jesus, which he never regarded as a real part of the end time, i.e., of eschatology. It is, however, much to be appreciated that Barth, after at first posing a philosophical, ahistorical opposition between time and eternity, worked out in his later years the historical character of eschatology ever more lucidly. He insisted, for instance, that we must accept that Christ will really come again.

Likewise *Cullmann,* renowned for his salvation-historical approach to the New Testament, also never allows for a radical, eschatological interpretation of Christ's earthly ministry. In his thinking, time and history push the person of Jesus into the background. For Cullmann, Jesus is the center and turning point of history—concepts, remarkably enough, that the Bible itself never applies to Jesus. But that Jesus is the end and the last, and that his earthly work is termed the last days, are facts which lie fallow in Cullmann's theology. According to Cullmann, who draws a sharp distinction between the kingdom of Christ and the kingdom of God, Christ's lordship began only at his ascension, after he had conquered the powers through his death on the cross. Cullmann explains statements which point to the eschatological nature of Christ's earthly ministry (e.g., Matt. 12:28: "But if it is by the Spirit of God that I drive out the devils, then be sure the kingdom of God has already come upon you") as anticipations *(Vorwegnahmen)* of the future. He declares that while Jesus came to achieve victory by his death, such anticipations were normal during his life on earth. As well as Matt. 12:28, he points to Luke 10:17 and 11:20. Elsewhere he asserts that Jesus regarded his own coming as the dawning of the end time. But it should be noted that for Cullmann end *time* is not the same as the end. Therefore Ridderbos correctly judges that this view does injustice to the significance of Christ's person before his death and resurrection.[2]

Pannenberg emphasizes that history is the place where God reveals himself. He rejects any distinction between salvation history and history, seeing the *whole* of history as the locus of divine revelation. Since history has not yet run its course, God has not yet completely revealed himself. What is at issue, therefore, is not merely that we are unable to survey the whole of history, but that God is not yet wholly revealed, especially in the sense of his being the almighty ruler. This will only be revealed in an absolute sense when history is complete. In answer to the question whether we can know anything of God and of the end, Pannenberg referred to Jesus as the "untimely born," he who proleptically appeared before the end, i.e., while history was still in mid course, and in whom, by his resurrection, God has given us certainty concerning the end.

Without attempting to pronounce a verdict on this view—in any case, Pannenberg himself is still wrestling with this problem—it seems that it disconnects Christ, to some extent, from the actual course of history. He becomes a sort of alien who has not yet given history its eschatological character. Needless to say, such a view cannot place the same stress as does this study on Christ himself being the last and the end and his entire history being real eschatology. To put it another way, Pannenberg does not treat in earnest the fact that the end has been reached in the one who is the end (Jesus) and that the last days are the days (the history) of this last One.

It is indeed remarkable—not to say alarming—that the message of Christ as the last and the end has on the whole exerted so little influence on eschatological study. Such early fathers as Irenaeus certainly mentioned the idea that Christ's very person is the last *(escha-*

---

2. O. Cullmann, *The Early Church* (1956), 150ff.; *The Christology of the New Testament* (1963[2]), 159; H. Ridderbos, *The Coming of the Kingdom* (1960), 96. Both Barth and Berkhof speak of Christ as the midpoint of history, thus failing to do full justice to Christ as the last and the end. In H. Berkhof's *Christ, the Meaning of History* (1966), Chapters 3 and 4 first regard Christ as the end of history and *then* as the beginning of history—a thought not encountered in the New Testament. (Cf. Heb. 1:2; 9:26; 1 Pet. 1:20.) Revelation knows Christ as the first and the last (not as the last and the first) and the beginning and the end (not as the end and the beginning). Cf. also K. Barth, *Kirchliche Dogmatik* (1932-1967) III/2, 553-54. The English translation (*Church Dogmatics* [1955-1969] III/2, 461) is shortened, and Barth's views on the close of the old age and the beginning of the new have been left out.

tos), the goal toward which all creation moves and the one who moves it toward its goal.[3] But this insight was not developed. Rather was it allowed to fade into the background of theological thought, where it could exercise little influence. With the rise of Scholasticism, eschatology was increasingly relegated to the closing chapter of theological texts, where it covered a number of such last "things" as the resurrection, the resurrection body, and immortality.

In modern Roman Catholic theology, the idea that Christ himself is the last does occasionally appear. *Schoonenberg,* in a chapter entitled Christ the Last, begins with the promising pronouncement that Jesus stands at the end of history, that he is without qualification the end, and that in this respect Christology expounds eschatology.[4] After devoting brief attention to the sense in which the end really dawned at the birth of Christ (referring to Mark 1:15; Gal. 4:4; Eph. 1:10; 1 Cor. 10:11; 1 John 2:18, etc.), Schoonenberg explains how it was that history went on as before after the birth of Jesus. He gives two reasons: because Christ, who was truly man, had himself to attain adulthood; and—carrying this principle further—because he had to attain maturity in his body (the Church), wherein he is still coming to completion. This will be accomplished at his second coming, when Christ himself will be complete, because all who are predestined to come to him by the Father will have done so. Thus will his body—i.e., his fullness—be realized. Then he will be the last in every way: the goal and the terminus of the world and its history. Only then can come the end promised in 1 Cor. 15:24.

By understanding Jesus as the last in this way (i.e., only at his return), Schoonenberg is unable to take seriously the fact that *Christ* is himself the last, since a specific section of his history, rather than his person, is viewed as the last. Only when Christ himself, his birth, ministry, crucifixion, resurrection, ascension, and working through the Holy Spirit, is understood as wholly and in every sense the last, have we heard correctly the Bible's message about eschatology.

A second Catholic approach, that of *C. Schütz* is even more important than Schoonenberg's. In a section dealing with the christological ground of eschatology, he presents a subsection on "Christology and Eschatology." He begins with the resurrection of Jesus as the one event which gave to Jewish eschatology a totally new dimension. For

3. C. Schütz in J. Feiner and M. Löhrer, *Mysterium Salutis* (1965-) V 565ff.

4. P. Schoonenberg, *Het Geloof van ons Doopsel* (1955-) III, 225-230.

the first time, eschatology lay in the future *and* in the past, and past eschatology (i.e., the resurrection) became decisively significant. Schütz even emphasizes that the earthly life and ministry of Jesus are intrinsic parts of his eschatological meaning.

In a section on *"Eschatos* and *Eschata,"* (i.e., The last and the last things) Schütz writes about the relationship between realized and futurist eschatology. In his view, in Christ the *eschaton,* and with it eschatology, are bound to a fixed point in history and have become a part of history and a fulfilled reality. In Jesus the *eschaton* has become the *Eschatos* (Jesus himself). Since the Christ event, the *eschaton* no longer lies in the future as a promise, but is bound to history. In the person of Jesus, a synthesis has been made between that which by its very nature always pertained to the future (namely eschatology), and a completed event in history (the ministry of Jesus). Because the *eschaton* is attached to a person, everything we say about the last "things" must be deduced from the last One, and must, moreover, be measured against him.[5]

As with the other theologians referred to, however, there is a short circuit in Schütz's reasoning. Instead of developing an eschatology based on the entire history of Jesus, he restricts himself to the "Christ event" (the *Christusereignis*). He includes only the earthly ministry, the death, and the resurrection of Christ. As a consequence, he has to extend eschatology beyond "christology" (the so-called Christ event), since there is of course a future aspect to eschatology— the work of the Holy Spirit and the second coming—which are not included in this "Christ event."

So it happens that Christ is again left by the wayside and an eschatology is developed without him. This is really not necessary, as the influence of Christ on eschatology need not be limited to the "Christ event," his ministry, death, and resurrection. Christ is his history—including his present work through the Holy Spirit and his second coming. All Schütz need have done was to have drawn the full consequences of his own viewpoint, namely that it is not possible to speak intelligibly about the last things apart from the last One. Had he done this, he would have given eschatology a new form and structure based on Jesus' whole history. As it is, his radically biblical insights concerning Christ as eschatology's foundation are ultimately unfruitful for the actual form he gives to eschatology.[6]

5. Schütz, 649-660.
6. The unfortunate trend appears from p. 660 of Schütz's work.

In stark contrast to these promising emphases among Roman Catholic theologians, *Karl Rahner's* dated and uninspired approach treats eschatology summarily in a brief closing chapter. Its first sentence declares: "This ninth chapter deals with Christian eschatology, or the doctrine about the *last things*." From that point Rahner develops eschatology solely from the perspective of anthropology. He leaves no room for a cosmic approach and allots no role to Christ.[7] It is a pity that Rahner finally adopted this position; in the 1960s his renowned essay on eschatology exerted a very positive influence on G. C. Berkouwer.[8]

DEFINING ESCHATOLOGY

In this and succeeding chapters we shall seek to apply the data of our first chapter to eschatology. This application will involve two considerations before all others.

The first is that the entire history of Christ is discussed in radical eschatological terms. In most cases, these terms are applied to all parts of his history so that no reason is left for limiting eschatology to any one part—as most authors do. The tendency is to confine eschatology to the future, particularly to those "last *things*" which have little direct connection with Jesus and his significance.

The second consideration is that Jesus himself is called the last and the end. Since his entire history is described in the same eschatological terms, he himself must be the *eschatos* (the last). The reverse is also true: since he himself is the *eschatos* and *telos* (end or goal), his whole history must be eschatology.

What does this mean? It became clear at the end of the preceding chapter that Jesus is the last, the end, and above all the goal of creation, that creation is therefore aligned toward him and directed to him; that it moves toward him, and that, united under his lordship, it will ultimately achieve harmony.

This means that we must use the term christology when we describe eschatology. Since Christ is the goal of creation and the Bible

---

7. K. Rahner, *Foundations of Christian Faith* (1978), 431-447.

8. K. Rahner, "The Hermeneutics of Eschatological Assertions," *Theological Investigations* VI (1966), 323ff.; G. C. Berkouwer, *The Return of Christ* (1972), 216ff.

describes his whole history in eschatological terms, we must focus on him and determine who he is in order to understand eschatology. This does not mean that eschatology is coextensive with christology; it deals with Christ only in the sense that he is the goal of creation and that in him creation achieves its purpose. Eschatology is teleological christology—goal-directed christology.

Implied by this understanding is that eschatology is not primarily a category of time. It begins with and has for its object a person and involves his whole history. Therefore we must be critical of two outlooks which often go together: that which restricts eschatology to categories of time (as does the salvation history school) and that which restricts eschatology to future time, whether the future in general or Christ's future.

Let us consider the second of these restrictions first. Moltmann defines eschatology as "Christology in an eschatological perspective."[9] Though this sounds encouraging, his work demonstrates that the "eschatology" in this definition is too one-sidedly preoccupied with Christian expectations for the *future*. Luther's contrasting emphasis is rather to be accepted: all christology is eschatological in character. He maintains that eschatology is thus no mere description of the future.[10] Since Jesus is the *eschatos* and the *telos,* eschatology may not be limited arbitrarily to any one portion of his history—in this case, that still to come.

We press our charge of unbalance at Cullmann as well, since his use of "eschatological" means no more than "of the end-time."[11] W. Kreck is another whose basic approach must be questioned. For him, eschatology is the doctrine of Christ's future and of the significance of his return for the redemption of mankind and the world.[12] What we criticize is Kreck's view of the future as the only—and so the entire—content of eschatology.

To a certain extent, this criticism applies also to Barth's escha-

9. J. Moltmann, *Theology of Hope* (1967), 192.

10. U. Asendorf, *Eschatologie bei Luther* (1967), 125 ("die Eschatologie ist . . . Auslegung der Christologie. . .": eschatology is the exposition of Christology), 46. Asendorf maintains that an eschatology dealing exclusively with the future is not possible, because this future is already in essence accomplished by Christ.

11. O. Cullmann, *Salvation in History* (1967), 172, note 3.

12. W. Kreck, *Die Zukunft des Gekommenen* (1961), 199. His title is promising, but the Christ *who has come* does not here receive the eschatological emphasis which the New Testament demands for him.

tology. It is true that he does not treat the future alone as the content of eschatology but also includes the three comings of Jesus—i.e., his first *parousia* (to Barth, the resurrection), his *parousia* in the outpouring of the Holy Spirit, and his third *parousia* (Christ's final return). Although Barth includes a much larger part of Jesus' history in eschatology than some others do, he still excludes Christ's incarnation, earthly ministry, and crucifixion. The New Testament does not so distinguish between the earthly life of Jesus and that which Barth calls his "different history since the resurrection."[13] And it is because Barth distinguishes between the incarnation (which he calls the "middle of time") and the resurrection (the "beginning of eschatology") that such passages as Heb. 1:2 and 9:26 are not fully recognized in his theology. In the final analysis, Barth, too, limits eschatology to a segment of Jesus' history.[14]

We turn now to a critique of the notion that eschatology is only or primarily a time category. The salvation-history approach of Cullmann, Kreck, and others tends to lay more emphasis on the passing of time (which—perhaps unwittingly—is equated with natural, earthly time) than on Jesus. Consequently these writers think primarily in terms of advancing growth and development, i.e., of new things emerging steadily until the fullness of consummation is reached— sometime in the *future*. Earthly time is thus made the yardstick of eschatology, and salvation history develops as the analogy of earthly time.

However, once *Jesus* is seen as the goal of creation and the *eschatos,* the consummation can be seen as reachable (in one sense, as already reached!) before the end of natural world history. This is possible because the *eschatos* is a person, not just a set of forthcoming *things*. In terms of the person of Jesus it therefore becomes possible to make the apparently contradictory statement that the consummation comes before the end.[15]

We would also set our critique against those who restrict eschatology to existential categories. As has been noted, such a restriction may represent a reaction to denials of the eschatological character of

13. K. Barth, *Church Dogmatics* IV/3, 295; III/2, 441ff.
14. This does not mean that Barth has no eye for the eschatological character of Jesus' earthly ministry. On the contrary, he grounds eschatology in Jesus and speaks of the incarnation and atonement as the *eschaton*. But afterward he limits eschatology decisively by including only a part of Jesus' history (from his resurrection onward) in his eschatological design.
15. I am indebted to Asendorf, 246, for this formulation.

Christ's first coming and especially of the interim between the first and second comings. Against this response (of Bultmann's school particularly) we rehearse the facts that *Jesus* is the *eschatos* and the *telos* and that he is a historical person with an (unfinished) history. Those who do not view the whole history of Jesus as eschatology—as does the New Testament—cannot make up for it by using existential categories. What is more, our objection to Cullmann's eschatology applies as well to Bultmann's: both arbitrarily restrict eschatology to less than the *whole* history of Christ. Bultmann confines it to the contemporary "Jesus event" and not even to history! So Braun, a student of Bultmann, proclaims that Jesus "wishes to happen again and again," certainly no adequate reflection of the New Testament teaching of Jesus' coming in the Holy Spirit.[16]

All these viewpoints have in common their restriction of eschatology to less than the whole history of Jesus. Against each limitation of eschatology to some part of Jesus' history we must affirm that Christ himself is the *eschatos* and *telos*. This means that from the beginning he was the goal of creation, and that he entered creation in order to bring it to this goal. Thus eschatology is the goal-directed history of Christ, or "teleological christology."[17]

An implication of this outlook on eschatology is that the goal of creation is in no way attainable apart from Christ. As the study of the last things, eschatology simply has no meaning unless it is Jesus who ushers in and accomplishes these things. Arresting and catastrophic events may occur, but they will not usher in eschatology (in which the *goal* is reached) without Jesus as their instigator and center. In consequence, we need not be exclusively supernatural in our eschatological expectations. Those things which are yet to happen may do so in a less conspicuous, more ordinary way than some people imagine. They need not be exceptional, supernatural, or catastrophic. Their criterion is whether God's creative purpose is achieved. Jesus' birth was like that—and it began a history which inaugurated the last days. Few extraordinary events took place; all that was to be seen were an infant in a crib, a few foreign astrologers, and a handful of local shepherds. Yet

16. H. Braun, *Gesammelte Studien zum Neuen Testament und seiner Umwelt* (1962), 335-336.

17. Incidentally we should note that here, indeed, is some sort of limitation. Eschatology is not simply christology; it is teleological christology. This means that not all aspects of christology will be discussed, but only those which are concerned with Jesus as the *telos* and the *eschatos*.

the event was eschatological in the fullest sense of the word, because that infant was *Jesus*.

We should emphasize that not every expectation about specific "last things" is necessarily illegitimate; there should be no tension between "personal eschatology" (eschatology with a focus on the *person* of Jesus) and the "last things" (as a component of eschatology). Though Berkouwer has correctly warned that our expectation must be fixed not on future events ("things") but on Christ, and that eschatology dare not lose for an instant this focus on the person, neither is it correct to object on these grounds alone to the term "last things"—as if depersonalization of eschatology lurked inevitably in the term itself. Though the term has an impersonal ring, as Berkouwer says, its purpose was always clear.[18]

Indeed, the term "last things" should be held up as a critique of personalism in eschatology. Personalism concentrates future expectations on the Christ in such a way that his "coming" and our "meeting" with him scarcely leave room for real things to happen in the future. Such an opposition between "person" and "things" leaves little room for the new earth or the resurrection of the body. Personal encounter absorbs "thing"-ness and causes an impoverishment of the eschatological hope.

What then can be left to hope for? It is one thing to reduce eschatology to nothing more than "things," quite another to hope for specific "things" inaugurated by a Lord who is the firstborn of all creation (Col. 1:15), apart from whom no single *thing* came to be (John 1:3), and under whom all *things* in heaven and on earth are united (Eph. 1:10) because for him all *things* are created (Col. 1:16) and in him all *things* exist (v. 17). In confessing Christ as the goal of creation, obviously we include all this. In fact there is no stronger defense against unbalanced personalistic expectations than confessing the resurrection of the body—*a thing!*

So when we declare emphatically that every eschatological expectation not focused on Christ's coming is unacceptable, we do not at all discourage attention to new *things*. As Berkouwer points out,

18. Berkouwer, 13-14. At this point Berkouwer (13, note 7) refers to P. Althaus, whose eschatology bears a strongly personal character and yet is entitled *Die letzten Dinge* (The Last Things). On the other hand, the concept of "last things" often fails to permit the expectation of Jesus himself to come into its full right—at least in popular theological books and discussions, in which far more is generally made of precisely what will happen, and in precisely what sequence, than of the coming of Christ himself.

every one-sided personalizing of eschatological expectation leads inevitably to the result that not only "things" but also, ultimately, the coming of the Lord itself vanishes from the horizon.[19]

In light of this bond between Christ—as the last and the end—and the last things, it should be clear that our characterization of eschatology as teleological christology does not restrict eschatology exclusively to the person of Christ. It is precisely because Christ is the goal of creation that it is not possible to contemplate his significance without considering "things" (i.e., created realities). Indeed, what he is and does, he is and does for creation. Christ is the goal of creation, and he accomplishes its purpose precisely because he forms mankind in his own image, so that he and his life are reflected in mankind. In fact, human beings are not only created in God's image but also remade in that image—and that image is Christ. In creation he gives himself form. As he lives his life through us (Gal. 2:20), we can live a new and holy life.

But there is another implication. It must be affirmed that because Christ is creation's goal, creation obviously reaches its goal when he comes—*every time* he comes! Jesus is not who he is, nor does he do what he does, for himself. He is Immanuel, God-with-us. He is *the* Human Being, representative to God for us all. Because he is neither

19. Berkouwer, 13-14. In reaction to horizontal eschatology (which does not take into account the vertical coming of Jesus in his second advent), Barth writes that Christ's return is not "merely the result of what Jesus Christ was yesterday and is to-day. It is again He Himself, His own person and work, in a new mode and form. . . . The New Testament does not look for an amelioration of present conditions or for an ideal state, but for the coming of the Lord—*Maranatha,* (1 Cor. 16:22)—in a definitive and general revelation; and therefore for the justification and redemption of individuals in judgment; for the end and new beginning of the cosmos; for the kingdom as the last thing corresponding to the first which was in the counsel of God before all times" (*Church Dogmatics* III/2, 486-487). Also, says Barth, we can legitimately speak of "the last things" so long as our expectation is concentrated on him who will come and, by his coming, bring them and establish them.

H. Lamparter, *Die Hoffnung der Christen* (1967), 9ff., can also be interpreted in this way, though he is noticeably more critical of "personalizing" than is Berkouwer, regarding it as neither fortunate nor helpful. Against this stands A. A. van Ruler, "Grenzen van de Eschatologisering," *Vox Theologica* 37 (1967), 181, who is convinced that the "things"—indicating reality—cannot sufficiently be emphasized. In *Ik geloof* (1968), 153, he expresses appreciation for the Confession's material emphasis on the resurrection of the body ("the flesh").

a human being nor God-with-us for himself, but always for us, God's purpose for us is always accomplished in him.

The difference between the return to life of Lazarus and that of Jesus is significant. Lazarus's return to life had no decisive effect on other people, living or dead. In fact, it had no ultimate effect on Lazarus himself. He died again. But the resurrection of Jesus means not only that death is finally behind him (Rom. 6:9-10), but also that *our* death is decisively affected by his. Not only is our future resurrection anchored in his rising from the tomb, but we have *already* been raised with him (Eph. 2:6; Col. 3:1). That is why Luther could speak of the resurrection and ascension of Christ "as if all the graves were already empty."

Luther went on to say that we should think of our own resurrection as if it has already taken place and waits only to be revealed.[20] He was acutely aware how difficult it is to put these realities into words. He acknowledged that old systems of thought are unequal to the task and asserted that we actually need a "new grammar" to express what it means to have been crucified, risen, and ascended with Christ. The rest of this study must be seen as a wrestling with this new grammar resulting in the three modes in which Christ has accomplished God's purpose: *for, in,* and *with* us and the world. Indeed, it is within such a structuring of eschatology that we shall attempt to come to terms with the truth that Luther spoke of: there is unity between the cross and final judgment.

If Jesus Christ is the last, then the end has already been reached in him; the end is even now being reached by him; and the end will yet be reached through him.[21] This is because he came, is with us now through the Holy Spirit, and is yet to come. This is the foundation of eschatology, as we see it, and perhaps this is a good place to outline how this approach will guide us in the rest of this book.

Since Christ himself is the last and the New Testament describes

---

20. According to J. T. Bakker, *Eschatologische Prediking bij Luther* (1964), 36, 51, Luther also draws attention to the contrast between Lazarus and Christ.

21. Something of this triple significance is also evident in G. Kittel's description of *eschatos* in *TDNT* II, 697: "The end began with the *coming of Jesus,* (Hb. 1:2; 1 Pt. 1:20). . . . But the early Christian writings also see their own *present* as the last time . . . [Acts 2:17; 2 Tim. 3:1; Jas. 5:3; 2 Pet. 3:3; Jude 18; 1 John 2:18]. At the same time there is also expectation of the *coming* last day. . ." (emphasis from the German original). The only point at which I differ from Kittel is that, with the birth of Jesus, the end has not only begun but has also been reached.

his whole history in eschatological terms, that history *is* eschatology and by it he accomplishes the purpose of creation. This means that there is no eschatology in the Old Testament: Jesus is the last and he was only born after the Old Testament period. In spite of the exceptional values it embodies, the Old Testament is on the whole a miscarried history in which the covenant failed. Jesus came for the very purpose of restoring the covenant.[22]

In order to build an understanding of the goal-directed, eschatological facets of Christ's work, we shall divide it on the basis of his three comings: his incarnation and earthly ministry, his coming in the Holy Spirit, and his return. While he is himself the purpose of God's creation, he accomplishes this purpose in a particular way in each coming:

Jesus *for* us: Jesus achieves the *eschaton* (God's purpose) *for* us chiefly by his first coming, particularly through his crucifixion and resurrection.

---

22. It is possible to view the Old Testament history as eschatological, in the very restricted sense in which Israel (the "remnant") did reach God's goal. Thus Abraham was justified through faith (Gen. 15:6), Moses was called the friend of God, and David was a man after God's heart. Something of God's goal for creation ("I shall be your God and you shall be my people") was indeed realized in them. But from the New Testament we know that this was in a proleptic and anticipatory manner before Christ, since apart from Christ no one is justified (Rom. 3:10). "For all alike have sinned and are deprived of the divine splendor, and all are justified by God's free grace alone" (Rom. 3:23-24). "For sins can never be removed by the blood of bulls and goats" (Heb. 10:4).

The phrase "I am the way" holds true for Old Testament believers (John 14:6), as does "no other name" (Acts 4:12). Therefore the faithful of the Old Testament lived to such an extent in hope of the future that Barth says, "Remarkably enough therefore, but also instructively, it was primarily the Old Testament background to the New Testament message which gave to the first Christian consciousness of time its forward direction and eschatological orientation, and to Christian life the form of a 'looking for and hasting unto the coming of the day of God' (2 Pet. 3:12)" (*Church Dogmatics* III/2, 497). "In the person of [God's] Son there has taken place the event towards which the history of the old covenant was only moving, which it only indicated from afar—the rendering of obedience. . ." (IV/1, 282).

This characteristic direction toward the future, greatly illuminated by contemporary Old Testament study, is so decisive for Old Testament history that in no respect can we speak of final eschatological reality before he upon whom it was focused had come. We can therefore speak of no more than a miscarried eschatology in the Old Testament and must view the exceptions as anticipations of the *eschaton* realized by Jesus. O. Weber's insights (*Foundations of Dogmatics* [1981, 1983] I, 292ff.) are particularly important.

Jesus *in* us: Jesus achieves the *eschaton in* us through the words and deeds of his earthly ministry, but primarily through his work through the Holy Spirit.

Jesus *with* us: Jesus achieves the *eschaton with* us at the second coming.

First, it is particularly in his earthly ministry, crucifixion, and resurrection that Jesus accomplishes God's purpose *for* us by being God's faithful covenant partner in our stead and as our representative. He ends our enmity with God, reconciles us with God, and brings peace between God and us. This he does without our aid—against our will, even, since he does it while we are yet enemies of God.

So we are not actively involved in this first mode of eschatology. But this does not mean that the accomplishment of God's purpose *for* us is imaginary rather than real. Nor does it mean that the end is not truly achieved. Because Jesus is the last and the end, the *eschaton* and *telos* are fully achieved by these acts of his on our behalf. He does not merely create a possibility for us to accomplish later on. The goal is actually reached by Christ for us—though still without us, of course. The enmity is really destroyed, peace is really established, and we are really reconciled with God. So the goal has been reached; Jesus is both God-with-us—Immanuel—and we-with-God—*the* human being as God's faithful covenant partner, not for himself, but for us. Yet the way in which this has taken place—without and in spite of us—requires that a further mode of action incorporate us actively.

Second, it is particularly by his presence and work through the Holy Spirit that Jesus accomplishes God's purpose *in* us, bringing us to faith in him, enabling us thereby to accept and experience the end of our enmity with God, and making us God's loyal covenant partners. In this second mode of eschatology, God's purpose is no longer achieved without us. Although the first mode, in which Christ realized God's purpose *for* us, is in no way deficient, of less value, or representative merely of a possibility, the second excels the first in that not only Christ in our place but now we ourselves become God's covenant partners.

Although we hold that the world was created with Jesus in view, we add with equal emphasis that he was not the only one in view. God had us in mind too when he created the earth. So the fulfillment of the covenant requires something rather more than that our representative should make peace with God for us but without us. It calls for the involvement of all of God's new humanity as his faithful covenant partners.

But precisely because we are actively involved in this second mode, the covenant is in this case not fully realized; those whom the Holy Spirit brings to faith in Christ do not achieve a complete break with their destructive hostility or consecrate their lives to God in total loyalty and trust. They live an amalgam of faith and doubt, trust and distrust, covenant-keeping and covenant-breaking. While God's purpose for us (in the first mode) is *fully* achieved on the cross and in the resurrection of Christ because it was done without us, in this second mode it is not fully realized *in* us because we are involved—and we do not cooperate fully.

Third, with us. Jesus will accomplish God's purpose *with* us at his second coming by eliminating the provisionality and incompleteness of the first two modes. The provisionality implicit in the first mode when he acted as our representative, and so reached the *eschaton* without us, is overcome by achieving God's purpose *with* us. The incompleteness of the second due to our active but defective participation is brought to perfection in the third: on one hand the goal is really reached *with* us, and on the other our hesitant faith and disobedience are excluded. In other words, Christ realizes God's purpose *with* us but not *through* us (i.e., through our responsibility).

Since, in order to achieve his covenant purpose, God created not only humanity but also an entire creation, there is a cosmic dimension to eschatology. Thus Jesus accomplishes God's purpose for us *and* for the world (the whole created order), in us *and* in the world, and with us *and* with the world. God brings about the goal of creation, which is that we should live on earth in fellowship with him, and he does this despite our sins and covenant breaking, by causing us to live as new beings on the new earth in his fellowship.

This does not mean that the end will be no more than a restoration of the original condition. There is an element of truth in that view; in the *eschaton* God does restore the covenant which was his original purpose in creation. But the accomplished goal is much more than the original. The resurrection body is a glorified body, and comparison of Adam with Christ (as we have seen) makes it clear that Christ is far superior to and more glorious than Adam. Just so, the new earth is much more than the garden of Eden. This is why Revelation 21 and 22 not only echo Genesis 2 but also use images far exceeding those of Genesis 2. One example is the tree of life, which on the new earth will bear fruit twelve times a year.

This account of the structure of eschatology might leave the reader dissatisfied, since it is presented without much substantiation. But its purpose has been to outline the whole picture before considering its details. This has necessitated touching on the chapters which lie ahead, in which the full substantiation of the three-part structure we have described will be found.

THE FOUNDATION OF ESCHATOLOGY

It is clear that there is an intimate bond between eschatology and Christ himself. He is the goal toward which everything moves, and the New Testament describes the whole of his history in "end" terms. He himself is called the last and the end. Therefore he is the obvious foundation for the entire doctrine of the end.

The important question now, however, is whether such a move in regard to eschatology is supported by theological reflection. It is one thing to show that certain statements in Scripture express a close link between Jesus and creation (e.g., Col. 1:16) and another to establish that these texts present Jesus as creation's goal in a comprehensive theological sense and, therefore, that it is right to say that creation's goal is realized in and through him.

To show that this is indeed the case, we shall investigate three relationships of Jesus Christ: to God the Father, to creation, and to the covenant. By investigating them we shall gain a broad theological perspective about the sense in which Jesus is the goal of creation and thus the foundation of eschatology.

Jesus and the Father

Why should the relationship of Jesus to his Father come up for discussion? Because there are also scriptural statements which present God (the Father) as the goal of creation. Indeed, it is remarkable that some of the important pronouncements about Jesus' relationship to creation are repeated verbatim in regard to the Father's relationship to creation. Thus beside Col. 1:16—"all things were created for . . . him [Christ]"—we can place Rom. 11:36—"from him and through him and to him [the Father] are all things." Other texts show similar seeming duplications. In 1 Cor. 8:6 Paul asserts that "there is one God, from whom all being comes, toward whom we move, and there is one Lord, Jesus Christ, through whom all things came to be." Then there is Rev. 21:6, which calls the Father "the Alpha and Omega, the Beginning and the End" (cf. Isa. 41:4; 44:6), designations elsewhere applied to Christ (Rev. 22:13) and very important in his relationship to creation.

The problem is therefore that specific terms used for Christ's relationship to creation are also applied to the Father's relationship to creation. What are their respective relationships to creation? To answer this question, it is necessary to examine briefly the relationship between *them*.

In my book *Here am I* (1982), I adopted the position that it is a mistake to attempt a doctrine of God from christology. Jesus is in the first instance the *mediator* between God and man. This means that he is both less and more than God. He is "less" in that he humbled himself by becoming a man and taking the form of a servant (Phil. 2:6-7). That means, indeed, that the Father is greater than he (John 14:28). Christ is "less" than the Father precisely because he is quantitatively "more" than the Father—i.e., because he is both God and man, while the Father is God only.

It is correct in principle to assert that in meeting Jesus we meet God. He is the revelation of God. He discloses to us what goes on in the heart of God concerning us. Yet we are not justified in attempting a doctrine of God by simplistic consultation of the biblical data on Jesus. Jesus humbled himself by becoming human. Those who attempt to work out a doctrine of God from christology forget the complexity of our problems with the relationship between Father and Son.

It nevertheless remains true that Jesus is the revelation of God. He must play a profound role in any doctrine of God. His disposition toward human beings and all creation teaches us what God's disposition is, and for the present we will confine our attention to this facet of their relationship.

The ontological element in the Church's confession that Jesus is truly God belongs properly to studies of christology. But that confession means at least that he is God's revelation, so that through his life, words, and deeds, we learn to know God. This has no more than a formal value if we do not go deeper into the history of Jesus, into his life and ministry. Only so can we learn to know God through him.

The question is: Who *is* the God who has made himself known in Jesus? The answer: Immanuel, God-*with*-us. This is the unmistakable direction of God's love in the activity of Jesus. Were his concern for the world and humanity subtracted from his history, nothing worthwhile would remain of the biblical Jesus. Were his words and deeds *for* humanity omitted, the biblical Jesus would disappear completely.[23] Jesus cannot be imagined apart from his existence and activity for the world and humanity. His healings, his miracles,)[24] his teachings, and his parables are all nothing else than an exegesis of Immanuel, God-with-us. From the fact that Jesus came to give his life for us, we learn that God does not love only those who love him or do good to only those who do him good. He is the one who does not impute to the world its own sin (2 Cor. 5:19-20) but himself pays its price (1 Cor. 6:20; 7:23; 1 Pet. 1:18-19) and, doing so, himself bears the burden of his own wrath against sin—our sin, under which we would have sunk for all eternity.

God is the One who in Jesus surrenders his life that we might live (John 10:11ff.) and moreover, who devotes himself to our health, safety, and happiness (as shown by the healing, feeding, and nature miracles). In the widest sense of the word, we learn to know in Jesus a God who is *for* us, who does not wish any to perish, but that all will come to repentance (Ezek. 33:11; 2 Pet. 3:9). He is the God who is good to all and whose compassion extends to *all* his works (Ps. 145:9). His wrath endures only for a moment, but his mercy is eternal (Isa. 54:7ff.; Ps. 30:6).

Even Jesus' sermons of woe and judgment are intended to save people. This does not mean that his wrath is less than real or that his warnings about hell are not to be taken seriously (Mark 3:5; 9:42ff.; Matt. 23; Luke 16:19ff.; John 5:28-29). But it does mean that he preaches thus in order to rescue people, to warn them, and to call them to repentance. Even when at his most emphatic in preaching judgment, he is still with us, still on our side, and still the Savior of the world. His wrath and judgment are in fact expressions of his love and mercy.

Thus Mark 9:42ff. really does call us to enter life maimed rather

23. This does not mean that God is subsumed in the history of Jesus, as if he did not also exist outside that history. Neither does it mean that Jesus is his own history and merely wants to happen again and again. Jesus is not his history; he makes his history. He is Lord of all history, including his own. This proposition merely emphasizes that God, in freedom, so bound himself to this history of Jesus that he could not just as well have made another history with different content. Who he is and will be we know *finally* in Jesus.

24. Here we must briefly refer to James Kallas, *The Significance of the Synoptic Miracles* (1961), a work which receives too little attention. He shows in a noteworthy manner how the miracles of Jesus are essential to the coming of God's kingdom, especially the exorcism of demons who have ruled the earth and made of it a chaos. We shall go into this viewpoint in the next chapter, when we discuss the kingdom of God more fully.

than be cast unscathed into hell. As Grosheide notes with regard to the end of Matthew 23, though the people reject Jesus, he wishes still to show them mercy.[25] The parable of the rich man and Lazarus (Luke 16:19ff.) means to summon people to hear Moses and the prophets (vv. 29, 31) and be saved. Jesus proclaims eternal judgment (John 5:28-29) in order to call people to embrace eternal life and so escape judgment (vv. 24-25).

In light of all this, it is not strange that there should be a correspondence between Jesus' relationship to creation and his Father's relationship to creation. Jesus reveals his Father and discloses what goes on in his Father's heart. Consequently there is an agreement between Jesus and his Father which includes their attitude toward creation. Both are positive toward creation; both care about it. Since God is the Creator and Christ also is Creator, creation itself is destined for a positive relationship with both of them. For this reason it can be said of both that all things are "for him" and that he (Father *or* Son) is "the beginning and the end."

Does this not imply the possibility of basing eschatology on the Father? No, because Jesus is "more" than the Father. Jesus is also human—in fact *the* human being. This makes it possible for him to stand in a relationship with humanity and all creation which the Father cannot. In Jesus we have to do with two parties: God and humanity. More important, in Jesus we have to do with a definite relationship between God and humanity. In Jesus, God is with us; that is to say, in Jesus, God stands in an explicit, fixed posture of love toward us. Further, in Jesus we have the one worthy and righteous human being. As a result, it is in Jesus that humanity stands in an explicit, fixed posture of love toward God. It is here that we touch on the deepest meaning of Jesus as creation's goal. In him, God is our God. In him, humanity is God's humanity. This is the covenantal relationship, the goal of creation. And this goal is attained in and through Jesus Christ.

God and Creation

There is no consensus on the relationship between God and creation. Because eschatology speaks of the goal of creation, we will need to investigate this relationship between Creator and creation more fully.

25. F. W. Grosheide, *Het Heilig Evangelie volgens Mattheus* (Commentaar op het Nieuwe Testament; 1954), ad loc.

In his doctrine of God, Tillich asserts that God is not a distinct being but rather the ground of being (i.e., of all that is) and, indeed, Being itself. Tillich suggests that it is equally atheistic to acknowledge God's existence as it is to deny it. To acknowledge God's existence implies that he is a being alongside or over against other beings and therefore one of a series, on the same plane as creation, and therefore no longer God.[26]

In this way Tillich attempts to show that God is different from creation. Yet in doing so he cannot escape a certain relationship of necessity between God and creation. He regards God as neither a part of creation nor apart from creation. God is the ground of being, or Being itself. But this means that Tillich is unable to declare without ambiguity that God was free to create or not to create, because in a sense God is bound to being or created existence. Naturally God is not dependent without qualification on being; if he were, he would not be God.

So Tillich assumes a middle position. On the one hand, creation is neither necessary nor indispensable. On the other, divine life is creative. Indeed, divine life and divine creative activity are identical. In this way Tillich avoids any necessity above or outside God which "drives" him to create.[27] What is unclear is just how Tillich evades any inner necessity or compulsion which drives God to create.

If divine life is by definition and in its being creative and if divine life is identical with divine creative activity, as Tillich asserts,[28] it follows that God cannot be God if he does not create, that God is not free *not* to create. Once one has adopted this position, it is mere quibbling to posit that God did not need to create. The result is that God is bound

26. "It is as atheistic to affirm the existence of God as to deny it. God is being-itself, not *a* being." "It is as wrong to speak of God as the universal essence as it is to speak of him as existing" (P. Tillich, *Systematic Theology* (1953-1963) I, 263, 262). A. J. McKelway, *The Systematic Theology of Paul Tillich* (1964), 123, note 8, correctly points to a statement by J. H. Hick which explains that "when Tillich says that God does not exist, he means that God does not exist in the way that man exists. He is simply trying to formulate a discrimination between the necessary and unconditional being of God and the contingent being of man."

27. "Nothing is necessary for God in the sense that he is dependent on a necessity above him" (Tillich, I, 280).

28. That Tillich indeed understands God in this way is clear from the fact that he encounters God's creative activity in the past, present, and future. He deals with God's originating creativity (I, 281ff.), sustaining creativity (290ff.), and directing creativity (293ff.) and bases this threefold division on one premise: "Since the divine life is essentially creative . . ." (281).

to creation and dependent upon it, making it impossible for the biblical teaching about God and creation to receive full justice.

Barth also speaks of the necessity that God be the Creator. If one understands the Son or the Word of God to be Jesus the Christ, true God and true man, from all eternity within God's counsel and so existing before creation, one will perceive with Barth that it is "not only appropriate and worthy but necessary that God be the Creator."[29]

The resemblance between Barth's view and Tillich's is only apparent, however. Indeed, it is not just a word game to characterize Barth's proposition with the term "free necessity." It comes down to this: If (read *since*) the manger, cross, and tomb are the realization of God's eternal counsel, then to create was more than a possibility for God; it was a necessity. But this "necessity" is one to which God bound himself in his free counsel, not one which resulted from the identification of his life with creative activity (as with Tillich). Thus Barth is able repeatedly to emphasize that creation is God's *free* act—a concept missing in Tillich.[30]

In the light of all this, it is clear why Tillich acknowledges no other specific purpose in creation than creation itself. He rejects both Calvin's view of the purpose of creation (God's glory) and Luther's (a communion in love between God and his creatures). In fact he prefers not to speak of any purpose at all, regarding "purpose" as a misleading term since creation has no purpose beyond itself. The Lutheran view of the goal of creation—a communion in love between God and his creatures—implies that God is in reality independent of creation, which Tillich rejects. In any case, real communion requires at least two parties who are not identical and who thus, in a sense, confront each other. In fact, any goal of creation requires such independence and distinctness between God and creation—and this, according to Tillich, cannot be.[31]

In truth, for creation to have any goal at all requires God to be the free Lord over it, not the necessary ground under it. We need to contend against Tillich's position that God was free to create or not to create, and therefore that the act of creation flows neither from some inner law (e.g., that divine life is creative activity) nor from some inner need for community. God was compelled to create by nothing other than his own free decision. As the one who freely loves, his act of creat-

29. Barth, *Church Dogmatics* III/1, 51.
30. *Ibid.,* 15, 95.
31. Tillich, I, 293.

ing is the overflowing of his love. Though his love is complete within himself (John 5:20), he freely decided to make a reality distinct from himself and allow it to participate in his joy and splendor. He created a being distinct from himself because he wished to be its God and to exist *for* it.[32]

Because this God who freely loves is he who made the world, Barth arrives at the conclusion that creation is grace.[33] Creation is neither a neutral basis for varying possibilities nor—much less—an imperfect, unworthy, meaningless start. We arrive at such a false conclusion if we begin with the created order and make our deductions from that beginning. Perception of the dark side of creation makes it impossible to say that creation is grace. But just as we cannot deduce from analysis of our own being that we are created and so must turn in faith to the Creator, so we must believe on the witness of Scripture that he is the One who loves in freedom and that his deed of creation is an act of grace.[34]

It may sound strange to say that creation is grace. Grace is normally associated with the forgiveness of sin, with reconciliation, and with our adoption by Christ as children of God. Of course this is all correct. Yet grace cannot be confined to those facets of the Bible's message. If grace is God's free favor to his creatures, then creation is grace. We could never merit being made by God; it was not necessary that he make us. He did not need us. So in making us, he bestows an incomparable favor on us: the opportunity to be his creatures, for whom he takes responsibility and for whom he cares. He makes it possible for us to enjoy his favor, love, and happiness by giving us the opportunity of living in his communion in love. Above all, he enables us to praise and adore him and give him glory. All this is conferred by a greater upon a lesser, by God upon us. It is nothing less than grace.

32. It is worthwhile to summarize a few of Barth's thoughts (III/1, 95). He says that in creation God freely willed and made a reality other than himself. The pressing question is what it was that God had in mind to accomplish by this deed. The answer is that he did not wish to be alone in his glory; he wanted another beside him. This can mean neither that it was unnecessary for God to create nor that he wished to satisfy a need in the sense of being lonely and unable to endure his loneliness. It can only mean that this work of God, otherwise incomprehensible to us, must be understood as a work of his love. He wishes, as Creator, to exist for his creation.

33. III/1, 95-97. G. von Rad, *Old Testament Theology* (1962, 1965) II, calls creation "a saving act of God."

34. Weber, I, 480-481.

We may call it creation grace in contrast with redemption grace, a distinction made by Barth.[35] Creation grace might be thought less marvelous than redemption grace, because it is not bestowed on a sinner who broke the covenant and rejected community with God but rather on a creature made in God's image. But it is grace nonetheless— God's sheer goodness in creating us to be his creatures and covenant partners.

This distinction is not to be equated simply with the Reformed distinction between common and special grace, nor should it be seen as a watertight division between two *different* things. Grace is grace, always God's favor toward human beings. What differs is the object (creature or sinner), and our amazement grows that God not only creates but also reconciles. Yet creation itself is grace, God's favor.

The Covenant as Creation's Goal

It may not be obvious at first that, since God's creative activity was a work of grace, the covenant was his goal in creating. Before we reach such a conclusion, we must answer two questions. First, could creation's goal be something other than the covenant? Second, could there not be different covenants and, if so, which would be the goal of creation?

Luther and Calvin are usually contrasted in the following way: the former is said to stress our salvation, the latter God's glory. But it has been pointed out in recent years that this dichotomy is false; our salvation does not compete with God's glory. A similar opposition has been posited in regard to their statements about creation's goal. But the glory of God (Calvin's view) does not preclude a community of love (Luther's view). For if we regard the covenant as creation's goal (which we shall do) and if the covenant is a covenant of grace ("I will be your God and you will be my people"), then covenant and community of love are one and the same.

The second question is whether or not it is the covenant of *grace* which is the goal of creation. There are many covenants in the Bible; what right have we to single out the covenant of grace?

In an earlier book I dealt at length with the covenant.[36] Here I shall use "covenant" as a theological rather than a historical term. From

35. IV/1, 8-9.
36. A. König, *New and Greater Things* (1988), chapter 4.

a historical viewpoint, there are many questions about the when, how, and what of covenant thinking in Israel's life. There are differing covenant traditions within the Old Testament itself (e.g., Abrahamic, Davidic, etc.). There is even some debate over whether or not "covenant" is an appropriate translation of Hebrew $b^e r\hat{\imath}t$.[37] But these are all problems for historians.

Theologically, I define "covenant" as a gracious relationship of love between God and humanity, a relationship in which God takes the initiative by creating the world to be the place where it can be realized, then creating human beings to live in it. He binds us to himself, giving us the right and responsibility to live in his love and to serve and glorify him in gratitude. Sin gives this covenant another dimension—that of salvation. God's created covenant partner is now also a sinner and, through God's redeeming work, is saved. But all this remains a part of the covenant of grace for which God created humanity.

The New Testament calls this covenant by two names: the new covenant and the covenant with Abraham. Whenever it is called the new covenant (e.g., Jer. 31:31; Heb. 8:8-9; Luke 22:20; 1 Cor. 11:25; 2 Cor. 3:5-18; Gal. 4:21-28) it is contrasted with the old covenant (the Law), which, as Judaism had come to interpret it, offered salvation through works.[38] And whenever it is called the covenant with Abraham (Rom. 4; Gal. 3) it corresponds to the covenant with Abraham in the Old Testament, which is seen as one of grace and in which God receives a person through faith. It can therefore also be called the covenant of faith. As for its contents, it goes back to Genesis 2, where the relationship between God and Adam is that of a loving, caring Father providing for his child, who should serve and honor him with gratitude in return. Genesis 3 comes as a shock because of the unexpected and unexplainable reaction of the recipient of grace against the gracious Father.

The covenant of grace plays a role from Genesis 2 onward, figuring prominently in all the major Bible traditions, until it is realized fully in a world made new (Rev. 21:1-8). Because of that, one is

37. See G. Hasel, *Old Testament Theology: Basic Issues in the Current Debate* (1982³), 118 for references.

38. In Gal. 4:21-28 Paul sets the Sinai covenant in a negative context. Hagar, Abraham's wife who bore Ishmael, is taken as an image of "the flesh" and of unbelief, representing the Sinai covenant. Her counterpart is Sarah, who bore the child of promise, the image of the Abrahamic covenant in which the congregation now lives. So again the old covenant is related to the Sinaitic law, not to the Abrahamic covenant.

justified in seeing the covenant as one way in which creation's goal can be defined. That through the ages different facets of this covenant are stressed (in the covenants with Abraham and with David, in the covenants of creation and of salvation) does not alter its central purpose: God's gracious communion with and care for humanity.

Christ and the Covenant

What is the relationship between Christ and this covenant? Our study of Scripture has shown that he is the last, the final goal, the point toward which all creation is directed and moves. Can Jesus and the covenant both be the goal of creation? It is possible for this to be so only if a specific relationship exists between him and the covenant—if he is, in some sense, the covenant itself. Is that the case?

At the end of our section on Jesus and the Father we mentioned that it is the covenant which takes form in Jesus. He is God, our God, God-with-us. "I shall be your God" is fulfilled in him. He is also The Human Being, God's covenant partner. "You shall be my people" is also fulfilled in him. We must now elaborate theologically on this perspective.

"I shall be your God" is the first part of the covenant—God's part, God's responsibility. What we hear and see throughout the Old Testament is confirmed in Jesus. In the covenant relationship, God is truly *for* us: he is neither antagonistic nor neutral toward his creation. In John 3:16 we read, "God loved the world so much . . . ," and in John the "world" is sinful humanity. God's love for the world is finally and fully revealed in Jesus. That is how God is, since Jesus is God's revelation, and that is how Jesus is. Jesus is *for* humanity.

His entire history on earth was a revelation of his involvement in our needs, we who had no just claim upon his care. This is the only history of Jesus; he had no other history except this history of love. In him we can learn to know God only as *our* God: "I shall be your God". He is *for* us, for *all* human beings. He is the Savior of the world (John 4:14, 42), the atonement for the sins of the whole world (1 John 2:2), the "Lord of all" (Acts 10:36; Rom. 10:12). As the goal of Israel's history, he is himself both the fulfiller and the fulfillment of God's covenant with Israel—and also the revelation that God's covenant with Israel was intended for and directed toward all people.

Every one of God's works (creation, providence, reconciliation, etc.) flows from his love for us (Tit. 3:4) and is directed toward the establishment, maintenance, and execution of his covenant with us. Because God is the covenant God whom we know in Jesus, reconciliation is his answer to our breaking of his covenant. Reconciliation is more than a reaction to faithlessness; it is the pursuit of God's original act, through which he intends to realize his goal, the covenant.[39]

"And you will be my people" is the covenant's second part, our part. The covenant puts humans under no obligation beyond gratitude—or short of it. Nothing further is required; in Jesus, God has done everything. It is through Jesus that the world has been reconciled with God, who no longer holds our misdeeds against us (2 Cor. 5:18-19). But nothing less is required, since God wills to be God-with-us and has from eternity renounced neutrality and created that he might be gracious. Our eternal destiny is to be none other than God's covenant partners, who must also, for our part, abandon neutrality and, as his children, depend on him.[40] The call to obey God's commandments is so urgent throughout the Bible because it is a call to gratitude, and it is really unthinkable that gratitude should not be the result of grace.[41] Though a person may have freedom of choice in the presence of idols, choosing whether to obey or not, we have no choice when God commands us. Obedience is the only possible response.[42]

39. Barth, IV/1, 34-39.
40. In *Man: The Image of God* (1962), G. C. Berkouwer regards our relationship to God as the essence of our humanity. The Bible views our being as "the man of God" (Berkouwer's title for chapter 10), and Berkouwer remarks in this connection that "the relation of man to God dominates the whole biblical picture of man" and "The man of God—that is surely the complete opposite of an abstract and neutral view of man" (350). "The man of God is man in this relation, from which we may never abstract him. This is man as he makes his way through the world, not enclosed in himself, not independent and autonomous, but as a man of God.

"This point of view is so central and dominant for the Word of God that it never gives us a neutral independent analysis of man in order to inform us as to the components and structure of humanness in itself" (196).
41. Barth, IV/1, 42.
42. Barth summarizes it, "By deciding for us, God has decided concerning us. We are therefore prevented from thinking otherwise about ourselves, from seeing or understanding or explaining man in any other way, than as the being engaged and covenanted to God, and therefore simply but strictly engaged and covenanted to thanks. Just as there is no God but the God of the covenant, there is no man but the man of the covenant: the man who as such is destined and called to give thanks. And it is again transgression, sin, if even for a moment we ignore this man who is true man, trying to imagine and construct a man in himself, and to regard his destiny to give thanks to God as something which is in his own

This is the obligation under which God places us when he says, "and you shall be my people." This is the obligation we have not met, but which Jesus (as The Human Being; see 1 Tim. 2:5) did meet. It is he who from the beginning has obeyed God perfectly. He submits to baptism to "conform in this way with all that God requires" (Matt. 3:15). He knows that humans cannot live by bread alone, but by every word which God utters (4:4). Therefore, his food is to do the will of the Father and to finish his work (John 4:34). The Father is with him and does not abandon him because he always does that which the Father wills (8:29). That is why he can say—and only he, in all the history of the world—"It is accomplished" (19:30).

Jesus is thus the man "for" God, the man who is on God's side. He is the "party of the second part" to the covenant which says "and you shall be my people." He became a human not for himself but for us, to be our representative before God. He came to stand in for us, for the faithless partner, enabling us to stand in his place at God's right hand. On our behalf he achieves righteousness and obedience. In our name he is God's true covenant partner, the beloved on whom God's favor rests (Matt. 3:17).

So it is that in Jesus God reaches his covenant goal for creation. As Schoonenberg encapsulates it in a single sentence, "Salvation consists in the covenant between God and man, and the God-man is the covenant in person."[43] Since creation's goal is the covenant, we can affirm with Mussner: "Because Jesus is the second and last (eschatological) Adam, creation reaches its culmination in Him."[44]

In this sense Barth, too, said that creation reaches its goal in Jesus of Nazareth—a goal toward which it was directed from the first. Barth

---

power, a matter of his own freedom of choice. The real freedom of man is decided by the fact that God is his God. In freedom he can only choose to be the man of God, i.e. to be thankful to God. With any other choice he would simply be groping in the void, betraying and destroying his true humanity. Instead of choosing in freedom, he would be choosing enslavement. By revealing himself in Jesus Christ as from the very first the gracious God, God has decided that man can only be grateful man, the man who takes up and maintains his place in the covenant with him, the gracious God" (IV/1, 43-44).

It is important to note the remarkable resemblance between the anthropology of Barth and that of Berkouwer. According to both, the being of the person lies in his or her relationship to God. But Barth puts the greater emphasis on the content of this relationship as thanksgiving and gratitude.

43. Schoonenberg, III, 224, my translation.
44. J. Feiner and M. Löhrer, II, 461, my translation.

was able to affirm this because he also affirmed that since Christ is "the content and form of the first and eternal Word of God," the covenant logically stands before creation as its "basis and purpose." The covenant is that promise of God "in which He binds Himself to man, and His command by which He pledges and binds man to Himself. At the beginning of all things in God there is the Gospel and the Law," which Jesus unifies in his own person, at once and completely comprehending both. He is the meaning and ground of the covenant, for he *is* the covenant, being in himself very God and very man.[45]

O. Weber explains, "Jesus Christ is the person in whom God's covenant finds its real partner, and he is simultaneously the one in whom this covenant itself is fulfilled."[46] The content of the covenant ("I shall be your God, and you shall be my people") is Jesus Christ, for both its parts are fulfilled in and through him. To say that Jesus is the content of the covenant does not imply that he replaces either God or humanity, but that he is truly both. In fulfilling the covenant he does not make humans superfluous; rather he will achieve for us, in us, and with us the goal God has in mind for us.

Creation and Consummation

How we have developed our argument to this point might leave the impression that the consummation is to be merely a restoration of the original condition of creation. Creation and consummation have indeed been strongly linked in theological thought for centuries, but there has been considerable dispute over their relationship.

Lutherans have regarded the consummaton as the restoration of creation, i.e., of the original condition in which man was created. They have pointed out that Adam was made in God's image—the highest level to which humans could attain. Therefore, the consummation could be nothing higher than that: the restoration of human beings in God's image—as is confirmed in the New Testament, especially by Paul.

Against this, Bavinck advanced the traditional Reformed view that, had Adam not yielded to temptation, he would have attained greater perfection. When created, he possessed freedom in only the formal sense. His freedom from sin consisted only of his capability of not sinning. Had he defeated temptation he would have become more

45. Barth, IV/1, 53.
46. Weber, I, 299.

perfect—he would have become incapable of sinning—which would have been a decisive step forward![47]

The Reformed view is preferable in that it allows for the entire historical development which, though it began at creation, certainly was not completed then. Creation was a *good beginning*. Both words must be stressed, but let us first examine the significance of "beginning."

Creation was only a starting point, not a final point. The Lutheran view is incorrect if it regards creation as an end point and Adam as complete, mature, and glorified. Earth was made as a place where covenant history could begin. In that history was to be the opportunity for God and man to live in covenant relationship and share each other's happiness. It stands beyond doubt that in the course of this history, humankind could become much more than it already was. Humankind could learn to know God and understand his will, enter more deeply into God's happiness and peace, and enjoy it all more fully. In this way, consummation must be seen as a great "plus factor" in creation.

But "good" is just as important. Creation is a *good* beginning. Bavinck accepts too readily the traditional distinction which says that it was possible for Adam before the Fall not to sin but not yet impossible for him to sin. This distinction makes it too easy to fit sin into a scheme and thus lose sight of its monstrous, shocking, and incomprehensible character. It is seriously misguided to expound Genesis 3 (as has become fashionable in some circles) in such a way that the serpent becomes a crafty master of psychological trickery. By so explaining the deception of Eve, the shocking unexpectedness of what happened is unconsciously toned down. But there was nothing sly or covert in the serpent's strategy. He set himself openly and insolently against God, made God out to be a liar, and left no doubt of his intentions. The attentive reader would naturally expect Eve to chase the snake away contemptuously.

That the opposite happened comes as a shock. There is no explanation for it. Eve had not the slightest reason to yield, least of all in the sense of having a formal freedom to choose between sin and obedience. The subsequent conversation with God makes it clear what he thinks of any "explanation" of Adam and Eve's sin. He ignores the excuses and punishes the sin. Sin can be sin (and deserve punishment) only when it is inexplicable, guilty transgression, which has but one "rea-

---

47. H. Bavinck, *Gereformeerde Dogmatiek* 1918[3]) II, 534ff. "Capable of not sinning," represents *posse non peccare*, "incapable of sinning," *non posse peccare*.

son"—not formal freedom, but the human being itself—we ourselves. Berkouwer is thus entirely right when he refuses to discuss the "origin" of sin and refers only to its *beginning:* an inexplicable and hence deeply guilty deed of the human being itself, a deed that went against everything expected from the goodness of God's creation (Gen. 2).

In this light Barth's strange expression has much to recommend it: sin is the "impossible possibility." It does far more justice to biblical data than does the philosophical distinction between formal freedom (the condition of the original human being) and material freedom (the condition of being unable to sin, attained only with the reaching of a higher degree of perfection). This shocking, unexpected character of sin arises from the fact that God made humans good—in his own image!

The scriptural proof usually given for the view that the consummation is to be nothing more than the restoration of the original condition needs to be understood in this light. Because creation had a good beginning, the prophets were able to reach back to the imagery of the creation stories for images to speak of the consummation. Many of the consummation images are reminiscent of Eden. For example, "To him who is victorious I will give the right to eat from the tree of life [cf. Gen. 2:9] that stands in the Garden of God" (Rev. 2:7). As this is a promise of the consummation, it is not surprising that Rev. 22:2 says that the tree will grow on the new earth and bear fruit. The meaning given this tree by Barth (a sign of God's presence and being, protecting humankind from death) reinforces our contention that creation was originally so good as to warrant use of its imagery to express the glory of the new creation.

"The river of the water of life, sparkling like crystal, flowing from the throne of God and the Lamb" (Rev. 22:1) is another such use of Eden imagery (cf. Gen. 2:10). In Ezek. 47:1 this stream is mentioned in connection with the temple, and this is worthy of special note since Barth has pointed out the connection between the temple and the tree of life.[48]

The most striking example of repetition is that of the covenant itself. Though the concept of covenant is not mentioned in the creation story, it is certainly found in Genesis 2—both the caring God ("I shall be your God") and obedient and grateful humanity ("you shall be my people"). It is no coincidence that the new earth is depicted in these very terms (Rev. 21:4). The Bible begins and ends with the same covenant of grace: this is one true insight to be gained from the idea that the consummation is a restoration of the original creation.

48. Barth, 281-283.

On the other hand it should be emphasized that consummation is to be far more than creation. Creation was the beginning, the necessary stage on which God could begin history with his creatures—with humankind in particular. History is a winding road along which occur genuinely new and unexpected events. Though the goal of God's work was known from the outset in the covenant, human response has been for the most part unexpected, incomprehensible, inexplicable, sinful, and guilty. The onward progress of this history has revealed more and more facets of God's character, sharply contrasting the brightness of his glory against the dark backdrop of humankind's faithlessness and sin. Thus is God's splendor more fully displayed than it could ever have been by life in the garden. And this superlative grace of God, growing richer as sin increased, produced at length the resurrection, the glorification, and the new world—far more than we could think or expect. So we read in Revelation 21 and 22 not merely of a restoration but of a new creation which far surpasses the old.

In Gen. 3:8ff., God *visits* Adam; in Rev. 21:3 (cf. TEV), he *makes his home* with humankind on the new earth. In Genesis 2 God builds a lovely *garden* in which for Adam to live and work; for the new humanity he builds a new *city* on a new *earth*. (In biblical terms, a city is immeasurably more than a garden; think of the safe, ordered convenience which city living meant in Bible times—in contrast with the savage, unprotected life of the open country.) In Genesis 2 we read of the tree of life; in Rev. 22:2 this tree becomes an orchard of "trees of life" (NAB), which bear not once but twelve times a year. And whereas humankind has always been absolutely dependent on the sun (Gen. 1:14ff.), even that will become unnecessary when the glory of God shines on us and the Lamb becomes our lamp (Rev. 21:23).

Naturally these images cannot be taken literally, lest the real glory to which they refer escape us. Taken literally, for example, the new Jerusalem itself could nowadays be built in large part by a developer, and by grafting, a pear tree can be made to bear fruit twelve times a year. But the meanings of these rich images must be interpreted in their context; when Revelation was written, they were unimaginably sumptuous. And their purpose was somehow to depict the marvels of promised glory—infinitely greater than the first creation's.

The most profound link between creation and consummation lies in Jesus Christ himself, who is the beginning and the end, the first and the last, the Creator and the Consummator. In his own person he unites creation and consummation. In him they are not two events infinitely separated from each other in time, but a single reality bound together in him, the living Lord by whose power creation proceeds to consummation and consummation comes forth from creation. All is created by him, and by him all is renewed.

And the Kingdom of God?

It is legitimate to ask why this book is theologically structured on a covenant framework rather than a kingdom framework. For the kingdom of God is certainly a central theme of Jesus—and of his apostles, for whom the confession "Jesus is Lord" conveyed the same content. And it is also true that the kingdom occupies a central position in the Old Testament, where it is signified by the declaration "Yahweh is king" and by the message that the power of other gods cannot be compared with his.

Indeed, the concept of the kingdom *could* assume the place occupied in this study by the covenant. It lends itself to an extremely wide perspective on creation and society. One could say that the two concepts are the sides of a single coin. Just as we can show that Jesus is the covenant in very person and that he fulfills it, we can show that he is the kingdom in very person and that he fulfills it too. The early Church confessed that he is himself the kingdom of God *(autobasileia);* it could not be otherwise, for in him the kingdom of God had come (Matt. 12:28). So he could say as he stood among the Pharisees: "The kingdom of God is among you" (Luke 17:21 NEB).

The concept of covenant is nevertheless to be preferred over the concept of kingdom for our purposes. Covenant is the broader concept in that it necessarily involves both God and humanity. Whereas the concept of kingdom tends to become impersonal, that of covenant necessarily involves two parties: God, the ruler and provider, and the human person, the obedient worshiper.

Some might object that for this reason the covenant is too intrinsically personal for the purpose at hand, that cosmic elements could be more easily included in the framework of the kingdom. I for one believe that this is not so, but if it were, one would have to include this broader aspect of the kingdom concept throughout, because one of this book's aims is to do justice to the cosmic elements which traditional eschatology neglects. The resurrection of the body and the new earth are parts of the eschatological message often hidden behind the more personal elements of eternal bliss and communion with God. But that is one-sided. Both personal and cosmic elements must be included in any biblical eschatology.

Chapter 3

CHRIST REALIZES THE GOAL FOR US

THE STRUCTURE OF ESCHATOLOGY

The first two chapters have examined Jesus Christ as the *foundation* of eschatology. The next three will deal with him as the *structure* of eschatology, reaching the goal of God for us, in us, and with us. In the first two chapters, everything revolved around the one upon whom this building stands, Jesus Christ; in the next three, it is the form of the building which we will consider, i.e., how eschatology is constructed and whether or not its various parts correspond to the foundation which has been laid. Since Christ himself is the foundation, it is obvious that the form must be determined by who he is and what he does.

We have seen that the three ways in which Christ accomplishes God's purpose, for, in, and with us, coincides more or less with the three phases of Jesus' history. What he does *for* us, he does chiefly during his first coming in his crucifixion and resurrection. What he does *in* us, he does chiefly in his work through the Holy Spirit in the interim between the ascension and second advent. What he does *with* us, he does chiefly at his return.

These are not watertight divisions. During his earthly ministry, Jesus not only fulfilled the *eschaton*[1] for us, he also did things in the lives of people. He healed them, drove out evil spirits, and forgave sins. Neither is his work during the interim restricted to what he does in us. For example, during this time he also appears on our behalf (for us) before God. Nevertheless, we shall see that it forms a useful construct to link together the three comings of Christ to the three ways in which he fulfills the *eschaton*.

1. Two forms of the same Greek adjective are used, one for Jesus himself to indicate his significance as the last (*eschatos,* as in "the first and the *last*"), and one for the goal of creation attained by Christ and the covenant he fulfills *(eschaton).* The word *eschato*logy is derived from this word and is traditionally related to the plural *eschata,* "last things."

One could draw up a very long list of *what* Christ does in these three comings. He dies for our sins, overcomes the forces which menace our lives, saves us, gives us new life, restores the relationships between God and us and between human beings, makes us children and heirs of God, and ultimately comes to raise us and give us eternal glory. The question now is whether it is possible meaningfully to relate all the things Christ does to the end, to God's creation goal, to the covenant? Could we say, for example, that in the things he does *for* us, he reaches the end, fulfills the *eschaton,* and attains God's creation goal? Could we also say that of all the things he does *in* us and *with* us?

When we analyze the things Christ has done, we do find that in differing ways they all fit together in the fulfillment of the covenant. A few examples will illustrate this point. Christ reconciles us and gives us peace with God particularly through his crucifixion (Rom. 5:6-10; 2 Cor. 5:14-21; Eph. 2:11-22). And in so doing it is indeed the covenant that he restores for us, since the covenant is the relationship of love and friendship between God and us—that in which God cares for us and we obey him as friends and covenant partners. Through reconciliation Christ terminates our hostility, makes us God's friends by removing the separation (sin) between God and us, and so restores the covenant. Thus he achieves God's purpose and fulfills the covenant *for* us through his crucifixion.

Christ attains the same goal through what he does in us. By coming to dwell in us and allowing us to dwell in him, he gives us new life (Eph. 4:20ff.). This new life includes our living in community with God, serving him obediently, and combating sin. And this is nothing less than another way of fulfilling the covenant, since the covenant is just that—community between God and us, in which we are God's true covenant partners, his own people who serve, love, obey, and glorify him. So also in the interim, through his work *in* us, Christ fulfills God's purpose or *eschaton.*

Similarly, Christ will fulfill the covenant in yet another way through his return. He will make the earth new, raise us, glorify us, and come with his Father to make his home with us. When that happens, God will truly be with us as our God and we with him as his people— which is the fulfillment of the covenant (Rev. 21:3). Then will his servants serve him while reigning as kings with his name written on their foreheads (22:3-5).

One can therefore say that Christ accomplishes God's purpose to fulfill the covenant in various ways. He fulfills the covenant for us by making peace for us with God, thereby restoring our broken covenant relationship with God. He fulfills the covenant in us by living in us and giving us a new life of covenant obedience. And he fulfills the covenant with us by renewing us totally and glorifying us eternally, in our covenant relationship with God on the new earth.

But another question arises: why should the goal be reached in three different ways? To answer, we could say that the three are linked, each flowing logically from the other, and yet the covenant is genuinely fulfilled in each.

The relationship between the various parts of Christ's work is an old problem. For example, consider the relationship between Jesus' crucifixion and his work in us through the Holy Spirit. Various ways of understanding this relationship have been employed. One suggests that Christ's atoning death established the *possibility* of salvation, which becomes a *reality* only when we come to faith. Another says that Christ *secured* salvation for us on the cross and now *applies* it through the Holy Spirit's work. Yet another speaks of objective salvation (the crucifixion) and subjective salvation (justification).

All these ways of understanding the relationship create their own problems. To demonstrate but one, because of Rom. 5:10; 2 Cor. 5:18-19; and Eph. 2:15-16, Christ's death on the cross cannot be limited to establishing the possibility of salvation, leaving his work through the Holy Spirit to effect its reality. These passages place a higher value on Christ's death than would be the case if they regarded it as establishing a mere possibility of salvation. According to Rom. 5:10 and 2 Cor. 5:18-19, we *are* reconciled by Christ's death—or, as TEV renders the latter, "God, whose enemies we were, *has* turned us into his friends." According to Eph. 2:16, "Christ *has* annihilated our enmity against him, and, through his death on the cross, has made peace." Verse 15 affirms that he already *has* "by his crucifixion created Jew and pagan afresh in one new humanity." Given these texts, it is impossible to regard the crucifixion as achieving the mere possibility of salvation. When enmity is done away, when peace is reached, and when we are made God's friends, then surely the covenant has been fulfilled, the covenant which consists of precisely those things: friendship, peace, and love between God and humanity.

But we must reiterate that by the cross and resurrection the covenant was fulfilled in a specific way: for us, but not yet in us. In fact, we were not yet born when the covenant was thus fulfilled. Paul had not yet been converted; he was still an active enemy of God when by his crucifixion Christ made him God's friend. This opens up interesting perspectives because, in another sense, Paul was crucified with

Christ (Gal. 2:20). But this became a reality only after the crucifixion, at the time of his conversion; at the time of the crucifixion he was still an enemy of God. That which had been done *for* him on the cross had later to be realized *in* him (Acts 9).

This means that the covenant is really fulfilled by the crucifixion of Christ, but only *for* us. It is necessary for the covenant to be fulfilled in us as well. This is the second form in which God's final goal is reached. The Holy Spirit conveys Jesus and all the riches he gained for us through his cross and resurrection into our lives. He brings peace and friendship into our lives by bringing us to personal acceptance of the peace and friendship of God, so that we actually experience that which he accomplished for us.

It is remarkable how this double realization of the *eschaton* is mentioned frequently in Paul's writings without any tension between its two facets. According to Rom. 5:10, we have already been reconciled by Christ's death but are only afterwards saved by his life. Through the cross we are truly reconciled, peace is really made, we are already God's friends—and yet this must take place in yet another way: we have still to be saved. This same duality is even more striking in 2 Cor. 5:18-20. First it is stated that God *has* reconciled the world through Christ's death; the exhortation then immediately follows "be reconciled to God." That which has already occurred must occur once again!

So it is clear that the covenant must be fulfilled in more than one way. According to Eph. 2:15-16, peace has been concluded by Christ's death. But according to v. 17, peace must thereafter be announced to those for whom it has already been established. Again, according to Col. 1:20-21, we have been reconciled by Christ's crucifixion. But v. 23 adds immediately, "only you must continue in your faith, firm on your foundations, never to be dislodged from the hope offered in the gospel which you heard."

By Christ's death upon the cross, the *eschaton* or goal is genuinely reached *for* us—but in such a way that need remains for another kind of fulfillment *in* us. What is lacking in the first (quite real) attainment of his goal through the cross is that we have not yet been actively involved in the process. This situation is repeated when, through the work of the Holy Spirit in us, Christ reaches the goal of creation in the second way. The covenant is actually fulfilled, we really receive a new life of thankful obedience, but still it is incomplete. Our gratitude and obedience are not yet perfect, and our new lives of covenant community with God must yet be lived out on an old earth which is devastated by sin.

This means that the second manner in which the *eschaton* is reached also cries out for a further fulfillment to eradicate these shortcomings. This will take place at Christ's second coming, when he will glorify us by giving us a life entirely under the Holy Spirit's lordship. This is the meaning of "spiritual body" in 1 Cor. 15:44. The world will be made new and we shall receive a glorified life in a glorified environment. Every form of tension within us (between our old and new lives) and around us (between our renewed selves and unrenewed society) will be completely ended.

Another important dimension of this discussion is the cosmic breadth of the *eschaton*. Does God's work with creation and the attainment of his goal revolve around us alone—as some of my chapter titles might suggest? The answer is a decisive "no."

Of course humanity is the most important part of creation. God made heaven and earth as a place in which to realize his covenant with humanity. It is for good reason that Genesis 1 presents a pyramidal structure with humankind at the pinnacle, for in that same chapter we are told that humankind alone is made in God's image. Indeed, humanity is the supreme concern of all creation. For this reason there is some justification for the use of "us" in my chapter titles.

But in no sense may eschatology be restricted to humanity. The Bible concludes with a new earth, with trees and rivers, and with a city of precious stones. In fact, in each mode wherein the *eschaton* is attained, we find an unmistakable cosmic element. Christ reconciles not only humanity but also the universe, "all things, whether on earth or in heaven" (Col. 1:20). In the same way, Christ's work *in* us is accompanied by what he does in creation and society. For example, he calmed a storm and formed a new community which did not fit within existing social structures. What he does *with* us is also an all-inclusive work which involves heaven and earth—the whole of creation.

And this cosmic facet of eschatology must be applied to humanity itself. It is a distortion of the gospel to think of salvation only in terms of the soul. The body is thus taken to be unimportant, "so long as one's immortal soul be saved." Paul could not accept this; in his view, denying the resurrection of the body jeopardizes the meaning of the entire gospel. This perspective, that of the human person as a whole, is part of eschatology's cosmic significance. Jesus did not just "save souls" when on earth. The gospels hold more accounts of miraculous healings than of forgiveness of sins. This means that the physical aspects of the human being must also be addressed by eschatology.

THE ESCHATOLOGICAL CHARACTER OF JESUS' FIRST COMING

The remainder of this chapter will focus on the eschatological significance of Jesus' birth, crucifixion, and resurrection. To do this, we must first account for the New Testament's description of these events in eschatological terms, so affirming their eschatological character. That done, we shall discuss the eschatological meaning of Jesus' first coming.

The Incarnation

Let us recognize again that most of us are not used to thinking of Jesus' birth as the end. That much is demonstrated by our custom of speaking of his "first" coming. This term separates his entire earthly ministry and resurrection from his return, the second coming. It is worth noting that the Bible never refers to a *first* coming. To do so would have created the wrong impression, that Jesus' birth and ministry were no more than the introduction or prologue to an ultimate eschatological victory in the future.

But is this not the approach of many of us? And is this not why we show so little understanding when the Bible praises the radical eschatological nature of Christ's incarnation? According to the New Testament, the incarnation is an event of decisively eschatological character, doubtless belonging to the end time, not a mere beginning or turning point in history. So let us look at the eschatological character of the incarnation, at the fact that already in his earthly ministry Jesus is seen as the last and the end and that, therefore, the end has already been realized in his birth.

Jesus announces his own arrival in the words: "The time has come; the kingdom of God is upon you" (Mark 1:15). Prior to Jesus' birth, Simeon *looked forward* to the consolation of Israel; now his own eyes *have seen* the deliverance which God has made ready (Luke 2:30). When Jesus reads in the synagogue at Nazareth the prophecy of Isaiah 61, it is no longer a promise because the fulfillment stands before the congregation (Luke 4:21). The reality of salvation has appeared in Christ so radically that the time of salvation is now (2 Cor. 6:2). Christ has come "in the fullness of time" (Gal. 4:4), and through him God speaks "in these last days" (Heb. 1:2), since he has appeared "at the end of the age" (9:26). Paul reminds his readers that "upon us the fulfillment of the ages has come" (1 Cor. 10:11). He also says, "When anyone is united to Christ, there is a new world; the old order has gone, and a new order has already begun" (2 Cor 5:17). Christ himself saw his exorcism of demons as a sign that "the kingdom of God has already come upon you" (Matt. 12:28), while Paul testifies that Christ, by his cross, "discarded the cosmic powers and authorities like a garment; he made a public spectacle of them and led them as captures in his triumphal procession" (Col. 2:15). He further affirms that Christ has "broken the power of death and brought life and immortality to light" (2 Tim. 1:10).

Berkouwer is absolutely correct when he concludes from these New Testament statements that the birth and earthly ministry of Jesus are "not just a highly significant phase that turns out to be relative after all, or a subdivision of the total time-continuum with the character of eternity. No, it is the 'hour of all hours,' because it has the weight of eternity." The events of the first coming are not merely a promise but rather the fulfillment, the end of the road, the accomplished purpose, the unique and decisive time. Indeed, Berkouwer goes so far as to call the time before Christ's birth—the history of Israel—"the period preceding the eschatological time of salvation."[2]

In light of all this, we can look again at several New Testament references which apply eschatological terminology to the incarnation. Heb. 1:1-2; 9:26; and 1 Pet. 1:20, as we saw in the first chapter, describe Christ's first coming with phrases like "in these last days." Jesus himself said that the kingdom of God had already come, that it was not merely an expectation for the future (Matt. 12:28; Luke 17:20-21). John 12:31 says that judgment is completed during the lifetime of Jesus, and John 3:36, that the believer already shares in eternal life.

There must be no watering down of these pronouncements—especially those in Hebrews and 1 Peter. It is particularly unjustifiable to allege that the plurals ("days," "times," etc.) look to the beginning of a period of time rather than the end. In Heb. 1:2 "these last days" does not mean the beginning of the "final age." As we have pointed out, the Greek words are a Hebraism representing the Old Testament form "in the last days," which is found, e.g., in Isa. 2:2 (cf. NIV) and

---

2. G. C. Berkouwer, *The Return of Christ* (1972), 99, 100. Despite this emphasis on the eschatological character of the incarnation as the decisive intervention of God in the world, Berkouwer has not worked out the eschatological significance of the incarnation, earthly ministry, crucifixion, and resurrection of Jesus—nor, for that matter, the eschatological character of the so-called interim.

indicates the *end* of the days or the *last* days, hence "the end." Thus the author of Hebrews regards the incarnation as the *end*.

The same is true of "the end of the age" in Heb. 9:26. The context of this expression leaves little room for doubt of its meaning. It is used as the opposite of "since the world was made." So we have the beginning and the end of the world, and the writer regards the incarnation and earthly life of Jesus as this end. Only two verses later it is said that Christ "will appear a second time" (v. 28). This does not mean that the "the end of the age"—the incarnation—is after all not that end. It is, rather, an indication just how free and unsystematic early Christian thought on this subject really was, how freely it could move when contemplating the end—precisely because, for those people, the end was a person and his history, not specific events called "the last things." This is just one more instance of how a single goal may be reached several times.

In 1 Pet. 1:5 and 20, we have a similar Hebraism for "the last days," which does not refer to the end *period*. Here too it is remarkable that the writer can view both the incarnation of Jesus (v. 20) and his return (v. 5) as the end. Once again, this is possible only because the last and the end is a person—Christ himself.

Probably no one has expressed the eschatological character of the incarnation more radically than John. How radical an eschatological statement we have in John 1:14 ("the Word came to dwell with us") and 16 can only be seen when we look also at Rev. 21:3: "Now at last God has his dwelling among humans! He will *dwell* among them and they will be his people and God himself will be with them."

John[3] thus notes the striking agreement between the coming of Christ to the old earth and the coming of God to the new earth. Both come to *dwell* with humankind. Because the Greek word translated "dwell" can also mean "erect a tent," faulty translation has sometimes proclaimed that Jesus' dwelling was temporary. Bultmann draws this conclusion in his commentary on John 1:14. He suggests that Jesus was only a guest who would later depart.[4] But Michaelis demonstrates

3. Though the authorship of Revelation is at issue, conservative scholars generally accept that it was John the Apostle, also author of the Fourth Gospel, who wrote it. Even more critical scholars acknowledge that Revelation's writer belonged to the same school as the Gospel-writer. And this offers adequate support for our underlying argument that a deliberate (or at least a conscious) parallel exists between John 1:14, 16 and Rev. 21:3.

4. R. Bultmann, *The Gospel of John* (1971), 67. How unnecessary and unjustified Bultmann's deduction is is evident from note 1 on the same page, in

that the sense of "dwell" in Revelation (7:15; 13:6; 15:5; 21:3) and John 1:14 is that of permanent residence; it is a figure of speech for abiding and gracious presence. Michaelis refers emphatically to the Septuagint of Exod. 25:8, which translates the Hebrew word for "dwell" with the same Greek word used in John 1:14. (Smelik also refers to Exod. 25:8, noting that God there expresses the desire to live permanently among his people.) In Michaelis's opinion, this means that the statement of John 1:14 (that Christ came to "dwell" among us) does not refer to a temporary visit of the Logos but rather shows that he is the presence of the Eternal in time. G. Schrenk correctly concludes from John 1:14 that the primitive Christian community were convinced, after the temple's destruction in A.D. 70, that in Jesus—God's presence on earth—they had the true temple. John 2:21 lends further support to this argument.[5]

It is quite clear, however, that as a result of widespread misinterpretation the eschatological meaning of John 1:14 does not have the impact on theology that it should. That Jesus came by his incarnation to *dwell* among humans and that God will *dwell* among them on the new earth certainly form a remarkable parallel. The concept comes directly from the Old Testament covenant "I shall be your God [dwelling among you] and you shall be my people." This describes the covenant as the goal of creation, which becomes a reality when Jesus, as God's revelation, comes to dwell among us (John 1:14), and again when God dwells among us on the new earth (Rev. 21:3). The goal is reached as much in the incarnation as on the new earth; in Jesus, God is with us as our God and we are with him as his people.

A further aspect of John 1:14's eschatological power is found in the way "glory," "fullness," and "grace" are emphasized. Jesus is among us *full* of *grace*—and "out of his full store we have all received grace upon grace." This fullness of overflowing grace is a strongly eschatological theme. The entire fullness of God is with us in bodily form (Col. 1:19; 2:9).

---

which he goes into the connection between *skēnoō* and the oriental concept of the salvation-bringing presence of deities among humans and the rabbinic concept of *šᵉkînâ*, a technical term for God's presence.

5. W. Michaelis, *TDNT* VII, 385-386; E. L. Smelik, *De Weg van het Woord* (1948), 31; G. Schrenk, *TDNT* III, 244. Cf. C. H. Dodd, *The Interpretation of the Fourth Gospel* (1953), 206-207, who speaks of the *visio Dei* in connection with the term *doxa* in v. 14.

The concept of glory *(kabōd)* has a markedly eschatological character in the Old Testament, especially in the Psalms and Isaiah. G. von Rad says that the appearance of the "glory of Yahweh" is an established part of eschatological expectation, and that the "appearance "of his glory will be the final realization of his claim to rule the world (e.g., Num. 14:21; Pss. 57:5, 11; 72:19; Isa. 6:3; 40:5; 43:7; 66:18ff.; Zech. 2:5).[6] In the New Testament, such expressions of glory are applied to Christ in Luke 2:14; Acts 7:2; 1 Cor. 2:8; Heb. 13:21; 1 Pet. 4:11; and Rev. 5:12ff. One could compare, for example, Isa. 40:5 ("Thus shall the glory of the Lord be revealed and all mankind together shall see it") with John 1:14 ("and we saw his glory") and 18 ("No one has ever seen God; but God's only Son, he who is nearest to the Father's heart, he has made him known"). So in John 1:14 we are dealing with nothing less than the goal attained: God is with his people as their God; they, represented by the man Jesus, are with God as his people.[7] ("Represent" indicates the particular mode in which the *eschaton* is realized by Jesus' incarnation—for us, not yet in us.)

These evidences that the incarnation is eschatological should come as no surprise. How could it be otherwise, since they refer to the incarnation of Jesus, the *eschatos?* Flückiger rightly says that eschatology *is* the life of Jesus.[8]

So must we understand the radical way in which the concept of "fulfillment" applies to Jesus' incarnation and work. G. Delling says rightly that the New Testament concept of fulfillment is summed up in the person of Jesus. According to Delling, the goal of Jesus' mission is

6. G. von Rad, *TDNT* II, 241-242.

7. It is necessary to refer briefly to Barth's strongly-contested idea in *Church Dogmatics* (1955-1969) III/2, 301 (inter alia) that in Jesus (and for Barth, especially in his resurrection) we have everything, so that nothing new is to be expected in the future (e.g., at the second coming). As a criticism of this, reference is generally made to the resurrection of the body and the new earth (e.g., J. Moltmann, *Theology of Hope* (1967), 229; U. Hedinger, *Hoffnung zwischen Kreuz und Reich* (1968), 152, note 13, pp. 176-182). It is doubtful that such criticism would impress Barth. He would probably stand by his conviction while acknowledging that our resurrection and the new earth still lay in the future—though it is unclear how he would have harmonized the two. But they can be brought into agreement by the eschatological structure developed in this study, for the *eschaton* is realized in more ways than one. It is realized in the incarnation, the cross, and the resurrection of Jesus, but in a particular way: *for* us. It is also realized at Christ's return, but again in a different way: *with* us. This latter mode would then include the resurrection and the new earth.

8. F. Flückiger, *Der Ursprung des christlichen Dogmas* (1955), 136.

fulfillment. In the same connection, he says that the characteristic feature of New Testament fulfillment, which distinguishes it from rabbinic doctrine, is its eschatological content. One of many examples is Matt. 5:17, "Do not suppose that I have come to abolish the Law and the Prophets; I did not come to abolish, but to complete." Here the Law and the Prophets stand for the whole Old Testament, the will of God revealed to his people.[9] Thus all promises are fulfilled in Jesus. C. H. Dodd (who placed special emphasis on the eschatological character of the first coming) declares that the writers of the New Testament "ransack the Old Testament to accumulate evidence that all that the prophets had said of the final issue of the divine purpose was fulfilled in Christ." According to Dodd "the sense of the preparatory, the provisional, the uncomplete, which is an inseparable element in all Old Testament prophecy, has no place in the New Testament. *The Lord has come.*"[10]

This radically eschatological emphasis on the incarnation of Christ is not merely the consequence of Dodd's realized eschatology, since it is to be found equally in H. Ridderbos, who wholeheartedly accepts future expectation as a part of eschatology. Ridderbos declares that from Mark 1:15 ("the time has come; the kingdom of God is upon you") "one thing is clear, viz. that these words summarized all that had been the object of Old Testament prophecy and of Israel's expectation of the future from the oldest times."[11]

Hedinger correctly interprets Barth in this connection, asserting that Christ and his community are the complete fulfillment of Old Testament promises. Barth refers to John 1:45 ("We have met the man spoken of by Moses in the Law and by the prophets: it is Jesus . . .") and declares that the entire content of the Law and the Prophets—of the whole Old Testament—is fulfilled in him.[12] Viewed from the conclusion we have already reached—that Jesus is the *eschatos* and the covenant as the goal of creation—it is only to be expected that the *eschaton*, the end-as-goal, would become reality in his incarnation.

Criticizing Schweitzer, who acknowledges no authentic eschatology before the final judgment, Flückiger correctly emphasizes that Christ's incarnation is eschatological.[13] We must guard against denying the real eschatological character of Jesus' incarnation and cross in

9. G. Delling, *TDNT* VI, 294, 296.
10. C. H. Dodd, *The Kingdom of God and History* (1938), 24-25.
11. H. Ridderbos, *The Coming of the Kingdom* (1960), 13.
12. Hedinger, 152. Barth, III/2, 583.
13. Flückiger, 107ff.

a one-sided reaction against such theologians as Dodd and Bultmann. What should be argued against them is only that eschatology is not *restricted* to the incarnation and the cross (and the *kerygma,* in Bultmann's usage), but that eschatology also includes the future (resurrection, new earth, etc.).

Perhaps Dodd's one-sided realized eschatology can even be explained to some extent as his reaction against a widespread tendency to deny the incarnation's eschatological character—especially since eschatology has traditionally been treated as no more than a last chapter in theology. *But in light of our investigation of the New Testament, it is clear that the incarnation is unmistakably eschatological.*

The Crucifixion

The New Testament also presents the crucifixion in eschatological terms. The evangelists place Jesus' famous eschatological discourse immediately before the crucifixion and then proceed to show how many of the events Jesus mentions in it as signs of the imminent end occur during the crucifixion. Jesus refers to people finding him scandalous and to love growing cold (Matt. 24:10, 12); all this comes to a head with his arrest, when the disciples forsake him and flee and Peter denies him (26:56, 69ff.). Jesus issues a call to watchfulness at the *end* (24:42) and then in Gethsemane enjoins it of his disciples (26:38). He speaks of a great persecution which will come at the *end* (24:9, 21), and of course that is what his cross becomes to him (26:39ff.; 27:46).

Jesus also prepared his disciples for strange phenomena in nature at the *end,* and during his crucifixion they occurred. The Old Testament prophets spoke frequently of judgment day as being accompanied by such extraordinary phenomena as the darkening of heavenly bodies (Isa. 13:10ff.; Joel 2:10, 31; 3:15) and earthquakes (Isa. 13:13; Joel 2:10; 3:16). When these very signs occur during the crucifixion (the sun is darkened, Matt. 27:45 [cf. 24:29] and the earth quakes, 27:51 [cf. 24:7, 29]), it is hardly strange that John declares the crucifixion to be the judgment (John 12:31). Furthermore, Jesus speaks of the treachery which will mark the end (Matt. 24:10), and before he is crucified he is betrayed by Judas (Matt. 26:14-16; Luke 22:48).

These prophesies about the end, fulfilled in a sense during Jesus' crucifixion, show just how definitely the New Testament writers saw the crucifixion in an eschatological light. Yet these prophecies are not fulfilled in every way at the crucifixion; they possess dimensions

which still await fulfillment.[14] This shows how unsystematically the
New Testament writers approach eschatology. Prophecies which refer
to the end can be fulfilled both at the crucifixion and later. This should
serve as a warning against taking a *narrowly* eschatological view of
the crucifixion, as though it excluded all future expectation.

In this respect we need to give some attention to John 19:28 and
30: "After this Jesus, knowing that *all was now finished,* said (*to fulfill* the scripture), 'I thirst'. . . . When Jesus had received the vinegar,
he said *'It is finished'*; and he bowed his head and gave up his spirit"
(RSV). Each of the three groups of words which we have italicized
translates a Greek word formed from *telos,* "goal." These are radically
eschatological statements. In Jesus' death on the cross, all is fulfilled.
The Scripture (and that altogether, not just certain of its prophecies),
is fulfilled in an absolute sense; Jesus declares without qualification,
"It is accomplished."

How right Barth is when he says that any limit placed on "It is
accomplished" would be utterly alien to the New Testament. Bultmann
affirms that with the completion of Jesus' work, the eschatological
events are fulfilled. U. Asendorf states that the eschaton has arrived
with the crucifixion.[15] Such statements do full justice to the absolute
manner in which Jesus, who is himself the *telos,* declares from the
cross that the *telos* has been attained and that all Scripture has reached
its *telos.*

The Resurrection

The eschatological nature of Jesus' resurrection must also be examined. The apostles lay particular stress on the resurrection as an
event of the end, as the beginning of the general resurrection of the
dead that is expected at the end of the world.

14. The promise and fulfillment schema is fully discussed in Chapter 5.
15. Barth, IV/1, 281, 306; Bultmann, 673-674, note 6; U. Asendorf, *Eschatologie bei Luther* (1967), 15. Barth declares, "Jesus knew what God knew in
the taking place of His sacrifice. And Jesus said what God said: that what took
place was not something provisional, but that which suffices to fulfil the divine
will, that which is entire and perfect, that which cannot and need not be continued
or repeated or added to or superseded, the new thing which was the end of the old
but which will itself never become old, which can only be there and continue and
shine out and have force and power as that which is new and eternal" (281; cf.
282-283; IV/3/1, 236).

In the first place, Jesus' resurrection is a part of—in fact the start of—the general resurrection. We tend to think of Jesus' and our own resurrections as widely separated events which therefore have little to do with each other. Some members of the church in Corinth evidently thought so, too. While they accepted the truth of Jesus' resurrection, they denied that there would be a resurrection of the dead (1 Cor. 15:12). According to Paul, this is impossible. "If there be no resurrection, then Christ was not raised" (v. 13). The apostle could only reason like this if Christ's resurrection is a real part of the general resurrection. Were they independent events, there might indeed have been the possibility that Christ could rise while others would not. Yet Paul repeats: "if the dead are not raised, it follows that Christ was not raised" (v. 16). The primary issue is the general resurrection. One who does not believe in that cannot believe in its beginning, Christ's own resurrection.

Paul assumes throughout 1 Corinthians 15 that there is a unity between Christ's resurrection and the general resurrection. In v. 20 he calls Christ "the firstfruits of the harvest of the dead" (see also v. 23). The concept of "firstfruits" comes from Old Testament sacrificial terminology. When crops had been harvested, the Israelites had to bring the first yields to the priest as an offering to the Lord. The entire harvest was sanctified by these firstfruits (Lev. 23:10ff.; Deut. 18:4; 26:1-10). Just as the first sheaf, part of the harvest, was cut when the ingathering began, so the general resurrection begins when Christ is the first to rise from the dead.

We can more easily understand this against the background of the future expectations held by Jews of that period. After the Exile, Jewish expectations developed strongly supernatural themes. This "apocalypticism" is most clearly represented in the Old Testament in the book of Daniel. Other apocalyptic books were not included in the Old Testament (e.g., 4 Ezra [= 2 Esdras]), and Revelation is the most prominent representative of apocalypticism in the New Testament.

The Old Testament prophets expressed Israel's future in historical images—other nations threatening or vanquishing Israel, natural disasters such as earthquakes or plagues sent by the Lord as punishments, and, conversely, other nations gathering at Jerusalem to worship the Lord. Such imagery is derived from normal experience and we have no difficulty imagining it as ordinary history.

But after the Exile the apocalyptic element developed, in which the future was expressed through unusual images. In Daniel we read of many-headed animals with horns, horns that speak and fight with each other. These are often difficult to understand, because the prophet was trying to describe unimaginable things. Such things simply do not happen within normal history with ordinary human actors; rather, what is portrayed is what will happen at the end of the world with supernatural participants, and, above all, through the direct intervention of God.[16]

One such apocalyptic expectation, developed after the Exile, was the resurrection of the dead. Though from early times Israel had confessed that the Lord had power over the dead (1 Sam. 2:6; cf. Deut. 32:39; Job 19:25), belief in resurrection developed only much later. Isa. 26:19 is sometimes referred to, but the first undisputed statement on this subject is Daniel 12:2: "Of those who lie sleeping in the dust of the earth many will awake, some to everlasting life, some to shame and everlasting disgrace" (cf. v. 13). As all Daniel, especially chapter 12, shows, this prophecy will be fulfilled at the supernatural end of the world.

The subject of resurrection came to the fore during the last few centuries before Jesus' birth; this is clear from the Jewish apocrypha (cf. e.g., 4 Ezra 2:16, 23, 31; 5:45). So it entered Jewish belief and came to be defended by the Pharisees against the Sadducees, a conservative group who rejected resurrection as a novelty (Matt. 22:23ff.;

---

16. There has been a revival of interest in apocalyptic writings in the past two decades, after they had suffered a long period of neglect. Since the rise of a new generation of systematic theologians such as Moltmann and Pannenberg, the apocalyptic element has been taken much more seriously (see Moltmann, *Theology of Hope;* W. Pannenberg, *Jesus—God and Man* [1968], 53ff.; *idem. The Apostles' Creed* [1972], 100ff.; K. Koch, *The Rediscovery of Apocalyptic* [1972], 98ff.).

Pannenberg assigns an exceptional role to the apocalyptic expectation of the resurrection of the dead at the end of the world. Yet the actual nature of apocalyptic thought remains a difficult question. The notion that it implies a radically pessimistic worldview and a consequent lack of concern with history (e.g., W. Schmithals, *The Apocalyptic Movement,* 33-49) places a question mark against Pannenberg's enthusiastic acceptance of apocalyptic thought—which stands alongside his acceptance of God's revelation in the totality of history and his zealous interest in history.

But R. J. Bauckham, "The Rise of Apocalyptic," *Themelios* 3 (1978) 19-22 questions whether a pessimistic view of history is essential to the apocalyptic viewpoint. He suggests that inadequate interest in history might rather be ascribed to the apocalyptic writings' appearance during the time in which Jews returned from exile and failed to experience the fulfillment of the Deutero-Isaianic promises. Discussion of this issue will doubtless continue for some time.

Acts 23:8). Those who defended it have always assumed it would be a supernatural occurrence which would take place at the end, when God would judge the world and remake the earth.

And now it happens to Jesus! After death and burial, he appears to certain women, brothers, and disciples (1 Cor. 15:4-8). It is striking that these appearances were interpreted by the apostles as Jesus having risen from the dead. They could have advanced other explanations. They could have said that they had seen the ghost of Jesus or his angel (Mark 6:49; Acts 12:15). But they choose an entirely unusual explanation, one known to them only from apocalyptic literature—resurrection. And since it was thought that resurrection would occur at the end, they were interpreting Jesus' resurrection as the beginning of the general resurrection at the end of the world.

Acts 4:2 has exceptional significance in this connection. This rather difficult verse says that the apostles were proclaiming "the resurrection from the dead—the resurrection of Jesus," that is, that resurrection from the dead had become a reality through the resurrection of Jesus.

Romans 1:4, too, is very important. Most translators do an injustice to the startling nature of Paul's assertion, giving the impression that it was on the strength of his own resurrection that Jesus was declared the Son of God. But the Greek phrase translated "in that he rose from the dead" is the usual one for the general resurrection at the end (Acts 17:32; 23:6; 24:21; 26:23; 1 Cor. 15:12, 13, 21; Heb. 6:2). Paul is saying here that it is the general resurrection which proves Jesus to be God's Son. One may say, "But this resurrection has not yet begun." "O yes it has," Paul would say, "in the resurrection of Christ!" In other words, Paul interprets Christ's resurrection as the beginning of the general resurrection.[17]

If the significance of this subject is to be clear, we need to appre-

17. A. Nygren, *Commentary on Romans* (1949), 50-51. H. Ridderbos, *Aan de Romeinen* (1959), ad loc. dismisses this exegesis with an unsatisfactory argument. Though he admits that the corporate significance of Christ is of real importance in Romans and places heavy emphasis on the corporate motif, he declares that Nygren places too much significance on the expression "resurrection of the dead," which does not have a corresponding use in Paul. This rejection is not convincing, because Paul argues in 1 Corinthians 15 from the fact that Christ's resurrection is part of the general resurrection. J. Denney, Romans in *The Expositor's Greek Testament* (n.d.), 586 points in the direction suggested by Nygren's exposition, and in *Die Letzten Dinge* (1957[7]), 18, P. Althaus declares that the resurrection introducing the new world has already begun: Christ is risen.

ciate the radical difference between the resurrection of Christ and the resuscitation of others.[18] Once or twice in the Old Testament we read of dead persons who come back to life (e.g., 1 Kgs. 17:22), and there are also a few instances in the New Testament (Mark 5:21ff.; Luke 7:11ff.; John 11; Acts 9:36ff.). But these examples are never related to the general resurrection at the end. Rather are they presented as the experiences of individuals who came back to life but would die again.

In contrast, the apostles place an entirely different interpretation on Jesus' resurrection. He does not return from the dead only to die again later on. By his resurrection he conquers death itself, so that "Christ once raised from the dead, is never to die again: he is no longer under the dominion of death. For in dying as he died, he died to sin once for all, and in living as he lives, he lives to God" (Rom. 6:9-10). Death is not represented here as a condition but as a power (as in Rev. 6:8, where death rides a horse). Just as in some places sin means evil deeds and in others the evil power which dominates human beings (see Rom. 6:14ff.), so death, too, has a twofold meaning for Paul. And the unique significance of Christ's resurrection is that he has defeated this evil power, Death, so that it can no longer rule over him. He has, in the ultimate sense, put death behind him.

That this is so appears repeatedly in the apostles' preaching. According to 2 Tim. 1:10 (TEV), Christ has "ended the power of death" and "has revealed immortal life." This means that believers, though daily in peril of death, can become victors through Christ (Rom. 8:36, 37), since death can no longer separate them from God (vv. 38, 39). Indeed Paul can even long to die (a desire unthinkable before Christ's resurrection, since death was seen as a terrible threat in Old Testament times), knowing that in death he will be with Christ (Phil. 1:23).

It is indeed Christ, the risen Lord, who here and now gives us victory over death; that is how Paul's classic chapter on Christ's resurrection ends (1 Cor. 15:57). The same message, expressed in apocalyptic language, is: "I am the First and the Last, and I am the Living One; for I was dead and am now alive for evermore, and I hold the keys of death and Hades" (Rev. 1:17f.). Here death and Hades are personified as evil powers prowling about with keys, with which they lock up the doors of death (as a condition) and Hades (as a place) behind people. But by his resurrection Christ has broken out of both the condition and the place and has taken away the keys from the warders, so

18. Pannenberg, especially, has attended repeatedly to this difference, e.g., *The Apostles' Creed*, 100.

that now he is able to unlock when he wills. The resurrection of the dead is in his hands, since with his own resurrection it has already begun.

It had been expected that this would be fulfilled at the end, when God would renew the old world. Apocalyptic literature abounds in affirmations that death (the power) will be vanquished and death (the condition) ended when the world is ended. But now it occurs through Jesus' resurrection! His resurrection acquires, therefore, an exceptional eschatological character, for in the light of such an event the apostles were sure to announce that his return was imminent. The end, after all, had already dawned. The resurrection of the dead had already begun. Given all this, it is simply inadequate to speak of Christ as the center, the hinge, or the turning point of history. Of course he is all these things, but he is much more. He is the end. Once he had risen, the apostles could no longer expect the end to occur in some remote future. As he had actually set the resurrection in motion, he had certainly appeared in the last days.

It will not do to speak with Pannenberg of Christ's resurrection as an anticipation of the end. To do so overlooks the fact that the end is not primarily a point in time but a person. Christ need not anticipate the end; he is the end. The end of time can only reach back to him. Indeed, the only reason we can expect a completion in the future is that he, himself the last and end, continues to live and so has a history into the future.

All things considered, it is now clear why Christ's entire life on earth (incarnation, crucifixion, and resurrection) is described in eschatological terms. With his arrival the end dawns; with his crucifixion all is fulfilled; and with his resurrection the general resurrection begins.

Now we can see what Jesus meant in his inaugural sermon by saying that "the time is at hand," as well as by his statements that the kingdom of God has come and is present among the disciples. We can also see what the apostles meant by using phrases such as "the last days" and "the fulfillment of the ages" in connection with Jesus' first coming. We usually begin the scope of eschatology too late; since Christ is the *eschatos,* eschatology begins with his incarnation, crucifixion, and resurrection.

THE ESCHATOLOGICAL MEANING
OF JESUS' FIRST COMING

Having established that Christ's first coming is entirely eschatological, we will devote the rest of this chapter to describing the way in which it is so and what this ultimately means, i.e., in what sense God's goal for creation was attained by Christ's first coming.

Christ is he toward whom creation was aimed from the start, of whom Adam before his fall was a type (so Bavinck), and who was himself God's goal for humans and for all creation. Therefore, God's goal for creation is reached in Christ. This goal is the covenant. And in his incarnation, Christ himself is the content and so the fulfillment of the covenant. He is Immanuel, God-with-us. He is the revelation of that God who is on the side of his creation ("I shall be your God") and is also the true and righteous man who is on God's side ("and you shall be my people"). Therefore God's goal for creation is accomplished in him and in every phase of his history, since throughout his history he is both God-with-us and the true man. God and humanity live in harmony in the person of Christ. In this sense he is the realization of God's goal in creation. Eschatology cannot be confined to the second coming or even be said to have begun at his resurrection (so Barth).

In his incarnation, crucifixion, and resurrection, Jesus really attains God's goal for us. He is really God-with-us and we-with-God. He attains that goal in a particular way: he leaves us outside the action, not yet involved in the *eschaton*. He attains it *for* us but not *with* us.

This does not mean, however, that we are left untouched. Christ never acts alone, and he is not what he is for himself. The term "firstfruits," already discussed, emphasizes this. The concepts "firstborn of the whole creation" (Col. 1:15), "head of the body" (v. 18), and "mediator between God and mankind" (1 Tim. 2:5) all point to this. To put it differently: because he is creation's goal, that goal is reached when it is reached in him—and in such a way that creation is really touched. Though we ourselves are not yet actively involved in the way in which God's goal is reached in the incarnation, cross, and resurrection of Jesus, neither are we utterly detached from it; that goal was set for us and is beneficial to us, and it alters the relationship between God and us radically and decisively.

The content of the goal which Christ attained for us by his eschatological incarnation, crucifixion, and resurrection can be nothing other than the covenant: "I shall be your God, and you shall be my people." Therefore, that Jesus reaches this goal means that he realizes the covenant for us. We broke it; we were God's unfaithful partners; indeed, we became his enemies. Christ now restores the covenant and attains God's goal by breaking down the enmity and making peace between God and us (Col. 1:20) and between us and our fellow humans (Eph. 2:15-16). This is called "reconciliation."

In this case reconciliation does not mean that two enemies are brought to peace, rather that humanity, which has become God's enemy, is brought to peace with him. God never became our enemy and so has no need of reconciliation. That God reconciles the world to himself in Christ (2 Cor. 5:19) means exactly this: he is not resigned to our breaking of the covenant but rather restores it, carries it through, and completes it. This he does by destroying our hostility, by reconciling us to him while we were still his enemies (Rom. 5:10), and by holding our misdeeds against us no longer (2 Cor. 5:19). So it is that we become friends of God, in fact his faithful covenant partners. And this is the *eschaton,* the realization of the covenant.

Christ's annihilation of our hostility (Eph. 2:15), his putting to death of our enmity by means of his cross (v. 16) and death (Rom. 5:10; Col. 1:20, 22), is rendered the more wonderful because he did this while we were still his enemies (Rom. 5:10). That is to say, he did it when we were not purposefully engaged in reconciliation through an altered disposition or an acceptance and experience of friendship.

Nevertheless it needs to be emphasized that the other side of the issue, the positive side, is equally true. Just as real as our hostility before reconciliation is the reality of that reconciliation. Our hostility is eradicated and, viewed from God's perspective, we are truly his friends since he no longer attributes our sins to us.

From this perspective, the atonement can never mean less than the realization of the *eschaton.* To characterize the atonement as a mere possibility to be realized later by our faith, or to regard it as objective— awaiting later subjective actualization (usually implying that this actualization is the decisive factor!) is to miss both the eschatological reality of the atonement and the radicality of a number of New Testament statements (e.g., John 19:28, 30; Rom. 5:10; 2 Cor. 5:18-19; Eph. 2:15-16; Col. 1:20; 2:4). Such statements concern nothing less than the peace which has been restored, the *eschaton* which has been realized, and the covenant, God's goal in creation, which has come into being. When God no longer holds our sins against us, when there is peace between ourselves and God, and when he has made us his friends, then he *is* our God and we *are* his people.

Yet we must remember that the *eschaton* thus realized is of one specific mode; they who have been made God's friends are still, viewed from their side, his enemies. And although God's side is dominant, this mode cannot be the final one. By its very nature it cries out for yet another, in which the same *eschaton,* the covenant, will be realized in yet another mode.

This implies no lack or inadequacy in the first mode. Its apparent shortcoming (that it is for us but without us)[19] is in fact a revelation of the grace which characterizes it. Since God is merciful, he first attained the *eschaton* in this way before later reaching it in us and with us. God's holiness and righteousness could not allow our covenant-breaking and hostility to go unpunished. He in his mercy first reaches the *eschaton* for us (and therefore without us) in Jesus, since we would perish eternally if his wrath descended on us.

But Jesus in his mercy bears the wrath of God for us, in our place. Indeed, God "made him one with the sinfulness of mankind," although he was innocent, "so that in him we might be made one with the goodness of God" (2 Cor. 5:21). "Christ bought us freedom from the curse of the Law by becoming for our sakes an accursed thing. . . . The purpose of it all was that the blessing of Abraham should in Jesus Christ be extended to the Gentiles . . ." (Gal. 3:13-14).

God's use of this mode is a disclosure of his mercy, which allows his wrath against our sin to descend upon Christ. Unwilling to accept the break in the covenant, he still wants, despite our hostility, to attain his creation goal with us.

So we are not describing a lesser mode to be grieved over, but a necessary and meaningful one for which we rejoice. In fact, had not the *eschaton* first been realized in this way, it could never have been realized in any other, since here was done for us what we could never do for ourselves. Here the burden under which we would have drowned

---

19. This "without us" has been expounded with unusual lucidity by Barth in a section which deals with Christ's sacrifice for us (IV/1, 229-230). He writes that Christ died for us—without this "for us" being covered by any "with us" (i.e., our communion with Christ). In fact, every "with us" is first based on this "for us," since all discipleship gains meaning and strength from what Christ did "for us." Discipleship, authentic oneness with Jesus, rests on the assumption that he was first "for us" without our being with him, while we (Rom. 5:6ff.) were still weak, godless, and hostile. Christ did not become "for us" only after we had somehow united ourselves to him; he was "for us" without reference to the question which this poses about our discipleship. The salvific event took place then, there, in him, for us.

forever is lifted. This load had first to be carried *for* us, before the goal could be attained *in* us.[20]

It is clear, furthermore, that we cannot be content with schemes which depict the fulfillment as "only just begun," to be completed eventually "at the end." Despite Luther's insistence on the eschatological character of Christ's cross and resurrection, the notion of a beginning, continuation, and final completion in the future still exerts a powerful influence on his thought.[21] Even Barth can be caught still writing in such terms, though his emphasis does fall on the full eschatological reality of Jesus' resurrection, not to be exceeded even by the second advent.

O. Weber draws attention to Luther's occasional use of traditional salvation-history terms, but Luther did find it a great problem that eschatology was expressed in terms of ordinary time-lapse (implying that each tick of the clock brings the end a second closer).[22] In Luther's opinion, this did injustice to the biblical vision of eschatology, time-lapse presupposing continuous growth and development, i.e., an unfolding characterized by the frequent occurrence of new things until "final consummation" is reached.[23] The crucial inadequacy of this salvation-history view of eschatology is that it elevates ordinary time to a guiding principle for eschatology. The influence this exerts on expectations for the imminence of Christ's return is everywhere apparent: once eschatology is deformed into an ordinary time category so that the end is reached merely in terms of ordinary time-lapse, delay becomes a problem.

But if eschatology is defined by the goal which God envisaged at creation—as Augustine said[24]—and is seen as fulfilled in Christ, then it is unacceptable to express eschatology simply in terms of time and the passage of time. We see once more how radically our understanding of eschatology changes once it is not restricted primarily to time categories but is understood to be a person. *He* is the *eschatos;*

20. We need not here examine the discussion about "satisfaction" or "propitiation" resulting from H. Wiersinga's *De Verzoening in de theologische Diskussie* (1971), since such technical questions are not relevant in this eschatological context.

21. Asendorf, 84, 87-89 says (my translation), "The beginning [of eschatology] has come [in Christ], and he aims at the consummation"; he is "the way to the eschatological consummation" (pp. 87-89).

22. O. Weber, *Foundations of Dogmatics* (1981, 1983) II, 671.

23. Asendorf, 246 (see also 47, 114-15).

24. *Ibid.*, 246.

in him the *eschaton* is already present, as well as being still in the future. "Beginning" and "development" are of little value here. Because this person has come, the *eschaton* has come; because this person will come again, the *eschaton* lies still in the future. Mere development and occurrence of new things are a wholly inadequate description of eschatology. Time, the passing of time, and development play their parts only because this person, Jesus Christ, has a history and lives it out in time. Eschatology cannot be subsumed into time-lapse, because the end cannot be restricted to a specific point of time or a period in his history. Because Jesus is the end, his whole history is the actualization of the end, the fulfillment, and the goal. Eschatology is not primarily interested in the end*time*, be it near or far, but in the End, a person. Therefore it is concerned with the manner in which he reaches the end or goal. He has reached it for us; he reaches it in us now; he will reach it in the future with us (and this of course involves normal time-lapse and thus the salvation-historical character of eschatology).

The delay in Christ's second coming moves to the periphery and becomes a problem of secondary magnitude.[25] Furthermore, schemes popularly employed to express the structure of eschatology are relegated to a subordinate position, having strictly limited use. Such schemes include: "already and not yet," "the hidden and the revealed," "passive and active," "the beginning and the consummation" (of the *eschaton*), "humiliation and glorification," "empty hands and full hands," "promise and fulfillment," and "faith and form."[26] All these schemes understand eschatology as primarily a time-category directly related to lineal time. It is apparent from our study thus far that their value is limited, because eschatology is primarily concerned with a person who is himself the end.[27] It is solely on the basis of his history that the linear passage of time reenters eschatology.

25. *Ibid.* The problem of Christ's imminent return must later be examined extensively.

26. Cf., e.g., J. T. Bakker, *Eschatologische Prediking bij Luther* (1964), 57, notes 67, 82, 103.

27. G. Sauter, *Zukunft und Verheissung* (1965), 173 also declares that because of its conception of time, salvation history shares in the problems of all linear models of time and history. His criticism (note 59) of Cullmann's concept of linear time is especially helpful.

The Incarnation

The eschatological terms in which the New Testament speaks of Christ's incarnation were discussed in detail earlier in this chapter. We discovered that the incarnation is spoken of in terms identical to those applied to God's presence among his people on the new earth, e.g., Christ "dwelt among us" (John 1:14) and "the dwelling of God is with mankind" on the new earth (Rev. 21:3).

The real eschatological meaning is that the fulfillment of the covenant relationship is announced by these words. Christ is bound to both God and us in a unique manner. He represents God (we confess him to be "true God") and he represents us (likewise, "true man"). Jesus reveals God as the God who cares, who comes to live among us, who shares our lot, who makes our lost cause his cause, and who adopts us as his children and heirs. Jesus also reveals the true human being, who serves God from love, who finds life's meaning in service to God and neighbor, and who exists for others. God's goal for his creation— "I shall be your God, and you shall be my people"—is our most concise summary of the covenant. In Jesus' life, both parts become a reality: he reveals the true God who loves us and the true human person who serves God in thankfulness.

Our attention is drawn to this remarkable fact: the covenant is fulfilled by Jesus' incarnation in such a way that we still stand outside. In principle, he was the only true human being. When he was born, crucified, and raised from the dead, he was the only one to whom we could point as an example of the fulfillment of the covenant between God and humanity. In him the covenant is really fulfilled. He is the true human being, fully obedient and faithful to God. "Behold the man!" And what of us? We are the people around whom all this revolves. He became a human for the sake of other humans—us. But in spite of his incarnation, we have not yet become God's faithful covenant partners.

For this reason it is not enough that the covenant is realized *for* us. This first mode demands a second; the goal must also be attained *in* us. We shall find this same need in the crucifixion and resurrection.

The Crucifixion

That the New Testament speaks of Christ's crucifixion in eschatological terms has already been established. God's goal—the same one, of course—must also be reached in the crucifixion. Our question is *how* the crucifixion does this. And the central concept which leads us to the answer is reconciliation.

In the apostolic preaching, in the Church's confessions, and in Christian experience, reconciliation occupies an extraordinary position. Reconciliation is proclaimed as the fruit of Christ's cross (Rom. 5:10; Eph. 2:16). It is through the cross that our sins are "blotted out" or forgiven (2 Cor. 5:19; Gal. 1:4; Eph. 1:7; Col. 2:14) and our hostility is ended (Eph. 2:13, 19ff.). Our mutual antagonism and enmity toward God comes to an end (vv. 15-16). Through the cross, Christ has brought us into the right relationship with God (Rom. 3:24), and God has accepted us as his friends (2 Cor. 5:18-19 TEV) because Christ, by his crucifixion, has made peace with God (Eph. 2:15). Through Christ's cross we become subjects in God's kingdom, members of his family (v. 19), members of Christ's body, and heirs of his Father (3:6).

We could list many more such radical statements. It is nothing less than the covenant's fulfillment and the attainment of God's goal for humankind that we should be his friends, children, and heirs, and that everything separating us from him should be done away. These are radical statements and they emphasize a single point: comprehensive peace has been made through the cross. Of course this was always God's goal for us. If we are made his people, his children, and his heirs, then the covenant is fulfilled and God's purpose is accomplished.

Yet we find here the same sort of realization of the covenant as before—for us but without us. Paul puts it clearly: "when we were God's enemies, we were reconciled to him through the death of his Son" (Rom. 5:10). In fact, all the marvelous things Christ gained for us on the cross, he gained while we were still his foes. The reconciliation, the peace, the forgiveness, the status of God's children, all were actually gained, but still without us—only for us.

This does not mean that real peace, forgiveness, and adoption did not truly come about. To suggest this would be to distort the preaching of the apostles. But it means that peace, forgiveness, and adoption must be realized in yet another way—in us—if we are really to accept our reconciliation (2 Cor. 5:20), begin to live in peace, and behave in this world as his children. But this is only attaining the same goal in another way.

Who is the "us" for whom Christ by his crucifixion attained God's goal? This is an important question. If "we" were an exclusive little group, it simply would not be true to say that God's goal in creation has been reached. God made heaven, earth, and all things living; his goal in creation is wide and includes more than a small group.

Now, it is remarkable that the apostles proclaimed reconciliation as something done for "us" or "you" on the one hand, while they emphasized its breadth and inclusiveness on the other. It is usually said that atonement was done "for us." Typical statements are "Christ gave himself for our sins" (Gal. 1:4) and "In him we have redemption through his blood" (Eph. 1:7). Yet John and Paul stand out by also making *the world* the object of the atonement (John 1:29; 3:17; 4:42; 10:16ff.; 11:52; 12:24, 32, 47; 17:18-20; 1 John 2:2; 4:14).

In 2 Cor. 5:18-19, e.g., "the world" is not opposed to "us." "Us" has no exclusive connotation and so can be placed beside "the world." This holds true for John, too, as is clear in 1 John 2:2. "Us" appears there too, but John stresses at once that "us" does not exclude the world.[28] So when the atonement is discussed, one must not oppose "for us" and "for all the world."

In fact, the New Testament never talks about the atonement as being limited in any way. It does not even hint that any specific group might not be reconciled, not even in the texts which say that Jesus gave his life for "many" (Matt. 20:28; Mark 10:45; Rom. 5:19; Heb. 9:28). It is incorrect to infer any limitation from the word "many." In the Servant Songs of Isaiah (e.g., Isa. 42:6; 45:22; 49:6; 52:14-15; 53:11-12), "many" refers to numerous heathen nations. It does so to stress salvation's inclusive character over against Jews who wished to limit salvation to Israel by excluding the Gentiles.[29] The meaning of "many"

28. Various facts indicate that in 1 John 2:2 we have an extraordinary contrast. S. Greijdanus, *De Brieven van de Apostelen Petrus en Johannes, en de Brief van Judas* (Commentaar op het Nieuwe Testament; 1929), ad loc., points out four words which make the contrast exceptionally sharp. In *hēmeteros* on its own, emphasis and opposition is disclosed; the participle *de* strengthens the opposition by its position (after *hēmeteros*); *monon* also bears special stress because of its position; and finally, *alla* points to a strong contrast. In fact the only other instance of *ou monon, alla* (without *kai*) in the same epistle occurs in 5:6, where it not only points in the direction of a strong contrast but also justifies Westcott's remark, *The Epistles of St. John* (1892³), 44, about the position of *de*: "The particle *(de)* marks the clause as guarding against error, not merely adding a new thought." In 2:2 there is thus a sharp reaction against any thought that Christ's reconciliation of us should exclude the world.

29. J. Jeremias, *The Eucharistic Words of Jesus* (1970), 179ff.; W. Michaelis, *TDNT* V, 74 note 115; J. Schniewind, *Das Evangelium nach Markus* (NTD; 1952⁶), 143; A. H. McNeile, *The Gospel according to St. Matthew* (1915), 290; H. Ridderbos, *Paul* (1975), 337-341. See also Jeremias, *TDNT* VI, 536-545.

is perfectly conveyed by Paul's famous phrase "Jews as well as Greeks."

So the message of reconciliation must go forth to "all the nations" with the call to repentance and faith. Only in this connection is any limitation of salvation or the attainment of God's goal implied—not in the first mode (the *eschaton* for us) but in the second (the *eschaton* in us). Only there do we hear of those who harden their hearts and are lost. But to the atonement itself, the first mode in which Christ reaches the goal, no limitations are applied.

The message of reconciliation is so deliberately formulated in universal terms that mention is made even of "the universe" ("all things") being reconciled by Christ. There are two reasons for discussing this remarkable topic now. The first is that it emphasizes the universality of the purpose Christ achieves for us; the second is that it provides an opportunity for investigating the cosmic (worldwide) sweep of the atonement and of eschatology.

Eschatology, as we have seen, is not merely a personal matter, as if only individuals (or, worse, only "souls") were saved. God made heaven and earth, and he makes a new heaven and a new earth. There is plainly a cosmic aspect to eschatology. Creation itself is ultimately the issue; more than humanity is at stake in the achievement of God's goal.

We find an important statement about reconciliation of the universe in Col. 1:20, "Through him God chose to reconcile the whole universe ('all things') to himself, making peace through the shedding of his blood upon the cross, to reconcile all things—whether on earth or in heaven—through him alone." *Gute Nachricht,* a German translation, renders this verse more or less as follows: "Through Christ all created things have regained peace with God. Through the blood Christ shed on the cross, God restored peace between himself and the world. This peace does not only pertain to humanity, but also to supernatural powers."

There is widespread discussion about this remarkable text, especially between theologians who teach an unlimited atonement and those Reformed theologians who teach a limited atonement. The latter deny that the text refers to evil powers being saved in any sense at all. They do so because there is no hint of such a thing anywhere else in the New Testament. Indeed, such a notion contradicts the New Testament's overall message that such powers are consigned to perdition. But all discussion between proponents of a limited atonement and an unlimited atonement seems to miss the real point of Col. 1:20—and indeed of the whole christological hymn of vv. 15-20. Colossians inveighs against the heresy of angel worship and preaches the unique preeminence of Christ. It does so first by announcing categorically, "his is the primacy over all created things" (NEB). Thereafter it reiterates at least six times "his primacy over all things." What strikes one about the structure of these verses is the presence of many details about Christ's primacy over all things and, in contrast, the absence of any details about the "all things" over which he exercises primacy. Paul refers in turn to Christ's supremacy in terms of creation (v. 16), providence (v. 17), resurrection (v. 18), revelation (v. 19), and salvation (v. 20). But he does not attempt to state who or what "all things" includes, save for the clear transition in v. 21 which stresses that the Colossians are included.

Therefore, it seems irrelevant to discuss precisely who or what is reconciled according to v. 20. When 2:15 deals explicitly with evil powers, the text makes it obvious that they have been defeated and humiliated through the cross. Just so, the meaning of v. 20 must be sought in that which the text makes obvious: who Christ is and what he has done have an all-inclusive significance. Creation, providence, and reconciliation—his work and his significance touch everything.

This is why Paul speaks of reconciliation and creation with equal breadth, deliberately including all things on earth and in heaven. Doing so reflects the sweep of God's creation goal and demonstrates that he wishes to attain it with all creation—and has attained it, in the first mode. He has attained it for us and for all creation in Christ. There never has been any notion of restriction in "for us"; his atoning work is as wide as his creation. In this sense the goal has indeed been reached through the cross.

The Resurrection

The resurrection of Jesus has an exceptionally important eschatological meaning. Indeed, Barth began his eschatology with Christ's resurrection. One criticism of this approach is that it bypasses the clearly eschatological nature and significance of Jesus' birth and crucifixion. But leaving this defect for the moment, there remain weighty reasons why Barth regards the resurrection as eschatology's beginning. We have already pointed out that the resurrection of Christ forms a unity with the resurrection of the dead. The latter began with the former. This means that in Christ's resurrection the end has already dawned. To this we must add another vital point. In Chapter 2 we explained that the consummation is to be more than a restoration of original condition. Part of the "gain" associated with consummation is glorification. But this begins only with the resurrection of Christ. His incarnation and—supremely—his crucifixion are still a part of "ordinary" history. He was born as a baby, like all other babies. He was judged and crucified, as have been others before and since. But his resurrection was unique. No one can compare with him in this—not even those whom he recalled to life. They faced death again; he vanquished death and put it behind him.

This is the point at which eschatology breaks through ordinary history and becomes apocalyptic. We now enter a realm of which we have no experience, for which we have no analogy. It is futile to doubt or deny the resurrection because we have no experience of dead people rising and so no analogies for Jesus' resurrection.[30] The apocalyptic sphere is that for which no analogies exist, the realm where radically new things happen. This explains why apocalyptic messages are so often couched in strange and unparalleled imagery, as in the book of Revelation.

For this reason, apocalyptic writings are indispensable: God is the God who is always doing new things. He has promised a glorious consummation, infinitely greater than the fragmented reality and history in which we live, and ordinary imagery is inadequate to express his promises. So it is obvious why Jesus employs Jewish apocalyptic imagery and why the last book of the Bible is its supreme apocalyptic prophecy.

This apocalyptic character of God's deeds offers important insights for eschatology. If Christ's resurrection is without parallel, we cannot fully explain or understand it. It is in principle impossible to explain matters for which no illustrative examples exist. In fact the term "resurrection" is itself a metaphor; even the Bible likens it to an awakening from sleep.[31]

Already in Isa. 26:19 there is talk of awakening from sleep. After

---

30. W. Pannenberg, *Basic Questions in Theology* (1970, 1971) I, 39-50. W. Kasper, *Jesus the Christ* (1976), 147. Pannenberg has done much to combat what he calls the "almighty analogy." From the nature of the Bible's God, theology derives an interest in analogy-free, new, contingent things.

31. Pannenberg has devoted considerable attention to this, and in the following few pages there is much which depends on his thoughts. See his *Jesus—God and Man,* 74ff.

the first sentence—which may refer to the resurrection ("But thy dead shall live, their bodies will rise again")—an explanation follows ("They that sleep in the earth will awake and shout for joy"), which uses the very imagery we are discussing. Similarly, Daniel (in the only generally accepted reference to resurrection in the Old Testament) employs the picture of sleeping and awakening: "Many of those who sleep in the dust of the earth will wake" (12:2). Paul and others continue this metaphor in the New Testament, applying it repeatedly to the departed, who "sleep" (Mark 5:39; 1 Thess. 4:13, 16; 5:10).

The use of imagery limits our knowledge of resurrection. But we have no alternative, since resurrection is without analogy. This restricts us to "negative knowledge," i.e., to knowledge of what it is *not* rather than of what it *is*. We have already said that resurrection is not merely becoming alive again; it is conquering death.

Paul tried to say something about this by comparing the earthly body with the resurrection body (1 Cor. 15:35ff.). But he, too, is forced to speak primarily in negatives. His comparison makes it clear that we can deduce nothing about the resurrection body from contemplation of our present bodies. "What you sow is not the body that shall be, but a naked grain . . . and God clothes it with a body of his choice" (vv. 37, 38). "The splendor of the heavenly bodies is one thing, the splendor of the earthly, another" (v. 40). Note the repetition in v. 41. Then follows a list of opposites: perishable-imperishable, humiliation-glory, weakness-power, animal body-spiritual body (vv. 42-53).

This means that there is no substantial or structural continuity ("correspondence") between earthly and resurrection bodies. Indeed, the overall impression left by this section (vv. 35-40) can be summed up in two words: "unknown" and "opposite." We do not know what resurrection bodies will look like (cf. with 1 John 3:2), but we know they will be radically different—in fact, the opposites of our present bodies.

This suggests that we should only discuss the nature and reality of the consummation with great reticence. Of course God's goal is quite clear: fulfillment of the covenant in Christ, and peace between God and creation. But about the actual form this goal will finally take, we must be tentative. At the best, we know what it will not be—though even this comes in apocalyptic language which we cannot take literally or exactly. We will look again later at our limited information on the consummation and view it from a different perspective, i.e., the manner in which biblical prophecy is fulfilled.

Granted the discontinuity between the two, there will be at least historical correspondence between our present and resurrection bodies. Paul highlights this at the end of 1 Corinthians 15, while dealing with the term "change." That "we shall all be changed" (vv. 51-52) and that "this perishable being must be clothed with imperishability" (v. 53) clearly presupposes a limited continuity. Obviously "this perishable" body is not *replaced* by a new, glorified one. Rather it is changed, and it is as a changed body that "this perishable" body enters glory. So there is at least historical continuity between the two; the same person, with the same name, history, and identity is glorified.

Much of this is evident from the resurrection appearances of Jesus. He is recognizable: "See my hands; reach your hand here and put it into my side" (John 20:27) and "Look at my hands and feet. It is I myself" (Luke 24:39). Of course, everything is different, too. Jesus can avoid recognition and open people's eyes to cause it. But one thing remains beyond doubt—it is Jesus the crucified who appears.

So there is historical continuity; in the long run, that is what matters. God does not abandon his handiwork or achieve his goal through some other creation. He does not annihilate fallen creation (earth or mankind) and create again from nothing. *"This* perishable being must be clothed with imperishability" (1 Cor. 15:53).

Earlier in this section we said that it is Jesus' resurrection which first exceeds our bounds of history and experience. We referred to his birth and crucifixion as parts of "ordinary" history. But in his resurrection we meet for the first time an event without historical analogy, which must consequently be described by imagery.

Of course that is only half of the truth; the other is that Jesus' resurrection casts a new light on his birth and crucifixion. They are described in eschatological terms because of his resurrection. His resurrection casts a new light over his entire life. No one would ever have characterized his birth as the last days or his crucifixion as the peace between God and humankind if he had not risen from the dead. Jesus' resurrection is the foundation of the disciples' faith because it vindicates his claims.

The Gospels are not disciples' diaries, written after each day with Jesus about the experiences of that day. They were written after his resurrection and express the meaning of his birth, words, deeds, and cross in the light of that resurrection. Had he not risen, no Gospels would have been written; because he did, it is clear that he is God's Son (Rom. 1:4).

Because he is God's Son, his crucifixion assumes a unique meaning: the reconciliation of the world. Again, because he is God's Son, his birth assumes a unique meaning: the last days have arrived. The resurrection of Jesus legitimizes his claims and deeds and gives meaning to his life and death. To this extent we can say with Barth that eschatology begins with the resurrection; yet Jesus' resurrection stamps so decisive an eschatological significance on his entire life that none of it can be excluded. Because he rose from the dead, the end has dawned; he is himself the end and the last. Thus his history is the last days, beginning with his incarnation.

It is easy to understand the apostles' emphasis on Jesus' resurrection. It legitimizes his claims and gives meaning to his life and works. Indeed, there is no gospel without it (1 Cor. 15).

SUMMARY

It is far from usual to expound Christ's first coming, cross, and resurrection in a book on eschatology, generally thought of as the doctrine of the "last things." But as we have seen, eschatology is a broader and richer subject than is generally supposed. The New Testament speaks of Jesus' incarnation, cross, and resurrection in fully developed eschatological terms.

God has spoken through Christ in the last days. Christ has appeared at the end of the age. In Christ's work, God's kingdom has come. Through Christ's crucifixion, all is accomplished. All this is known in the light of his resurrection, which is the beginning of the resurrection of the dead. Since the Bible speaks in such terms about Christ's first coming, it is impossible to discuss eschatology without devoting considerable attention to the way in which the end has already been reached and the goal attained by his first coming.

Through his incarnation, crucifixion, and resurrection, Christ has reached God's goal by making peace for us with God, by ending our hostility toward God, and by fulfilling for us God's covenant goal in creation. In him the covenant is fulfilled. He is God-with-us and we-with-God. In him, God is our God and we are God's people.

Christ attains God's goal for us in this way because, by our sins, we have called down God's wrath upon our heads but are unable to bear it. Christ therefore takes our places and does for us what we could not do for ourselves. Had God determined to reach his goal directly *with* us, rather than *for* us through Christ, we would have perished under his judgment. Christ excludes us at first; he acts for us but without us to make a place where we can stand so that he can attain God's purpose in a second way: *in* us.

Two matters are of paramount importance in connection with this first realization of the goal. First, it is really achieved. Though it has been accomplished without us, hostility is utterly ended, peace is truly concluded, humankind is actually reconciled, and death is surely vanquished. All this is part of God's goal for creation, the covenant. So Christ's first coming is no mere introduction; it is real eschatology because it is he, the *eschatos,* who comes.

Second, this way of reaching the goal calls for yet another to attain the same end *in* us. Indeed, though hostility is at an end, it is thus far only *for* us, in our place and name, that it has been ended. We have yet to accept this peace. We are not yet living as reconciled people, we do not yet experience God's friendship. That is why the goal must be reached in another way, enabling us actively to be involved and to live in it. That is the subject of the next chapter.

Chapter 4

CHRIST REALIZES THE GOAL IN US

WHY IN YET ANOTHER WAY?

Our need for the goal *(eschaton)* to be reached in yet another way flows from the manner in which Christ achieved it for us. On one hand, the goal was actually achieved for us through Christ's incarnation, crucifixion, and resurrection. Our enmity was brought to a radical end, and the world was so radically reconciled that God no longer reckons its sins. On the other hand, the way in which this *eschaton* was achieved for us is incomplete; it took place when we had not yet accepted the putting away of our enmity or the reality that we were dead to sin and alive to God. From our viewpoint, we were still God's enemies—when in fact he had ended our hostility. We persisted in disloyalty and disobedience when he had already accepted us as his true covenant partners in Christ.

So the *eschaton* realized for us has yet to be realized in us.[1] We must be brought to the point of accepting the end of our hostility toward God; we must begin to experience our freedom from sin and freedom for God and neighbor; we must begin to live actively as God's true servants and offer our lives for his service. This is the second way in which God's goal must be reached.

We emphasize again that although creation's goal has yet to be realized *in* us, this in no way suggests that it was not truly achieved when it was realized *for* us. What was then realized was not less than God's purpose, nor was it realized only in part. The complete *eschaton,* the covenant as the goal of creation, was indeed realized—but in a par-

---

1. In *De Vervulling van de Wet* (1947), 218, van Ruler speaks of *"een ingaan van het heil in de existentie"* (a penetration of salvation into existence) and further—speaking in pneumatological terms—of *"de vereeniging, de verbinding en de vermenging van het heil met de existentie"* (the union, the binding, and the mixing of salvation with existence).

ticular mode, i.e., for us. Because God takes us quite seriously and has no wish to complete everything without us, he repeats what he has done for us in such a way that it takes shape in our lives, that we accept his peace and friendship, and that we experience the goal *in* ourselves.

Now, it is striking that this second mode demands yet a third. Precisely because we are involved in it actively—by responding, believing, giving thanks, and serving—we exert an influence upon the way in which this second mode, unlike the first, is realized. Since our response, belief, thanksgiving, and service are imperfect, the mode itself is imperfectly realized, and God's goal in us incompletely achieved.

Naturally we must guard against the misconception that it is we who must achieve the *eschaton* in its second form. It would be wrong to describe the first mode as God's part (the "indicative") and the second as our own (the "imperative"). Once again, it is Christ who reaches the *eschaton*. But while in the first mode mankind was only acted upon, in the second we are involved in Christ's work in us (justification and sanctification) and in the world (mission). It is our very involvement which contributes this element of incompleteness, making it necessary to achieve the goal in yet a third manner, "with" us.

In the next chapter we shall see that in the third mode God through Christ reaches his goal once more without us—and for that reason, perfectly. It is obvious that whenever God achieves his goal through Christ alone, in no matter what specific form, he does it perfectly. It is that one time when we are actively involved that he achieves it imperfectly.

But now we must examine more closely the unique nature of the second mode, "in" us. It is clear from many New Testament passages that it is in this mode that our final decision to be saved or lost falls. In the first mode, God's goal is universally achieved in a salvationhistorical sense, i.e., for all people, Jews and Gentiles. In it there is no talk of limitation. Christ is "the remedy for the defilement of our sins, and not our sins only but the sins of all the world" (1 John 2:2). Since God in Christ reaches his goal for us, there can be no talk of limitation or exclusion.

But where our wills are involved, where Christ calls us to have faith in him, there a warning echoes to remind us that we can remain standing outside. Thus there is talk at this point of the decisive nature of faith: "he who puts his faith in the Son has hold of eternal life, but he who disobeys the Son shall not see that life; God's wrath rests on him" (John 3:36).

This might leave the impression that the goal is not really achieved in the first mode, that Christ's work for us is no more than a possibility which only later turns to reality through our faith—exactly the opposite of what we said repeatedly in the previous chapter. To clarify this point, let us note that the New Testament never discusses a theoretical meaning of the atonement for the lost. The reality and salvation-historical universality of Christ's atonement are proclaimed in a radical manner. At the same time, however, the call goes out for faith and repentance, in the absence of which the accomplished goal will not be the unbeliever's lot.

For this reason, 2 Cor. 5:19 and 20 stand together in the Bible—in a single breath. The call in v. 20 ("be reconciled to God") is no abrogation of the radical message of v. 19, which says that God no longer holds our misdeeds against us. Yet neither does that message of v. 19 eliminate the decisive character of v. 20. Anyone who neglects this call is lost—despite the achievement already of the goal.

We should keep in mind the flexibility with which the New Testament writers handle this topic. A striking example is the parable of the unforgiving creditor (Matt. 18:23-35). The warning of this parable is that the unmerciful creditor, himself forgiven by *his* creditor, discovers that his debt has returned. This means that being forgiven and forgiving others ("doing unto others as we would that they did unto us") are so interwoven that neither can happen without the other. What is done *for* us is inextricably bound to what is achieved *in* us.

We should never try to think in a more "purely" theoretical manner than the New Testament does. For its authors, there is no problem concerning the significance of destroyed hostility and established peace for those who are lost. Hostility is indeed eradicated; peace has indeed been made—for all! But the unbeliever is lost. To ask whether or not such a person was indeed reconciled is to raise an illegitimate question.

We read in 2 Pet. 2:1 of those who, by their conduct, are "disowning the very Master who bought them and bringing swift disaster on their heads." Here again, simultaneous mention is made of a completed reconciliation and of the disobedient who are lost. Luke, too, writes of someone who was forgiven and yet had no love (7:42). The implication is that he was not really forgiven (v. 47) and that this becomes apparent in his lack of love.

For this reason, Jesus taught his disciples to pray: "and forgive us our trespasses, as we forgive them who trespass against us." He continued, "For if you forgive others the wrongs they have done, your heavenly Father will also forgive you; but if you do not forgive others, then the wrongs you have done will not be forgiven by your Father"

(Matt. 6:12, 15; cf. 1 John 4:7, 9-11, 19-20). Paul preached the same message. In Col. 1:22-23 he proclaims completed reconciliation and then warns, "Only, you must continue in your faith . . . so that you are never dislodged from the hope offered in the gospel." So the New Testament writers did not think it strange to teach both that the goal has been reached and that decision falls within the province of faith, because faith lives entirely from the achieved goal.

However, the true significance of the second mode does not lie in the decisive character of faith, but rather in our active involvement in what Christ is doing now in and through the Holy Spirit to achieve God's purpose in this mode. Christ did not work only in the past (in the incarnation, crucifixion, and resurrection); he will not work only in the future (in the second coming and the new earth); he is also at work now. What characterizes his present work, however, distinguishing it from his past and future work, is that he involves us—by doing it in us and through us to reach God's goal.

Jesus is present in the Holy Spirit and continues his work because it is not yet finished. It is our glorious, God-given privilege to be his fellow workers and thus to have a share in salvation history. In fact, so gracious is God that he does not do all his own work, we remaining mere objects.

He grants us, his servants, time and space beside him. No mere onlookers but rather covenant partners, we reap with him a harvest produced by the seed of the cross. Nor does God violate his nature by doing this. From all eternity, he decided to create beings who were other than himself, who would live in covenant with him, so that he would be their God and they his children. Therefore he does not wish to speak his last word without us or even, as to mere objects, *to* us. Rather, especially after the failure recorded in the Old Testament, he wants us to participate in his work.

All this would have been impossible had God allowed Christ's final coming to occur immediately after his resurrection. Such a plan might seem better to us. But there would then have been no time or space between the first and last forms of his coming, and no time or space for a reconciled world to be involved in his redeeming work. There would be no rejoicing congregation, no witnesses, no one other than objects and spectators. It is the time and space between Christ's first coming and his return which is the great opportunity he gives us to serve him freely.[2] Since God never wishes to make of humankind

2. K. Barth, *Church Dogmatics* (1955-1969) IV/3/1, 323-367.

an object, but rather his child and so a cooperating subject and covenant partner, Christ does not reach the *eschaton* only for us, but also in us— with us actively involved in the goal already reached for us.

Though this chapter will direct our attention primarily to the work of Jesus in and through the Holy Spirit in the interim between Jesus' ascension and return, we shall also deal with his earthly activity, i.e., his preaching and miracles. This is because Jesus had already begun to achieve by them God's goal *in* human lives and the world— that same goal which was achieved by his incarnation, crucifixion, and resurrection *for* us. So both of these facets of his history must be discussed here. The first half of this chapter will discuss his earthly work in preaching and miracles, the second his work through the Holy Spirit.

THE EARTHLY ACTIVITY OF JESUS

Because Jesus is the last and the end, he achieves the purpose of God for creation in all parts of his history. Knowing the radically eschatological character of his incarnation, crucifixion, and resurrection, we are hardly surprised to find that his earthly activity also has a thoroughly eschatological character and that in this part of his history, too, he reaches God's goal.

The Background of the Kingdom of God Concept

The concept chosen here for introducing the eschatological significance of Jesus' earthly ministry is "the kingdom of God." Today the general consensus is that Jesus' earthly ministry (and indeed the whole New Testament message) can be summarized in that key concept.[3] As we shall see, the meaning of the kingdom is intimately connected with the meaning of the covenant: God is our God (our king and that of all the universe) and we are his people (subjects of his kingdom, the universe).

It is remarkable that John the Baptist, like Jesus, began to preach

3. In *Teleios: The Idea of Perfection in the New Testament* (1959), 148ff., P.J. du Plessis provides references. What now follows leans heavily on H. Kleinknecht, G. von Rad, and K. L. Schmidt, *TDNT* I, 568ff.

by proclaiming that the kingdom of God was near (Matt. 3:2; 4:17).
This means that the concept was extremely important to them both.
But it is equally remarkable that neither of them elucidated what he
understood by "the kingdom of God." Nor did either devote any effort
to convincing his audience that such a kingdom existed or that it would
come. All this John and Jesus assumed. They even assumed that their
audiences were expecting the kingdom, since they announced simply,
"the kingdom of God has come near." What notion of the kingdom
would audiences of John and Jesus have had? To discover this, we must
investigate "the kingdom of God" in the Old Testament and in the rabbinic and apocalyptic literatures, and thereafter the particular content
which Jesus gave to this concept by his preaching.

It is in the New Testament, mainly, that we read about the kingdom of God. (Matthew usually calls it the "kingdom of heaven.") In
the Old Testament we encounter the concept very seldom (apparently
only 1 Chr. 29:11; Pss. 22:28; 103:19; 145:11-13; Dan. 4:3; Obad. 21).
In fact the concept developed later, in post-Old Testament Judaism.
The Old Testament preferred indicative verbs over abstract noun forms
(e.g., "the Lord reigns," over "kingdom of God" or "kingdom of
heaven"). This should remind us that the kingdom of God does not
refer to a specific area or country where he reigns, but to his active
rule— the Lord *reigns*.

As early as Exod. 15:18 we read, "The Lord shall reign for ever
and ever." Israel sings this song of praise as an expression of gratitude
for the mighty deeds by which the Lord liberated the people from
Egypt. This liberation is how they came to know him, and, much as
the exodus remained in the center of Israel's faith, God remained its
king and ruler. Israelites did not stress the territory over which their
God was king as much as his liberating acts in their history. Neither
did they stress his office as king, but rather his function—that the Lord
was he who liberated and protected them.[4]

Two other ideas developed at a later stage of the Old Testament,
first, that the Lord was king of other peoples as well, indeed, of all
peoples (e.g., Pss. 22:29; 97:1, 6; 98:3, 9; Jer. 10:7, 10).[5] A number of
Psalms, especially the "enthronement" Psalms, celebrate the worldwide rule of the Lord (e.g., Pss. 47; 93-99). Psalm 145 assumes a

4. R. Schnackenburg, *God's Rule and Kingdom* (1963), 1f. A considerable
number of the insights which follow were gleaned from the first two chapters of
this book.
5. T. C. Vriezen, *An Outline of Old Testament Theology* (1958), 348-350.

special place among Psalms which sing of the breadth and depth of God's sovereignty, e.g., v. 13, "Thy kingdom is an everlasting kingdom, and thy dominion stands for all generations."

The second development was the conviction that God reigns not only over humankind, but over all creation. Isaiah (6:3ff.) sees the Lord seated on a high, exalted throne and hears the seraphim crying, "the whole earth is full of his glory." He rules even over the "flood" as king (Ps. 29:10). Indeed, "the Lord has established his throne in heaven, his kingly power over the whole world" (Ps. 103:19). Even the heavenly beings bow before the Lord in recognition of his power (Isa. 6; 1 Kgs. 22:19).

In the time of the great prophets, Israel experienced its worst reverses and catastrophes. Matters reached the first level of their nadir when the northern kingdom was exiled in 722 B.C. and the southern kingdom was threatened with the same fate. A strong expectation for the future developed during this period, central to which was confidence that the Lord would reappear as king, prove his might, liberate Israel from its enemies, and rule in glory over them from Zion in Jerusalem.

It is significant that all three aspects of the Lord's kingship were now incorporated into a future expectation. He would rule over Israel at Jerusalem (Mic. 2:12ff.), over all peoples (who would stream to Jerusalem—see Isa. 2:2-4 and Mic. 4:1-4), and over all creation, to restore the peace of paradise (Isa. 9:6-9; 35:1-10).

During the exile—for Israel a great humiliation which shook its faith in the lordship of God—Deutero-Isaiah proclaimed a message of consolation: the Lord would reappear as the great king; as of old in Egypt, Israel would experience an exodus which would lead her to Jerusalem. This prophet proclaimed repeatedly that the Lord was certainly king and that he would come to reign (Isa. 40:10; 41:21; 43:15) at the second exodus (43:16 f.). Nor did he restrict future expectation to one of national victory for Israel alone. All flesh would see the salvation of God (40:5) and God's house would be a house of prayer for all people (56:7), so that, wherever they were on earth, they would sing together a new song to the Lord (42:10-12).

Later (intertestamental) Jewish writings fall readily into two categories: rabbinic writings (the more "official" Jewish viewpoint) and apocalyptic writings (perhaps the more "sectarian"). It is under the influence of rabbinic literature that the sense of the indicative verb form, "the Lord is King," comes to be expressed in the abstract noun form, "kingdom of heaven." But this does not result in any abstraction of meaning, nor is the reference to a "territory" over which God rules. The same holds true for the Hellenistic Jews associated with Philo: the original meaning "the Lord is King" remains intact.

Another important development in post-Old Testament Jewish literature was that it became a regular feature of prayers to ask that the kingdom of God be revealed. The Targum speaks frequently of the end time, in which the Lord would reveal his kingship. Furthermore, the rabbis came to see the concept "kingdom of heaven" as wholly eschatological.[6] They did not deny that God was King in the present, but he was so in a *hidden* fashion. So they could explain his people's continuing servitude after the exile, and so they looked anxiously for the last day, when he would *reveal* his kingship in power.

Further, they looked forward to a messianic kingdom and were convinced that through their study and observance of the Law, through penitence and good deeds, they could hasten the messiah's coming. Thus the nationalistic expectations of Israel became more and more bound up with the messiah's coming.

The apocalyptic expectation of God's kingship took its own direction. Of particular importance are its suprahistorical character and the place within it occupied by demon powers.

In the Old Testament the future expectation was strongly nationalistic. Its concerns were for Israel and Israel's future, and its perspective derived chiefly from such ordinary historical events as Israel's victories in war. But apocalyptic expectation eventually became strongly suprahistorical, supernatural, and universalistic. The book of Daniel is a good example of this development, for Daniel expects the heavenly kingdom to include all peoples. Daniel 2 expounds the dream of Nebuchadnezzar; after describing four world kingdoms, it prophesies that God will create a kingdom to overthrow all others and stand forever (v. 44). To make it clear that this will not occur through ordinary war, v. 45 states that a stone (the kingdom of God) is loosened from a mountain "without human hands" and smashes the other four kingdoms.

Daniel 7 makes it even clearer that the supernatural kingdom will arrive in suprahistorical fashion. After describing four animals (the kingdoms of ch. 2), there appears in a vision "one like a son of man coming with the clouds of heaven" before the Ancient of days, and kingship is bestowed upon him so that *all* revere him. His kingship is eternal and will never be destroyed. Clearly we are dealing here with

6. K. G. Kuhn, *TDNT* I, 574.

a heavenly being, who appears in a supernatural manner and receives a heavenly kingdom. Therefore we are concerned with far more than the redemption of Israel from its enemies.

The coming judgment plays a special role in this apocalyptic expectation. God will make his lordship known by judging, by annihilating the ungodly, by restoring for the faithful the original paradise of earth—or by destroying the earth and removing the faithful to heavenly glory.

Kallas believes that one can never correctly interpret the kingdom and eschatology in Jesus' preaching and ministry (as in all the New Testament) without viewing it against a background of demonology.[7] For example, we can never grasp why Jesus devoted so much attention to exorcism—relating it directly to the coming of the kingdom—if we fail to grasp the apocalyptists' conclusion that the world has been stolen from God by evil powers which must be overcome before God can rule again on earth. This conviction had its roots in the Old Testament.

According to the Old Testament Yahweh is the only true God, but he is nowhere portrayed as the only supernatural being. There are seraphim, cherubim, angels, archangels—and even many other gods (Pss. 82; 86:8; 95:3; 96:4; 97:7, 9; 135:5; Exod. 15:11). Old Testament monotheism consisted not of presenting God as the only spiritual or heavenly being, but rather as he who rules over all other heavenly beings and who alone among them is truly God. Further, the Old Testament teaches that God makes use of them. Sometimes he uses them to bless, sometimes to punish humankind (as by "the destroyer" of Exod. 12:23). Not all these spiritual beings are obedient to God, however; Satan, e.g., is the antagonist of God's children (Job 1:6-12; 2:1-6; Zech. 3:1; cf. 2 Sam. 24:1; 1 Chr. 21:1).

Conviction of the Lord's kingship is strong throughout the Old Testament. But increasingly it becomes a problem to prophets and people why God (good, powerful, and ready to help) should tolerate suffering and injustice. The book of Job wrestles mightily with that question; why should a righteous child of the King suffer? (See also Ps. 73.)

This struggle crystallizes during the intertestamental period in the apocalyptic writings. Here the conviction takes shape that Satan and the evil powers oppose God radically (more by far than in Job 1–2 and

---

7. In the exposition which follows, considerable use is made of J. Kallas, *The Significance of the Synoptic Miracles* (1961), especially Chapter 4.

Zechariah 3, where the impression lingers that Satan is God's servant) and that *evil powers rule the earth.*

The more deeply this awareness penetrates, the more God's lordship becomes a *future* expectation. For now, Satan rules; he is the prince of this world (John 14:30). But God is its true king; one day he will reveal his dominion to all by vanquishing the evil powers. According to Kallas, this means that not only humankind but all the world must be freed from Satan when God's kingdom comes—i.e., when he rules on earth. Kallas's interpretation is supported by the fact that statements about the fall of the angels and the rebellion of the evil powers against God are rare in the Old Testament, while in Jewish apocalyptic literature of the intertestamental period they abound.

Given this background of the concept of the kingdom of God, it is clear that Jesus' audiences could have a variety of ideas about it. Some could hold the narrowly nationalistic expectation that God would send a political messiah to liberate Israel from Roman oppression and restore the nation to former glory. Others could entertain apocalyptic images of a supernatural intervention by which God would execute his judgment, destroy the earth, and remove the faithful to heavenly glory.

What is common to all these interpretations is that God reigns invisibly at the present; in the end, his kingdom will burst forth to usher in a new epoch. It is clear why Jesus' proclamation ("the kingdom of God is at hand") projects such a strong, eschatological character. If God has come to rule on earth, the end has arrived. The goal ("I shall be your God, and you shall be my people") has been reached.

Jesus Christ the King

Jesus did not merely announce God's kingdom and then remain aloof. On the contrary, there is a direct connection between his ministry (especially his exorcisms of demons) and the coming of the kingdom (see, among other texts, Matt. 12:22-29). Although there are problems in this regard, one must ultimately accept that Jesus himself acts as the king who makes God's reign visible and exercises it concretely. In order to grasp the nature of his lordship, however, we need to examine what misunderstandings existing among his contemporaries Jesus rejected.

The first of these was the misconception of his kingship, that he came to rule in Caesar's place (John 6:15; Luke 23:2; Acts 17:7). In fact Jesus' kingdom did "not belong to this world" (John 18:36-37) and so had no boundaries like that of an earthly kingdom which might oppose another kingdom such as Rome. God's kingdom is his unbounded rule over all other kingdoms (1 Tim. 6:15).

Jesus failed to fall in with nationalistic expectations that he would restore the bygone glory of Israel at the expense of other peoples. Instead he came to rule over Israel *and* all other peoples. His real enemies were Satan and the powers of evil—as the demons themselves were evidently aware (Matt. 4:8-9).

But this in no way implies that Jesus came to erect a "spiritual" kingdom. Evil spirits had enslaved *earthly* humans far too literally for any purely *spiritual* liberation to be helpful or possible. Further on we shall place considerable stress on the earthliness of God's kingdom, illustrating by Jesus' miracles that God's kingdom liberates people (not their souls only) and creation itself.

There were other misconceptions which Jesus had to dispel. Part of the populace thought it could make Jesus its king, though he had come simply to reveal the eternal lordship of God, to exorcise evil powers from God's creation, and to summon the world to share in God's lordship and blessedness (Luke 2:14). In this way he fulfilled the Old Testament eschatological expectation, which was that the Lord would make his dominion *known,* not that he would *become* king. We can therefore appreciate why Jesus would not allow the people to make him king.

The inscription "king of the Jews" above Jesus' head on the cross reveals the same misunderstanding. There is bitter irony in the fact that this accusation was intended as Jesus' indictment, while in fact it was his vindication that he *was* king of the Jews—and of the whole world. Yet though he was the king who ruled his people and creatures only for good, some of his opponents saw in him a threat to Caesar.

Jesus' statement that his kingdom did not "belong to this world" (John 18:36) must be read against this background. It does not mean that he takes no interest in this world. It does not mean that he brings peace only to our souls, ignoring real storms, handicaps, politics, and demon possessions. God is God of heaven *and earth*!

What John 18:36 does mean is that Jesus concerns himself with a different order of politics than that of earthly kings. He has no desire to proclaim his kingdom in opposition to the Roman or any other kingdom. He is king of kings (Rev. 17:14; 19:16). No Roman emperor need renounce his office to accept Jesus as king. The whole world belongs to God; Jesus has come to announce and restore his dominion, one in which there is room for all earthly authority which is obedient to him.

Jesus did not want to be *made* king; he already *is* king! The Synoptics name him king in various ways, among them "king of the Jews" (Matt. 2:2; 27:11, 29, 37; Mark 15:2, 9, 12, 18, 26; Luke 23:3, 37ff.; John 18:33, 37, 39; 19:3, 14-21), "king of Israel" (Matt. 27:42; Mark 15:32; John 1:49; 12:13), and simply "king" (Matt. 21:5; 25:34, 40; Luke 19:38; John 12:15). This means that there is a direct connection between Jesus and Yahweh, who is king of the whole world. This is why there is an equivalence between Jesus (the king) and the kingdom (lordship) of God. The kingdom of God has come because Jesus has come.[8]

Matthew 12:27 is extremely important in this connection. Here Jesus decisively relates the coming of God's kingdom to the expulsion of demons. Now, the remarkable fact is that he is not the only one to exorcise. He himself refers to pupils of the Pharisees who practice exorcism. As we pointed out in Chapter 1, it is therefore not the mere fact of exorcism of demons which shows that God's kingdom has come. It is shown, rather, by the fact that it is Jesus who drives them out—or, as Matthew tells us, that he does so by the "finger" of God, not by the magic formulas of exorcists.

This identification of Christ with the kingdom also emerges from comparisons of certain parallels in the Synoptics: e.g., of Mark 11:10 ("the coming kingdom") with Matt. 21:9 and Luke 19:38 ("him who comes as king"), of Mark 10:29 ("for my sake") with Luke 18:29 ("for the sake of the kingdom") and of Mark 9:1 with Matt. 16:28. By the Hebrew parallelism in Acts 8:12, the phrase "name of Jesus Christ" explains "good news about the kingdom of God." In the light of these equations between Jesus and the kingdom, we must affirm with Origen that Jesus is the *autobasileia,* the kingdom-as-person.[9]

This casts much light on why Jesus stands at the center of the

---

8. The manner in which T. van der Walt divides his treatment of Kingdom and the Son of Man in *Die Koninkryk van God—Naby!* (1962) already indicates a certain parallelism:

KINGDOM	SON OF MAN
The Kingdom *has come*	*The Son of Man* has come
The Kingdom *will come*	The Son of Man *will come*
The Kingdom between one coming and the next	The Son of Man *between one coming and the next*

9. K. L. Schmidt, *TDNT* I, 589, mentions "the actual identity of the kingdom with Christ." The texts mentioned and the pronouncement of Origen are derived from Schmidt's article.

gospel. He comes not to proclaim some*thing* but some*one*—himself! Our future is decided by our relationship to *him*. Everyone who does not gather with him scatters (Luke 11:23). Whoever confesses him is safe. Whoever denies him is lost (Matt. 10:32-40). Jesus does not say, "By losing your life, you will gain it," but "By losing your life for *my* sake, you will gain it."

Jesus is the king in whose person and work lies the world's last great decision. God's kingdom comes in him; in him God reveals his dominion over the world. Jesus is the king. In him God's expected lordship over the earth is revealed. Therefore we rightly confess Christ as he "by whom the Father governs all things" (*Heidelberg Catechism,* answer 50).

Though we have not mentioned nearly all that the New Testament contains concerning the kingdom of God, it is already clear that we must cautiously approach Cullmann's suggestion that there is at least a temporal difference between the lordship of Christ *(regnum Christi)* and the kingdom of God *(regnum Dei).* For Cullmann, Christ's lordship begins with the ascension and will conclude at the inception of the world to come.[10]

Both Berkouwer and Ridderbos point out that this does injustice to Jesus' ministry before his crucifixion.[11] His sayings about the presence of the kingdom cannot come into their own if they are seen, as Cullmann suggests, merely as anticipations. Cullmann himself admits that distinctions between the lordship of Christ and the kingdom of God cannot be applied consistently in the New Testament.

It is not consistent, either with the doctrine of the Trinity or with the concept of salvation history, to draw a sharp distinction between the lordship of Jesus and the kingdom of God. The New Testament applies pronouncements about Yahweh to Jesus, and Jesus identifies his own person with the kingdom of God. In fact, Cullmann's own view of the place and revelatory function of the Son militate against any such distinction.

The New Testament doctrine of Christ as the *eschatos* offers even less evidence for Cullmann's case. If Jesus' earthly ministry is not the arrival of the kingdom but only of a provisional reign, then Jesus cannot be the *eschatos,* and his incarnation and earthly work are

10. O. Cullmann, "The Kingship of Christ and the Church in the New Testament," *The Early Church* (1956), 105ff.
11. G. C. Berkouwer, *The Providence of God* (1952), 110f. H. Ridderbos, *The Coming of the Kingdom* (1960), 95ff.

not eschatology. And if this is the case, then eschatology can start only after the second coming and judgment, when this provisional lordship will be replaced by God's kingdom (1 Cor. 15:28). And only at that point would God's goal be reached.

Were this so, Cullmann would be correct not to present the earthly work of Jesus as eschatology. But the witness of the New Testament is decisively against him, for we have shown that Jesus *is* the *eschatos*. The goal lies in him and is therefore attained in every phase of his history—including his radically eschatological incarnation and earthly ministry.

Only now is it clear just how radically Cullmann's linear view of time affects his whole outlook on the New Testament. For him, New Testament eschatology is more a matter of time categories than of a person. That is why he finds it so easy to fit Jesus into a series of *things* which must happen. Jesus and his kingdom are only one more step toward a consummation which draws ever nearer, as certain new things happen.

In the light of this, we can appreciate better than ever how right and timely is Weber's reaction (see Chapter 3) against equating eschatology with the passage of secular time *(Verlaufszeit)*. Once the end, the *eschatos,* and the goal are viewed as a person, the distinction between Christ's lordship and God's kingdom falls away.

Because Jesus is the revelation of God and his reign aims at achieving the purpose of God, the *eschaton* is attained in Jesus' kingly acts. His royal call, "Follow me" (Luke 5:27, etc.), is the summons of a God who from all eternity has willed to be for us, has bound himself to us, has made our cause his cause, and has bound us to him. When this call is answered in faith and obedience (Luke 5:28, etc.), God's goal is reached in our lives, and what follows is a feast, because that which was sick is healed, the unrighteous has been called, and the sinner has repented. This is how Jesus attains God's goal in us, even during his earthly ministry. He comes to live beside his own possession in total identification with the lot of humanity. He is their God and calls them back from their straying so that they can be his people.

The Extent of Jesus' Lordship

For many reasons, we should expect God's kingdom (i.e., Christ's lordship) to be widely inclusive. The Old Testament anticipates a revelation of the Lord as king of the whole earth. The Old Testament concept of peace is a comprehensive one, a salvation which specifically includes earth and the things of earth. The Old Testament calls for nature to praise God (Pss. 19; 96:11-13; 149; Isa. 43:20, etc.). All of the data supports the expectation that the kingdom of God will encompass much more than "the spiritual." Furthermore, the covenant is creation's goal and God is the God of heaven and *earth*. This same cosmic breadth is to be expected of Jesus' kingship.

This consideration is prominent in the earthly ministry of Jesus. He comes not only to save souls but to save people, to save the world, and to renew the earth. Thus he not only forgives sins but also heals people. Exorcism is an important part of Christ's cosmic dominion. Its importance becomes apparent when the intertestamental background is considered. People of that time regarded Satan as the master of this world, the ruler and ruiner of God's creation. Old Testament prophets had promised, however, that a day would dawn in which God would reveal his lordship to everyone.

This happens in the acts of Jesus. Demons flee before him. When they see him they cry out, fall down, and implore. They know who he is: the Son of God or the Holy One of God. According to Matt. 12:27-28, exorcism assumes an exceptional place among the deeds of Jesus. It indicates that he is king and that the kingdom of God has come in him. Jesus' exorcisms are remarkably comprehensive. They affect both people and nature. Let us probe more deeply into this cosmic aspect of God's kingdom in Jesus' ministry with some specific examples.

The healing of the crippled woman (Luke 13:10-17). This woman has been unable to stand upright for eighteen years. The cause: a spirit of infirmity. To avoid all misunderstanding, Jesus states that it was Satan who has kept her prisoner (v. 16). Therefore, it is in breaking the dominion of Satan over her life that Jesus heals her (v. 16).

The Gadarene demoniac (Mark 5:1-20). This event presents a gripping example of the misery into which demons plunge people. The man is totally under their control. He has become a beast. He lives among tombs and snaps the chains with which people try to restrain him. Yet he is a human being, whom God has destined to be his happy servant. Jesus expels this legion of demons, which at once wreak havoc on the environment, causing two thousand pigs to stampede into the sea. But what a transformation! There the untamable savage sits, clothed and in his right mind. Jesus breaks the power of demons and heals what they have damaged, because he is king. In this exorcism he reveals his lordship openly; the kingdom of God has come—because the king has come.

Jesus stills the storm (Mark 4:35-41). Here is an arresting example of what the kingdom of God (i.e., the lordship of Jesus) means in the realm of nature. According to Kallas, this miracle shows that, for Jesus, a storm is no normal happening of nature but rather the work of Satan, who seeks to drag not only humans but also nature into chaos. That is why Mark uses words so frequently uttered by Jesus when driving out demons: "He stood up, rebuked the wind, and said to the sea, 'Hush, be still'" (4:39; cf. 1:25; 3:12; 9:25, etc.). So we can see that Jesus views the storm as a threat to human life and the work of a demon. He expels the demon from nature and so destroys the evil power which threatens human life.[12]

He is at work restoring God's dominion over the earth and bringing true peace to the world. This is much more than peace for our souls; it has cosmic significance. Not only humankind, but also the world humankind inhabits, is being saved. Is it not God's world (Ps. 24:1) which God himself has made (Gen. 1:1)?

Through the centuries, this cosmic significance of Jesus' ministry and lordship has frequently been misrepresented in the Church's preaching. Even today, his stilling of the storm is interpreted in ways which have nothing whatever to do with that event's function in the Bible. Richardson shows how Tertullian took the ship to be a figure of the Church, the sea to symbolize the world, and the waves to represent persecutions and temptations.[13] That Jesus stilled the storm, Tertullian took to mean that he wishes to bring peace into our hearts.

According to Richardson, Tertullian was but one of many of the Fathers who upheld this view. Richardson himself sees two meanings in this and other miracles. Primarily, they reveal just who Jesus is. In the Old Testament, it is Yahweh who rules over nature. His power over storms is a recurrent theme in the Psalms (107:23-30; 89:10, etc.). So Richardson sees the primary meaning of Mark 4:35-41 to be that Jesus has the power of Yahweh.

Secondarily, posits Richardson, they offer consolation. This particular miracle is meant to bring comfort to a storm-tossed Church in a hostile world. The message to Christians, toiling against huge waves and head winds of persecution, is that Christ brings peace to our hearts amidst the storm.

When Richardson, following Tertullian's lead, declares that this is what Mark meant beyond any reasonable doubt, he joins the age-old

12. Kallas, 65.
13. A. Richardson, *The Miracle Stories of the Gospels* (1941), 93.

ranks of the "spiritualizers." Even though he counts consolation a secondary theme, it appears from his treatment of the text that—for him—this is its ultimate meaning. Indeed, when at the end of his book he presents a summary of his views in "The Religious Value of the Miracle Story for Us," miracles receive short shrift as literal events. We are told that miracles, beyond making Jesus known as the fulfillment of Old Testament eschatology, "speak to us of the gracious dealings of Christ with our sick, hungry, and tormented souls."[14]

Kallas reacts sharply to such spiritualizing. Indeed, it is at this point that he differs essentially from Richardson. Both agree that Jesus sees the storm as Satan's work and calms it by the same means as that by which he exorcises demons.[15] But Kallas emphatically denies Richardson's "secondary" meaning—which in the end becomes the one real meaning in Richardson's presentation.

Kallas does not deny the fact that, through the ages, Jesus has protected the Church on life's sea of temptations and persecutions. Nor does he doubt that Jesus wants to still the troubled heart and life. He considers these messages valuable and their proclamation necessary—but they do not constitute the meaning of this miracle. Anyone who suggests that it is fails to perceive the real drama of the attack Jesus launches against the demons of the deep.[16]

But the real problem in the interpretation of this miracle is not the choice between "spiritual" and "literal." After all, Richardson does acknowledge that the spiritual is secondary. The real problem is that the literal cannot function in Richardson's application of the miracle, but is totally overwhelmed by the secondary.

Truth to tell, this is the problem with the way in which miracles are commonly proclaimed in today's Church. Literal meanings are scarcely ever denied or explained away in moderate circles. But the moment they are applied to the situation here and now, they are spiritualized. H. van der Loos correctly observes, "when the fishing boat which was once in distress on the Sea of Galilee is converted into the 'ship of the church,' it should be realized that this conversion is effected purely and simply in the ship-yard of the imagination."[17]

But another problem lies on a yet deeper level: it is the question

14. *Ibid.*, 136.

15. Kallas, 91: "St. Mark in iv. 39 implies that Jesus is casting out the daemon of the storm since the words . . . are parallel to the words in Mark 1:25."

16. *Ibid.*, 89-90.

17. H. van der Loos, *The Miracles of Jesus* (1961), 649.

of whether or not Jesus really saw demonic power at work in the storm and so acted against an evil spirit. Van der Loos denies that this can be said with certainty and maintains that as Jesus elsewhere gave orders to inanimate objects, he could here have been doing so to the sea (cf. Mark 11:14, 23). But what then, for example, could that miracle mean in which Jesus curses an unfruitful fig tree? Is Jesus necessarily commanding an *inanimate* object?

The withered fig tree (Mark 11:12-14, 20-26; Matt. 21:18-22). This miracle has presented great difficulty throughout history. First, it is Jesus' only "negative" miracle. Second, he seems to give an order to an inanimate tree—or to pass sentence upon it. Third, he curses the tree for not bearing figs, though Mark says explicitly that "it was not the season for figs."

Richardson, who usually at least *begins* with the literal meanings of miracles, here abandons any attempt at literal interpretation in favor of the suggestion (based on the parable in Luke 13:6-9) that this "miracle" was created by later tradition. Others hold that the report is so full of inaccuracies and corrections that its meaning can no longer be discovered. Most agree that its meaning is symbolic, that Jesus was targeting the Pharisees—or the people of Israel in general—who celebrated many outward ceremonies but bore no fruits of inward repentance.[18]

Exceptions to this rule are all the more striking because they are few. F. W. Grosheide denies that there is any application here to Israel's formalistic religion, seeing the miracle's purpose as one more proclamation by Jesus to his disciples of the power of faith. E. Lohmeyer goes a bit further, seeing in it Jesus' declaration that anything which does not serve humankind is unworthy of life (cf. Luke 13:6ff.) and, further, that Jesus is nature's Lord. Kallas finds himself in basic agreement with this, though he places this miracle in a much broader context.[19]

Kallas's view is derived particularly from his understanding of the kingdom of God, which we earlier discussed. God made the trees to feed people (Gen. 1:12, 29; 2:16). Rev. 22:2 deliberately alludes to

18. E.g., E. P. Groenewald, *Die Evangelie volgens Markus* (1948), ad loc.; J. Schniewind, *Markus* (NTD; 1952⁶), ad loc.; van der Loos, 696ff. A. Richardson, 57, draws out the symbolism to mean that the mountain was "the mountain of Jewish unbelief."

19. F. W. Grosheide, *Het Heilig Evangelie volgens Mattheus* (Commentaar op het Nieuwe Testament; 1922), 320; E. Lohmeyer, *Das Evangelium des Markus* (KEK; 1963¹⁶), ad loc.; Kallas, 96ff.

the account of the garden of Eden in its description of the tree of life, "which yields twelve crops of fruit, one for each month of the year." This means that trees were intended to produce an uninterrupted supply of food; the very existence of seasons is part of the chaos sown by Satan.

The curse Jesus placed on the barren fig tree is, then, in Kallas's view, a prophetic glimpse of the future. On the new earth, there would be no season about which Mark could say that it was not the season for figs. Every trace which Satan's touch left on God's creation would be eradicated. So it is that the withered fig tree is a sign of the coming of the kingdom, since Jesus regards its lack of fruit as a work of the devil.[20]

The sea and other natural forces. Let us reconsider the meaning of the storm which Jesus stilled. As mentioned, van der Loos denies that one can safely assert that Jesus addresses the storm as a demon because, he says, Jesus addresses an inanimate fig tree in the same way. However, it is possible that Jesus saw the storm and the fig tree as two evidences of demonic work, so that, in cursing them, he cursed Satan. When we place against their full Old Testament background the miracles of stilling the storm, walking on water, and (perhaps) cursing the fig tree, there seems little doubt that Jesus sees in these phenomena of nature the work of Satan and responds accordingly.

In his exposition of Gen. 1:9-13, Barth pointed out that the sea is as hostile to the land as darkness is to light.[21] Like darkness, the sea is a figure of the forces of chaos which menace God's creation. The sea has a certain affinity for the chaotic which God repudiates. Just as

20. This does not solve all problems. The question remains whether it would not have been more meaningful had Jesus caused the tree to bear fruit twelve times a year, or at least caused a rich fig crop to appear there and then. But in the first place, it is surely not our task to provide reasons why Jesus acted as he did. In the second, it is meaningful to refer to the parable of Luke 13:6ff., where the unfruitful tree is given a year's reprieve before being cut down. In both cases the principle remains that a tree which does not do its work ought not to be tolerated.

Taken as a whole, Kallas's exposition is the most meaningful, partly because it does not attempt to explain away Mark's statement that "it was not the season for figs." It is clear that this miracle has always been a cause of difficulty and that there is little hope of ever reaching any consensus about its precise meaning.

21. Barth, III/1, 141-156.

at creation earth is not altogether freed from darkness (night), neither is the land entirely freed from chaos (the sea). This will occur only with the new creation (Rev. 21:1, 23; 22:5).

In fact, one can speak of more than an affinity between chaos and the sea. In the Old Testament there is some identity between the sea and the forces of chaos, especially Rahab and Leviathan. In Ps. 74:13-15 the sea, sea monsters, and Leviathan are parallel concepts (see also Ps. 89:10ff.; Isa. 27:1; and Hab. 3:8, where God's wrath is directed against the sea). So it is hardly strange that Jesus does not distinguish clearly between the sea and the demon in it when he stills the storm.

More than once in the Old Testament, we find God's act of creation represented as a contest with the forces of chaos. This harmonizes with the views we have just considered. In Ps. 104:5ff., we are told how waters covered the earth, a reference to the state of things before Gen. 1:9. The psalmist goes on to say: "At thy rebuke they ran, at the sounding of thy thunder they rushed way." Gen. 1:9 can also be compared with Job 38:8-11; Pss. 74:13; 77:17; 89:11. The concept of boundaries is important in these texts. "You fixed them a boundary which they (the waters) might not pass" (Ps. 104:9; cf. Job 38:8-11). So long as the waters remain within their boundaries, they perform a service for God's creatures. The psalmist bears witness to this in the verses which follow (vv. 10ff.), and, elsewhere in the Bible, the waters display a much friendlier disposition. There is even talk in the New Testament of the "water of life" (John 4:14; 7:38; Rev. 22:17; etc.; cf. Isa. 55:1).

Nevertheless, water—and especially the sea—remains such a threat, a figure of powers which are hostile to God, that J. H. Kroeze actually calls it an enemy of God (cf. Isa. 17:12ff.; 50:2; Pss. 18:5; 46:2-4; 65:7; 69:2-15; 124:2ff.; 144:7ff.).[22] Of course this does not mean that the sea can break out uncontrolled. We have already pointed out that God has set a boundary for the sea, and within this it serves the life of humankind. Furthermore, the sea is summoned along with the rest of creation to praise the Lord in the words: "The Lord is King" (1 Chr. 16:31-32).

But when we recall the menacing character of the sea (and never far away, its monsters Rahab and Leviathan), it is hardly strange that, though dwellers by the sea (Judg. 5:17; Gen. 49:13), the Israelites

22. J. H. Kroeze, *Het Boek Job* (Commentaar op het Oude Testament; 1961), 291. (See also his exposition of Job 7:12.)

never took up seafaring. Their few attempts ended in disaster (e.g., 1 Kgs. 22:49ff.; Jonah). In fact they ranked sea voyages with desert caravans, imprisonment, and disease as chief among the human miseries (Ps. 107:23ff.), from which afflictions it is the will of God to save them.

Barth proceeds from such observations to this important pronouncement: "It is thus the more noteworthy that the most striking Messianic deeds of Jesus [we would say: two among the most striking such deeds] are His walking on the sea in royal freedom, and His commanding the waves and storm to be still by His Word." Therefore, "in the new heaven and the new earth . . . there will be no more sea, i.e., man will be fully and finally freed from each and every threat to his salvation, and God from each and every threat to His glory."[23]

There can no longer be any doubt that Jesus acts against the sea as against a demon. The demonic character of the sea, hostile to God and threatening to humankind, is evidenced throughout the Bible. But Jesus, the king, has arrived to destroy the works of the devil (1 John 3:8). He compels the sea (and its monsters) to silence and so protects the lives of his disciples. And when he walks on the waves (Mark 6:45ff.), he exhibits his power and dominion over "God's enemy" (Kroeze).

There is much in this to support Kallas's explanation that Jesus regarded the barren fig tree as Satan's work. Fruit trees are to produce food for humankind; when they do not fulfill their purpose, they should no longer clutter the ground (Luke 13:6ff.).

In view of this, we can only welcome reactions against spiritualized interpretations of the nature and healing miracles. Jesus' acts—and through them God's kingdom—exhibit decisively cosmic structures. That Jesus comes to save both humanity and the world agrees fully with the earthly character of the Old Testament concept of peace and with Paul's statement in Rom. 8:19ff. But let us conclude by considering another of Jesus' nature miracles.

The feeding of the multitude (Mark 6:30-44; 8:1-9). The two miracles of the multiplication of loaves and fishes have long expositional histories. Schweitzer mentions speculation that Jesus showed hidden baskets of food to the crowds. But rejecting this theory, he propounds his own. Schweitzer accepts the entire matter as historical, save only the narrative remark that all were satisfied. To him, the event's significance lies in Jesus' thanksgiving prayer and in that all received

23. Barth, III/1, 149.

a little piece, making the meal a typical messianic meal. According to Schweitzer, this sharing of food is more than a sharing of love and community; from Jesus' standpoint it is a sacrament of salvation.[24]

Even among conservative expositors and preachers such unacceptable spiritualizing often occurs, especially in sermons. Jesus' giving bread and fish to the crowds is usually interpreted as his wish to give spiritual nourishment to satisfy spiritual hunger.[25] His words, "Let me have them," referring to the loaves and fishes (Matt. 14:18), are taken to mean that even such meager abilities as our own can achieve much, if we put them in his hands. All these applications are true *in themselves* and are spoken of *elsewhere* in the Bible. We read of spiritual hunger and of bread in John 6:50ff. and of what can be done with our feeble abilities in Phil. 4:13 and 2 Cor. 12:9-10. But we read nothing about spiritual hunger, spiritual needs, or human talent in a miracle where hundreds are fed from a few loaves and fishes. Here the people quite literally received bread and fish from Jesus, and it is precisely in the *literal* reality of the event that its *spiritual* meaning lies.

Crowds are following Jesus. He pities them because they are like sheep without a shepherd (v. 34), and untended sheep are always in danger. That they are so is the work of Satan; but Jesus helps them. First he satisfies their spiritual hunger by teaching them "many things," then their physical hunger by giving them bread. He does this because their physical hunger is as much of Satan as their spiritual hunger. God made the earth to yield food for humans; when famine or other disasters lead to starvation, this is one more sign of Satan's assault on God's creation. Satan is resolved to destroy God's handiwork and to visit suffering on those whom God meant to be his glad partners in covenant. This is why Paul regards hunger as a weapon in Satan's hand (Rom. 8:35) and why famine is so important a part of Satan's onslaught against God's world (e.g., Mark 13:8).

In this light, we can understand why Jesus pities the hungry and feeds them; this is a sign from him of God's kingly rule. God provides lavishly for his creatures. Note that in each instance, far too much bread

24. A. Schweitzer, *Geschichte der Leben-Jesu-Forschung* (1913[2]), 430. (This section is not included in the English translation.)

25. A. Richardson (*op. cit.*, p. 98) has elaborated the "spiritual" meaning to a great extent. He sees the inclusion of two feeding miracles as signifying that the gospel is not for Jews only, but also for Gentiles. Indeed, the site of the first feeding does presume a Jewish gathering, while that of the second feeding presumes a Gentile gathering. Thus "the disciples need have no anxiety concerning Christ's ability to supply spiritual food to the whole Gentile world."

results. The same thing occurs in John 2:1-12, where Jesus makes more wine than the guests can drink. Again in Luke 5:1-11, Jesus provides such an abundant catch of fish that the boats almost sink. Wherever Jesus appears and makes known the dominion of God, there we find real, literal abundance.

One other important circumstance of the feeding miracles is that they most probably take place in the desert (compare various translations of Mark 8:4; Matt. 15:33 and Matt. 4:1; Luke 4:1). If they do take place in the desert, the destruction of Satan's work is even more forcefully evidenced. For throughout the Bible, deserts are terrifying places (Isa. 21:1ff.; Ps. 107:1ff.; Exod. 14:11; Num. 14:2; 16:13). Indeed, the devils live there. Jesus goes into the desert to be tempted by Satan (Matt. 4:1), and the Old Testament identifies the messianic age as one in which the desert will blossom and yield fruit (Jer. 33:11ff.; Joel 2:22; Isa. 35:1ff.; 41:19ff.).

So when Jesus performs a food miracle in the desert, he is stating that he regards the desert as a caricature of God's good and fruitful earth drawn by the devil. The miracle thus becomes something of a prophecy that there will be a new earth without deserts, since God intended the earth to yield food.

It is noteworthy that Mark stresses here again the overthrow of Satan's work. After describing the miraculous feeding, he tells us at once of Jesus walking on the water. This astounds the disciples, particularly when the gale abates as Jesus boards the ship. And Mark links their astonishment to the fact that "they had not understood the incident of the loaves; their minds were closed" (Mark 6:51-52). Had they grasped the significance of the miracle of the loaves, i.e., that God used this means to destroy Satan's misdirection of the earth and to show his care for his people, they would also have understood the miracle of the calm. For here, too, Jesus thwarted Satan, who jeopardized human life by means of the storm.

To sum up, we affirm that Jesus' ministry—particularly his miracles—shows that he did more than bring salvation to souls. The kingdom of God which emerges in his deeds, like the *eschaton* which he realizes in us through that ministry, is directly involved with the whole person (including bodily needs) and with the earth in the cosmic sense. The natural order is not disrupted by Jesus' miracles, though a surprising number of people are of this opinion. It is Satan and his evil powers who upset the natural order, so that the waters which ought to serve humanity (Ps. 104:11) threaten it, trees which should feed people bear fruit only at certain times, humans become beasts through demon possession, and the fruitful earth becomes a barren wilderness. Jesus the king begins his rule by *restoring the natural order:* by healing the sick, by feeding the hungry, by stilling the storm, by walking on the waves, by clothing the naked, by restoring minds, and by cursing the barren tree as a sign that it shall have no place in the new earth.

God's kingdom and the *eschaton,* which Jesus reaches in us through his deeds on earth, are truly cosmic in character. They embrace the whole person and the whole earth. Jesus' miracles affect a disordered nature: since we must someday rise *bodily,* the *earth* must be remade. Jesus begins this already during his earthly ministry. The kingdom is his gracious dominion for the salvation of his entire creation. Such is the wideness of God's purpose for his handiwork. Thus it is not surprising, as was emphasized in Chapter 3, that the goal Christ attains for us (the atonement) is just as wide; it includes all of creation.

It is therefore one-sided and causes misunderstanding to say that Jesus' kingdom is spiritual and heavenly by comparison with earthly kingdoms, or that God's kingdom consists only of his lordship over the hearts of his subjects.[26] Such comparisons are deceptive. The kingdom of Jesus is far more creation-directed, i.e., concerned with earth, than are earthly kingdoms themselves.[27]

But for as long as this real earthliness of God's kingdom—underscored so heavily in the New Testament—is not allowed its rightful place in our faith and lives, Buber's complaint (that Christians commit treason against the earth by not grasping the Old Testament's earthly character) will be fully justified. But were Buber to level this change against Jesus and the New Testament, the misunderstanding would be on his side.

The *eschaton* is beyond doubt realized, or at least begun, in Jesus' earthly work through which God's kingdom begins to come. This he does not achieve *for* us, or on our behalf—as he does by his crucifixion and resurrection—but *in* us and in the world, calling people to repentance and discipleship by his words and deeds. These show that the king has come and with him the kingdom. By expelling Satan from nature and from human lives, he begins to reach God's goal and to restore order to God's creation.

Clearly, Jesus' earthly ministry is but the beginning of the *escha-*

---

26. E. Roels, *God's Mission* (1962), 280.
27. In *The Return of Christ* (1972), 211-212, 225-228, G. C. Berkouwer has emphasized this same perspective in connection with the future expectation.

ton's second mode. Kallas expresses it thus: "in the demon-controlled world, there were small islands. There, where Jesus worked, were small places where the power of God recreating the world was already manifested."[28] This beginning was continued by Jesus' ministry through the Holy Spirit when his disciples began to make the good news known throughout the world. Here again we cannot ignore the cosmic structures (see, e.g., John 14:12; Acts 3:7; 5:15, 16; 9:40).

But although in Jesus' earthly ministry we see only a beginning, it is clear that his concern is nothing less than the attainment of the *eschaton,* the goal which God has set for creation. "For Jesus, the Kingdom of God meant exactly that—the reign of God over this world and its inhabitants. It meant the driving out of Satan, the cleansing of this world's ills, and the restoration, the *re*creation, of the garden where man could walk with God in the cool of the evening and God could say, 'It is good.'"[29]

Jesus' Dominion over the Evil Powers

We have seen again and again that Jesus' victory over evil powers plays an important role in the coming of God's kingdom. From the emphasis placed by Jesus on exorcising demons, it is clear that he shared the apocalyptic conviction that demons dominate the world and try to plunge it into chaos. God's kingdom can only come if these evil powers are vanquished. Against this background we can understand why Jesus should devote so much attention to the battle with these forces and to gaining victory over them. In fact the matter is so important that we must look even more closely into it, since the apostles persisted in attending to it after the ascension.

In the previous chapter we examined the "reconciliation" of these powers. Despite exceptional problems over exactly what Paul meant by his statements, we found that it implied at least their subjugation.

Precisely what are they? A whole range of terms is applied to them. These include "authority," "power," "might," "dominion" (Eph. 1:21), "sovereignty," "evil spirits" (6:12), "thrones," "potentates," "principalities," and "powers" (Col. 1:16), all used without any system. In Rom. 8:38ff. other terms are used, and some assert that Rom.

28. Kallas, 75. On the other hand, it is clear that Kallas makes too little of the already-realized character of the kingdom (p. 66), evidently because the idea of limited areas ("small islands") dominates the central concept that Jesus himself is the kingdom of God.

29. *Ibid.,* 74-75.

13:1ff.; 1 Cor. 2:8; 6:1ff.; Gal. 4:1ff.; and Col. 2:8, 16-23 refer to the same powers. In any case, it is clear that sin (Rom. 6:14), death (6:9), and death's domain (Hades; Rev. 6:8; 20:14) are numbered among them.

There is no consensus on the nature and character of these powers. Cullmann, for example, detects a limited relationship between them and their instrument, human authority. Berkhof describes them exceptionally broadly as the framework of creation which preserves it from general collapse, or, as do the dikes of his native Holland, restrains chaos and keeps it from flooding the world.[30] Cullmann's and Berkhof's descriptions make clear that it is possible to view these powers favorably.

Indeed they are not always spoken of negatively in the New Testament. In Col. 1:16 we read that the powers were "created through him [Christ] and for him." But there is also a direct relationship between the powers and Satan and his evil spirits.[31] Perhaps we should accept that there are good powers and evil, and that angels rank among the good ones (Heb. 1:14).

When we try to identify these powers in society, we must consider a broad spectrum of phenomena which range from personal powers to structural ones. On the individual level, we point to the worldwide renewal movement's emphasis on individual subjection to evil spirits and on exorcism as the Spirit's gift—though certainly many misuses and even ridiculous practices occur.

With regard to social structures, Berkhof's viewpoint is well-known. He holds that God appoints such powers to keep society running along orderly lines. The state, the family, general moral principles, public opinion, tradition, and many other forces are examples of this. When they obey God, they bring many blessings to society and protect life from various dangers and miseries.

30. O. Cullmann, *The State in the New Testament* (1957), 65f.; *idem., The Early Church,* 105ff.; H. Berkhof, *Christ and the Powers,* chapter 3. In *Christ and Time* (1964), 195, Cullmann says that "the actual State authority is thought of as the executive agent of angelic powers."

31. Paul relates "the devices of the devil" directly to "cosmic powers . . . authorities and potentates of this dark world" (Eph. 6:11-12). Elsewhere he speaks of the subjugation of authorities and powers in the same sense that Jesus speaks of his expulsion of demons and his victory over evil spirits (Col. 2:15; Matt. 12:28ff.). Even death is named as one of these, indeed, the most important (1 Cor. 15:26), and a close link is observed between death and Satan (Heb. 2:14-15). For the hostility of the powers to God, see especially G. Delling, *TDNT* I, 482-484.

But when they exceed their bounds and break away from God's rule, these powers leave chaos and calamity behind them. The absolutist state brings misery on those it oppresses—and on itself, as its leaders lose their humanity. The lapse of strong public morals brings lawlessness in its wake. Fragmentation of the family results in dislocation and loneliness. Traditions not formed by the gospel experience tremendous strain when it is proclaimed and received. Capitalism may exploit workers to favor a few who were born to wealth. Communism may enslave an entire populace to the service of those few who wrest power at times of revolution.

It is not at all farfetched to see evil powers at work in these systems and structures. Slavery was beyond doubt one such demonic power whose corruption went beyond the individual. It allowed the slaveholder to be a committed Christian, behaving humanely toward slaves while he or she was yet a part of a sinful and inhuman system. If Christ is the vanquisher of all powers (Col. 2:10, 15), then evil powers in private life and social structures must bend before him. So it becomes the Church's task to subject society's structures to the continual scrutiny and test of the gospel: to discover the demonic in them and to proclaim Christ's lordship over them.

The New Testament witness to Christ's victory and lordship over powers contains two sets of statements on the subject. The first announces his victory emphatically; the second, however, warns of continuing danger.

The first, the announcement that Jesus expelled demons, is a primary focus of the Synoptics: the demons were powerless before him, able only to cry out, beg, or flee when he spoke (Mark 1:23-34; 3:11; 5:5-13; 9:26); their response proves that the kingdom (lordship) of God had come in Jesus (Matt. 12:28ff.; Luke 11:20ff.); Jesus "watched how Satan fell like lightning" (Luke 10:18). Elsewhere we read that Jesus proclaimed "now shall the Prince of this world be driven out" (John 12:31); that Satan has been judged (16:11); that, disarming the cosmic powers, Christ "made a public spectacle of them and led them as captives in his triumphal procession" (Col. 2:15); that God "did not spare the angels who sinned, but consigned them to the dark pits of hell where they are reserved for judgment" (2 Pet. 2:4; Jude 6); that Christ is therefore the head to whom "every power and authority in the universe is subject" (Col. 2:10); that Christ is enthroned "above all government and authority, all power and dominion, and any title of sovereignty which can be named, not only in this age, but in the age to come" (Eph. 1:21-22); and that "angelic authorities and powers" have submitted to him (1 Pet. 3:22). Jesus himself declared: "Full authority in heaven and on earth has been committed to me" (Matt. 28:18). This first set of statements, culled from various parts of the New Testament, confirms the literal meaning of Jesus' use in Matt. 12:29 and Luke 11:21-22 of the image of a strong man (Satan and the evil spirits) being overcome, disarmed, and bound by a stronger man, Jesus the vanquisher, who then divides the spoils.

But the other set of statements indicates the danger still posed by Satan and evil spirits to the faithful and speaks of the promise that they will be annihilated, but only in the future. Eph. 6:11ff. talks of wrestling "against cosmic powers, against authorities and potentates of this dark world, against superhuman forces of evil in the heavens." John speaks of Satan as "the ruler of this world," warning that "the whole godless world lies in the power of the evil one" (1 John 5:19). 1 Pet. 5:8 warns that the devil goes about like a roaring lion, seeking someone to devour. We read in 1 Cor. 15:25 that Christ is "destined to reign until God has put all enemies under his feet." Phil. 3:21 speaks of Christ's "power which enables him to make all things subject to himself."

Two matters are clear at once. First, the New Testament places more emphasis on the message that Christ is the head who subjugates the powers (indeed, that Satan and his spirits are powerless against him) than on the message that Satan and the evil spirits still threaten the faithful. Nevertheless, that threat is affirmed; it would be fatal for the faithful to ignore such warnings just because it is also true that Christ rules over all powers already. Satan is still a roaring lion, seeking to devour. The combat in which the faithful are locked is portrayed as a struggle for life.

But the other side is equally true: they who heed only the warnings about Satan's power are not for that reason to be considered more pious; they neglect the joyful news of Jesus' lordship over the subjugated Satan. By not praising Christ for his victory, they deny him the honor which is his due. This means that the faithful must remain faithful to how Scripture distributes the emphasis in this matter.

The false conclusion can be drawn that these two sets of statements contradict or exclude each other. Does not one set affirm that Christ is the head to whom all power has been committed, so that he has conquered every "authority and power"? Did not the demons without exception cry out, plead, and flee at his appearance and command? What can remain here of a wrestling match, a roaring lion, or the prince of this world? Is there any purpose to urgent warnings if they are directed against a disarmed enemy, over whom Christ has triumphed and of whom he is making a public spectacle (Col. 2:15)?

For an answer, we must notice how the New Testament handles the subjection of evil powers. When Jesus exorcises demons in Luke 11, explaining by the analogy of a strong man bound that he is disarming and binding Satan that his house might be plundered and its inhabitants—God's people—freed (cf. Matt. 12:29), he adds, "He who is not with me is against me, and he who does not gather with me scatters" (Luke 11:23). So the conflict is not yet past. The decisive question is whether or not we are with Jesus. Luke goes on to relate the parable of an unclean spirit who is expelled but returns with seven more wicked than he to reoccupy the "house." He reclaims the house because it is unoccupied, "and the last state is worse than the first" (Matt. 12:44).[32]

The meaning of this parable is clear: though evil powers are overcome, disarmed, and expelled, they will return to him from whom they were driven—unless he is otherwise inhabited. This is to say, only if he is possessed and filled by Jesus can Satan's repossession be prevented. This parable highlights the specific way in which Satan has been defeated. That Jesus binds, disarms, conquers, and drives him out does not stop Satan from seizing every opportunity to mislead whom he may. But he avoids Jesus, who is the stronger and from whom he always flees. With Jesus and in Jesus, we are completely safe from Satan (see the *Heidelberg Catechism,* answer 127).

The second set of New Testament statements supports this; the warnings show that the conflict with Satan is not hopeless. The statements about Satan's power and the struggle's intensity (Eph. 6:10ff.) not only give a warning but also move the faithful to put on the whole armor of God. This will equip them to stand firm against the devices of the devil (v. 11), to remain standing when things are at their worst (v. 13), and to quench all the flami`g arrows of the evil one (v. 16). Similarly, 1 Pet. 5:9 says that, steadfast in the faith, they can and must resist the devil.

So both sets of statements reach the same conclusion. Powerless against Jesus, against the whole armor of God, and against faith, Satan is defeated. Warnings to the faithful are intended not to focus their consciousness on Satan but to remind them that their only victory is in Jesus.

---

32. Berkhof, chapter 4, has arresting things to say about this, especially about de-Christianized culture.

Despite these clear statements, there are still many who deny that Jesus has in any sense already overcome Satan on earth and bound him. They appeal to specific statements in John, e.g., that Satan is the "prince of this world" (John 14:30), and that "the whole godless world lies in the power of the evil one" (1 John 5:19; cf. 1 Cor. 2:6-8; 2 Cor. 4:4; Eph. 2:2).

It is important to note that in John 12:31 where Satan is referred to as the prince of this world, we read: "Now is the hour of judgment for this world; now shall the prince of this world be driven out." This expulsion is compatible with the exorcisms in the Synoptics. According to John 12:31, then, Satan is driven out of the area over which he rules—that is, the world he has plunged into chaos. According to the Synoptics, this is the pinnacle of all that Jesus did during his ministry. Evidently Jesus thinks in John 12:31 of his crucifixion; hence the future tense of "*shall be* driven out." Paul agrees (Col. 2:15). This perspective coincides with the idea of God's kingdom coming through Jesus' expulsion of demons and of his liberation of humanity and nature from the chaos into which demons had dragged them.

One can deduce nothing, therefore, merely from the phrases "prince of this world" and "god of this passing age" (2 Cor. 4:4), "this passing age" and "its governing powers" (1 Cor. 2:6; Eph. 6:12), or "the spiritual powers of the air" (Eph. 2:2). These are rabbinic terms for Satan which Jesus and early Christians adopted. The real thrust of their use in the gospel proclamation is that the ruler of this world has been disarmed, subjugated, bound, and driven out.

Though the powers have been conquered *already,* they will be conquered *again.* It is difficult to formulate the distinction between the two. For example, we read of death's power being already broken (2 Tim. 1:10) and being again abolished at the resurrection (1 Cor. 15:26). Satan's power, too, was broken by Christ's death (Heb. 2:14); yet he will be cast into hell only when Christ returns (Rev. 20:10). In trying to understand this, we should in the first place remember that Christ, the last and the end, achieves victory over the powers throughout his entire history, in the same way that the "last days" and the end extend through his whole history. Thus he conquers the powers during his earthly work (as in the Synoptics), during his crucifixion (as in John, Paul's epistles, and Hebrews), in his resurrection (Rom. 6:9), during his present work through the Holy Spirit (demonstrated by the apostles' deeds in Acts), and again at his second coming.

However, one should also note that the New Testament writers distinguish between the way in which powers are subjugated now and how they will be subjugated on judgment day. We have dealt with the manner in which Christ has already bound them, though this does not relieve us of responsibility to resist them in the present (1 Pet. 5:9). But in the end, Satan, death, and Hades are to be hurled into the lake of brimstone, "there to be tormented day and night forever" (Rev. 20:10, 14). Then "every knee shall bow [before Jesus] and every tongue confess him Lord" (Phil. 2:10-11). And "every kind of dominion, authority, and power" will be abolished (1 Cor. 15:24).

But in referring to our present situation, the New Testament almost never refers to Satan's subjugation as his "abolition" or "destruction." It thereby implies a more radical, comprehensive victory at the last judgment. Then God will be all in all, or as John puts it, the sea (representing evil powers) will be no longer, neither will there be any darkness or night (Rev. 21:23; 22:5). There will be nothing but perfect fellowship with God (21:1-7). Every tongue will confess him and every knee bow before him (Phil. 2:10-11). Then there will be no opposition to God, no threat to the faithful, and no need for them to wrestle. This is how we must distinguish between the present subjection and the future destruction of the powers.

Death provides a good example. It is already conquered—in that we are liberated from the slavery resulting from our fear of it (Heb. 2:15), in that victory is already ours through Christ (1 Cor. 15:57), and in that even death cannot separate us from the love of God (Rom. 8:38-39). For believers it is true that even though they die, they will live (John 11:25), because death's terror and victory have been abolished (1 Cor. 15:55ff.). That is why Paul could yearn for his departure from life as for something far better (Phil. 1:23).

Yet only at Christ's second coming will death be cast into hell; that is why we still die. Death is still an enemy which Christ must yet destroy (1 Cor. 15:26) and which still causes sorrow for Christians. We have already seen that the same situation holds for Satan and the evil spirits in Ephesians 6 and 1 Peter 5. In contrast to these warnings, we read that the gates of the New Jerusalem will never close—a symbol of perfect safety and the absence of any threat (Rev. 21:25).

Once again the eschatological character of Jesus' whole history is confirmed by the way in which the powers are conquered throughout that history. Indeed, the apocalyptic expectation was that God's kingdom would finally come through his conquest of the evil powers.

The Millennium

Our findings lead us inexorably to Revelation 20, where we read of Satan being bound so that he can no longer mislead the nations. We must begin by saying a few words about our method of expounding this chapter, which is of decisive importance to chiliasm (belief in a future thousand-year reign). We shall elucidate obscure, difficult passages with clearer, easier ones; we shall expound poetic, apocalyptic, highly symbolic sections with prosaic sections. As both Matt. 12:29 and Rev. 20:1-2 tell of Satan's binding, and as numerous other verses speak of Satan's subjugation by Christ, it is obvious that the clear, direct language of Matt. 12:29 ought to be considered in any exposition of the highly symbolic, apocalyptic style of Revelation 20. Another sound principle is to test our expositions of isolated or obscure statements in Scripture against more central, widely-attested truths. It happens that the binding and subjugation of Satan and his evil powers are recurrent New Testament topics, constituting one of the most important aspects of Jesus' earthly work. The binding of Satan for a thousand years is mentioned only once in the Bible (Rev. 20), yet the whole structure of chiliasm (= millennialism) depends upon one possible interpretation of this isolated passage.[33]

It is unacceptable to launch out from Revelation 20 in an attempt to explain the clear doctrine of the New Testament (that evil powers have been conquered, subjugated, and bound) by the light of this obscure, highly symbolic text. Actually, the history of chiliasm coincides with the history of the interpretation of Revelation 20. So far as I can determine, no one ever was a chiliast who did not espouse a specific, futuristic view of Revelation 20.[34] Overdue is a test—indeed, scholar-

33. See Berkouwer, *Return of Christ* (p. 301), on Berkhof's statement that only Revelation 20 describes the thousand-year reign "expressly and in detail" (Berkhof, *Christ, the Meaning of History* [1966], 153). This does not mean that chiliasts use only a few other Scriptures to develop their point; quite the opposite is true. But it does imply that their position (or its core, since there is much difference of opinion on details) is based on Rev. 20:1-6. That the position is called "chiliasm" (or "millenialism"; *chilioi* and *mille* means "one thousand" in Greek and Latin respectively) and that this is the only place where there is talk of a thousand years are signs of chiliasm's absolute dependence on Revelation 20. (See also J. A. Heyns, *Die Chiliasme of die Duisendjarige Ryk* [1963], 12, 27.)

34. For a short review of chiliasm's history, see H. A. Wilcke, *Das Problem eines messianischen Zwischenreichs bei Paulus* (1967), 13-17; K. Hutten, *Seher, Grübler, Enthusiasten* (1960), 12-15. For an unusually comprehensive exposition, see K. Dijk, *Het Rijk der Duizend Jaren* (1933), 11-180.

ship requires one and chiliasts should welcome it as much as anyone—of their interpretation of Revelation 20 from the perspective of other, clearer Scriptures. But before we proceed, let us form some notion of the chiliastic and anti-chiliastic positions.

Despite their great variety, all schools of chiliasm teach basically that a thousand-year reign of peace on earth will dawn at some future date. During this period Satan will be bound, no longer having his present freedom to tempt and devour people like a roaring lion (1 Pet. 5:8). Though not all people will necessarily be believers, neither will Satan be able to tempt them (Rev. 20:3). Consequently there will be a time of exceptional peace on earth, over which Christ and his faithful will reign.

This view is opposed by anti-chiliasts, whose conviction is that we are even now living in the millennium: that Satan and his evil powers have been bound by Christ's victory (Col. 2:15), and that he will be released for a short time at the end of our age to mount a final rebellion against God (Rev. 20:3, 7ff.). This position explains Satan's present bondage (vv. 2-3) in a way which does not suggest that he is impotent or inoffensive, but does insist that we have complete safety in Christ, because Christ has defeated him. Thus the joyful gospel of redemption is proclaimed throughout the world. And as the nations hear and accept the liberating gospel (John 8:32, 36), Satan is unable to mislead them.

But it is doubtful whether either of these positions does justice to the Bible witness. Both ascribe convictions to the author of Revelation 20 which he did not have. Both interpret the chapter—as they tend to do with all of Revelation—as if it were a product of the twentieth century rather than the first. They fail to consider the purpose of the chapter itself and of the book as a whole.

Broadly speaking, the circumstances under which Revelation was written were these: The young churches of Asia Minor were subjected to persecution and martyrdom (Rev. 2:9-10, 13; 3:10). This made them confused and doubtful, because the gospel as it was taught to them asserted that Satan had been defeated (Col. 2:15; Matt. 12:28-29; Luke 10:17-18; 11:20-22; John 12:31). Why then were they under attack? Had not Christ conquered Satan by his life, death, and resurrection? Neither chiliast nor anti-chiliast takes proper account of the confusion being experienced by the Asian Christians. Revelation 20 is often explained in a way which would have conveyed nothing to its original recipients—as if it were really written to us. John never expected that one or two thousand years would elapse before Christ returned. Jesus himself forbade all calculations of when he would return (Matt. 24:36-50; 25:13; Mark 13:33-37). Further, both Christ and his apostles taught that his return was near (1 Cor. 7:29; Jas. 5:8-9; 1 John 2:18; Rev. 22:12). In 1 Thess. 4:15 Paul clearly considers it possible that he will be one of those to see the second coming.

So John did not write Revelation as advance history of the twentieth (or any other) century; it is not a forecast of specific events.[35] He was called to write a message of comfort to troubled people of his own time. Our first question is therefore what Revelation 20 meant to Christians of the late first century. Only after answering that question should we ask what God intends it to say to us now.

Revelation 20 could have offered no consolation whatever to those original readers if the thousand years were meant either literally (as chiliasts contend) or symbolically (as their opponents do). How could it have helped the confused, persecuted congregations of ancient Asia Minor to learn that Satan would be bound at some remote, future time? They needed help then! This means that futuristic chiliasm is unacceptable.

But what comfort, either, could those Christians have derived from anti-chiliasm? It would have them think that John was only reiterating the New Testament message, i.e., Satan has already been bound. Yet their problem was why they suffered persecution and martyrdom if he was bound. John would certainly have supplied no answers to their questions by reaffirming that Satan had indeed been bound but would once again, later on, be *un*bound "for a short while."

This would have amounted to John, their comforter, telling them that their present trouble was nothing to what they would experience when Satan was unbound again. Further, if the thousand years of Revelation 20 really is a symbolic figure, as anti-chiliasts insist, this would mean that the period might end at any moment. Now, as this would have consoled hardly anybody, the anti-chiliast interpretation is as unacceptable as the chiliast—though there is doubtless some use in symbolic approaches to the text.

If we are to find an acceptable exposition of Revelation 20, we shall have to note specific connections between this symbolic picture of the conquered powers and the rest of the New Testament position

---

35. The distinction between, on the one hand, promise or prophecy and fulfillment vs., on the other hand, forecasts which come true has arisen several times and will be fully dealt with in the next chapter.

on the powers. Both Matt. 12:29 and Rev. 20:2 make much of the binding of Satan. Both passages mean that they who were in Satan's power are released by Jesus, as Mark's account of the Gadarene demoniac so vividly demonstrates. Similarly, Revelation 20 affirms that Satan is bound "so that he might seduce the nations no more." This is not necessarily the same idea we find in Matthew and Luke, but that remains a possibility (especially with respect to the Gentile missions). It even becomes a probability when we consider the connection between Revelation 20 and John 12:31. And this we shall do presently.

The binding of Satan and evil spirits is mentioned also in 2 Pet. 2:4 and Jude 6. There we are told that the angels who sinned are cast into hell and consigned to "fetters of darkness" (eternal chains), there to be held for judgment. These verses have obvious connections with Rev. 20:1-3, where we read that Satan is bound with a great chain and thrown into the abyss, which then is sealed over him.

Precisely because all these statements employ imagery, we must look, too, at Col. 2:15. There the theme is Christ (or God) discarding authorities like garments and making a triumphant public spectacle of them. ("Triumph" here evokes the image of a Roman general binding leaders of his conquered foe to his chariot in chains, then dragging them in procession through the streets of Rome.) Matt. 12:28; Luke 10:18; 11:22; and Col. 2:15 all serve to support our contention that Rev. 20:1-3 speaks about that same binding of Satan and his powers which is a frequently recurring New Testament theme.

W. Hendriksen compares Rev. 20:1-3 with John 12:31 and indicates the coincidences of circumstance in which these statements occur. John 12:31 follows from the request of "certain Greeks" to see Jesus. Jesus says two things: (1) that Satan is expelled from his sphere of power and (2) that Jesus will draw all people to himself. This, says Hendriksen, means that Jesus will make disciples of all nations through his worldwide mission, which indicates that Satan is bound and unable any longer to seduce them—the precise thought of Rev. 20:3. "Hence, through the death of Christ, the power of Satan over the nations of the world is broken."[36]

36. W. Hendriksen, *More than Conquerors* (1949[5]), 223-229; *idem., Commentary on the Gospel of John* (1967), 202. 1 John 5:19 (". . . the whole godless world lies in the power of the evil one") is not in conflict with Hendriksen's comments, but agrees fully with the salvation-historical vision of the New Testament concerning the kingdom of God. Jesus broke the evil powers during his earthly ministry as well as by his crucifixion and resurrection—but in such a way that,

Hendriksen emphasizes the enormous difference between the position of the nations before and since Christ's coming. Now his triumphal procession reaches them all (Col. 1:6, 23; 2 Tim. 4:17). Satan's loot has been "divvied up"; because of Christ's victory and worldwide mission, Satan can no longer seduce the nations (Rev. 20:3). So to expound Rev. 20:1-3 in terms of Christ's victory (through his cross, resurrection, and work during the interim through the Holy Spirit) is completely in harmony with the whole New Testament.

Then what do the concepts "a thousand years" and "a short while" mean? G. C. Berkouwer proposes that these do not indicate time but rather symbolize power.[37] "A thousand years" symbolizes the absolute defeat, binding, and total subordination of Satan and his forces which are clearly taught by the rest of the New Testament. "Thousand" does not refer to time at all; it demonstrates the completeness of Christ's victory over Satan.

Berkouwer rightly asserts that this explanation is faithful to the motives which underlie Revelation. In fact Revelation revolves around Christ's triumph, which is to be the churches' source of consolation. This is why the wars described in Revelation (which—because of widely organized hostility to God—appear on the surface to involve massive conflict) accomplish nothing against God's people. Frequently that conflict turns out to be negligible, little more than the instantaneous extermination of his enemies by the Lord's breath.

Similarly, the "short while" of Rev. 20:3 is not a literal period of future time. It is entirely foreign to the New Testament to imagine that the Satan who has been radically defeated should suddenly be *un-*

---

as his work continues, ever more of those under Satan's (broken) power are snatched away as loot by those who are *for* Jesus and so gather with him (Matt. 12:30; Luke 11:23).

The coming of the kingdom runs through all of history. It is not completed in a moment. In this sense the world (which in John 12:31 is opposed to the Church) is still in the power of the evil one. This is the portion of the spoil still to be taken, i.e., that part of the world which is still to become the Church.

37. G. C. Berkouwer, in *The Return of Christ* (chapter 10), is so far as I know the first person ever to interpret "thousand years" and "short while" in this way. It agrees so remarkably with the rest of Revelation and of the New Testament that here indeed is a case for remembering Calvin's famous retort to the Roman Church that it is not heads (votes) which must be counted but arguments that must be weighed. All the same, compare this with Max Warren in *The Truth of Vision* (1948), 135, to whom the millennium is a symbol "for the vindication of God in history."

defeated for a while, or that Christ's work should suddenly lose its effect and the world be delivered once more to Satan.

But given the circumstances of first-century churches and the implications of the millennium as a symbol for the subordination of Satan, it is certainly meaningful to interpret "short while" as a symbol for the limited danger Satan still poses to the Church. What John is trying to say by "short while" is that Christians' suffering and martyrdom do not mean that Satan is on the loose. He has truly been bound, as proclaimed by the symbol of the millennium; he nevertheless remains a limited threat, tempting and seducing the faithful.

The amount of slack allowed Satan is strictly limited (a "short while" vs. a "thousand years"), so John's congregations need not fear that present persecution will get the best of them or that Satan will ever be the victor. He has been defeated. The history of Jesus' earthly work proves this. Persecution takes place only within the *restricted* space which Satan and his powers still have, before they are destroyed at Christ's second coming—or, in Revelation's imagery, before they are cast into the lake of fire and brimstone. Indeed, this limited suffering can tend toward the strengthening of Christians' faith, as in Jas. 1:2-4 and 1 Pet. 1:6-7 (where, again, testing lasts a "little while"); 4:12-13.

But the "short while" of Rev. 20:3 does not encourage the Church to underestimate its conflict with evil powers. The New Testament speaks often and earnestly of this combat, as we have seen. However, it also wishes to reassure the Asia Minor churches—and Christians of all ages—that a continuing battle is not a losing battle, nor are we by any means defenseless defenders. The battle bears a strictly limited character.

Christians of all ages can find encouragement therein for their struggles and sufferings. They fight on, knowing that the victory is won already and that they are now engaged in a mopping-up operation. This is why Paul can paint his own conflict in such light, joyous colors (2 Cor. 4:16-18; Rom. 8:18, 37). He can endure his struggles with such optimism because he knows that he is on the winning side, that Satan is totally defeated (i.e., bound for a thousand years), and that he can do no more than launch an occasional sortie (a "short while") against the Church.

It is remarkable how this interpretation of Revelation 20 agrees with the main message of Revelation and even with its details. For instance, the principal message of Revelation is that Christ is the conqueror. Hendriksen calls it "The Victory of Christ and his Church over the Dragon (Satan) and his Helpers." In support he cites Rev. 1:13-18;

2:8, 26-27; 3:21; 5:5-9; 6:2, 16; 7:9-10; 11:15; 12:9ff.; 14:1, 14; 15:2ff.; 17:14; 19:11, 16; 20:4; and 22:3, 16.

The exposition of chapter 20 offered here fits far better with the message of Revelation than do any of the chiliastic or anti-chiliastic explanations. That Satan and his powers are vanquished agrees well with the message that Christ is their vanquisher—better, in fact, than the notion that Satan has yet to be bound (chiliasm) or will one day be again unbound (anti-chiliasm).

As far as the details of Revelation are concerned, it provides signal agreement between chapters 12 and 20. Revelation offers seven overviews of history, each from a different perspective (beginning with chapters 1, 4, 8, 12, 15, 17, and 20).[38] Chapter 12 begins the fourth of these overviews with an account in symbolic terms of Jesus' birth, Satan threatening his life in the person of Herod, his ascension (v. 5), the subjugation of evil powers ("the dragon and his angels") to Christ the king (vv. 7-10), and the vicious attack of Satan on the Church and the world (vv. 12-17). These last verses are of special importance to us. It seems at first glance that they contradict the New Testament message that Satan is bound; indeed, we are told of great persecution. But the core of their message is of a piece with the rest. Despite Satan's wrath and terrible zeal for persecution (Eph. 6; 1 Peter 5), the remarkable fact is that the Church is maintained in safety.

Clad in all its symbolism, the passage reads, "the woman was given two great eagles' wings, to fly to a place in the wilds where for three years and a half she was to be sustained, out of reach of the serpent" (Rev. 12:14). A raging Satan is thus powerless against the protected Church. Even when he launches another attack, we read that "the earth came to her rescue and opened its mouth and swallowed the river which the dragon spewed from his mouth" (vv. 15-16). Once more a furious Satan is impotent to harm the protected Church. In fact the most striking statement is the first part of the verse which follows: "At this the dragon grew furious with the woman, and went off to wage war on the rest of her offspring." This is an image of powerless fury; because the offspring "keep God's commands and the witness of Jesus Christ," the king will protect them (vv. 14-16).

So Revelation, like the rest of the New Testament, presents Satan and his powers as furious but subjugated—dangerous only to those outside of Christ. To decide that Rev. 20:3 refers to a different binding—for the nations—than that of chapter 12 for the Church is to

38. Hendriksen, *More Than Conquerors*, chapters 2, 4.

forget that John contemplates history from seven different viewpoints, repeating his message with a different emphasis each time. In fact, Hendriksen shows clearly that the binding of Satan in Revelation (as in all the New Testament) is a limited binding, closely associated with worldwide gospel proclamation.[39]

Furthermore, it is quite clear that the remainder of Revelation teaches a distinction between Satan's present subjugation and his future annihilation. So we read of the white horse and him who rides forth upon it, "conquering and to conquer" (6:2). Duvenhage notes tellingly that the red, black, and pale horses remain but outriders of the conqueror on the white horse. In 19:11ff. they disappear completely as the white steed marches forward, the host of the redeemed following him.[40] It should be clear that our understanding of 20:1-10 intrudes no alien element but rather harmonizes with the rest of the book and the rest of the New Testament.

Now let us return to the traditional distinction between chiliasm and anti-chiliasm. We have seen already that neither is completely supportable. The underlying reason for this is that both defend in principle the same position: that by decoding Revelation correctly we can write history in advance. Chiliasts believe that Revelation teaches that at a specific, identifiable future moment Satan *will be bound* and later released for a short period. Anti-chiliasts believe that Revelation teaches that Satan *is already bound,* but that at a specific, identifiable future moment he will be released for a short period. The only point at issue between them is that one expects Satan's binding to happen in the future; the other believes that it happened in the past.

Both regard Revelation as history written in advance. That is why neither can be accepted and why we advance an alternative— without claiming that we do total justice to every detail of Rev. 20:1-10 or that we have broached (much less solved) all the problems connected with the millennium.[41] We are content to claim that our

---

39. *Ibid.,* 225ff. Heyns, 31, has shown that even chiliasts must admit Satan's binding during the millennium to be only partial, since some unbelievers will not be converted even then. Of course this makes it remarkably similar to our own time! Thus even chiliasts must acknowledge that "so that he might seduce the nations no more"(Rev. 20:3) implies that people might still be lost.

40. S. C. W. Duvenhage, *Voor sy troon en hier benede* (1960), 41-42.

41. It is indeed a serious question whether the writer of Revelation meant to give a particular significance to every minute aspect of his message. Yet it falls to the exegete, not to the systematic theologian, to discover what is message and what are supporting details meant—as in Jesus' parables—only to complete a picture.

exposition does greater justice than anti-chiliastic or chiliastic approaches to the primary intentions of the author of Revelation and Bible authors, and that it offers a meaningful coherence between Revelation 20 and the rest of the New Testament.

The alternative proposed by chiliasm does not appear promising. For its explanation of Revelation 19 and 20 it hunts accommodations in the rest of the Bible.[42] Quite apart from the awkward chronology to which its explanation forces it,[43] chiliasm's efforts to portray Jesus and Paul as teachers of a thousand-year reign of peace on earth remain unconvincing.[44]

Berkouwer has pointed out a number of chiliasm's essential characteristics which underline the unacceptability of its theses.[45] First, there are its double expectations. It expects both a millennium—and a new Jerusalem to come after it; both a "first consummation" amidst death, tears, and sin—and a "second consummation" without the same; both a first return of Christ and a second return of Christ; and both a first resurrection (of the just) and a second resurrection (of the ungodly). Berkouwer calls this the "reduplication of fulfillment."

42. In *Das Tausendjährige Reich* (1955), e.g., H. Bietenhard starts out to expound Rev. 19:11–20:10 and only then launches his search for the thousand-year reign in both Testaments.

43. Berkouwer, *The Return of Christ*, 303f. W. Hendriksen has also demonstrated the unreliability of this exegesis at length and in detail (*More than Conquerors*, 53-54). Certain points in Bietenhard's exegesis of Rev. 19:11–20:10 (see previous note) support this; he frequently interprets events mentioned earlier as anticipations or prolepses of those mentioned in 19:11–20:10.

For example, in 19:11-16 he notes that an anticipatory (proleptic) description of the coming of the Son of man is given in 14:14. Similarly, according to him (p. 23), 20:4 is linked to earlier happenings in 6:9 and 13:8. Thus, in his view (p. 25), we have in chapter 7 a similar anticipation (*Vorwegnahme*) of chapters 20 and 21, because the apocalyptist regards those who must undergo persecution as they who have already attained the end. Likewise the full force of 19:18b (". . . the flesh of all men, slave and free, great and small") does not emerge, because he expounds (p. 21) chapter 20 in chronological order after chapter 19—and 19:18 cannot therefore be the final battle.

This strained exegesis is unnecessary when the principle is accepted that Revelation is divided into seven main sections, each reflecting history from the beginning, and each with a new emphasis. To do so renders prolepses and forced chronological sequences superfluous. (See Hendriksen, chapter 4.)

44. Wilcke, 150, has demonstrated convincingly that Paul did not know of such an interim kingdom. Bietenhard admits this (p. 88), though he goes on to plead that there is room in Paul's teaching for such a kingdom.

45. Berkouwer, *The Return of Christ*, 316.

He then draws our attention to the predominating pessimism with which chiliasts view this life. Berkouwer finds that they give the impression that evil is an autonomous, undefeated, and all-governing power, to which Christ's victory has made virtually no difference, and to which it could make no difference before his second coming. Chiliasts simply write off the world as incorrigible, painting a one-sided picture of total decay spreading over the entire world. Little room is left in their view for a gospel that includes the promise of victory— even in this life. So it is not strange that they fail to do justice to the coming of the kingdom in the ministry of Jesus, or that Bietenhard, like Cullmann, calls Matt. 12:29 an anticipation of the future.[46]

Against chiliasm (and, to a certain extent, against anti-chiliasm, too) we insist that there is no difference of time or essence between the kingdom of God which came in Jesus and the so-called thousand-year reign. The latter is a figure employed by John to convey the truth that Jesus has overcome Satan and ever increases his kingdom in triumph despite the repeated assaults of a Satan who goes about as a roaring lion, against whom the Church is so safe that the gates of hell will not prevail against it (Matt. 16:18).

Conclusion

The kingdom of God is the specific manner in which Jesus begins to attain God's goal in us and all things created during his ministry on earth. Jesus' proclamation is part of the kingdom; indeed, the kingdom (lordship) of God came not only by Jesus' deeds but also by his words. And just as surely as his actions were intended to save not only souls but also whole persons (hence healings) and even to restore nature, it is also true that his coming has altered our relationship with God. Especially by preaching the forgiveness of sins and by actually forgiving them, Jesus inaugurated the eschatological time of salvation.

In conclusion, as far as the eschatological significance of Jesus' earthly ministry is concerned, it represents the beginning of his attainment of the *eschaton* in the second mode, i.e., in us. Though this mode is realized chiefly through his coming and work in the Holy Spirit, it cannot be confined to the interim; Jesus began already to realize the kingdom of God during his ministry. He summoned people, they came to him, and they listened to his words. So they began to become God's

46. *Ibid.*, 320-321; Bietenhard, p. 89.

true covenant people and, in thankful obedience, to "forsake all and follow him" (Luke 18:28).

Although Jesus' earthly ministry was but the beginning of the realization of this mode, the *eschaton* was nevertheless truly fulfilled in this period, and its radical eschatological character ought not to be mistaken or relativized. Because this mode is continued in Jesus' work in the Holy Spirit, the rest of this chapter is devoted to the way in which this second mode of realizing God's goal in creation is accomplished during the interim.

JESUS' WORK THROUGH THE HOLY SPIRIT

Why is this section needed in a book on eschatology? To answer we must return to the foundation of eschatology, which is the *eschatos,* Jesus himself. He alone makes eschatology. Only where he is are the end and goal attained. Eschatology does not exist simply because "things" happen; when and where Jesus comes onto the scene and *makes* them happen, there is eschatology.

This brings us to the problem of the period between the ascension and second coming. Is Christ not absent during this interim? Do we not speak of his first coming and then of his second? Do we not now live in a period when he is in heaven at the Father's right hand, interceding for us—and so not here among us? Do we not live in an interim during which the world must depend on our witness, if it is to come to him? Do we not inhabit that time of which Jesus said: "the time will come when the bridegroom will be taken away from them, and on that day they will fast" (Mark 2:20)?

If the answer to these questions is "yes," then clearly we cannot call this interim "eschatological." When Jesus the *eschatos* is absent, there is no eschatology; no end-as-goal can be reached.

But the answer to all these questions is an emphatic "no!" The interim is not a time when Christ is away or missing (Matt. 28:20). The world does not depend on our witness to bring it to faith (John 16:8-11). We are not substitutes for Christ (Acts 2:47). The interim is not an absence of the bridegroom or a fast for wedding guests. Most important of all, though the covenant is not realized apart from us during the interim—for which we thank God profoundly!—neither is it realized apart from Christ (Heb. 12:2)—and for this we are a thousandfold more thankful!

But the questions remain, how is Christ present with us and how does he reach the *eschaton* in us during the interim? After all, we know that the disciples saw him taken away from them up to heaven (Acts 1:11).

The Relationship between Christ and the Spirit

Expectations of the Holy Spirit's coming in the end time play an important role in the prophets' messages. They presume that the Spirit will not descend just on individuals as was characteristic of Old Testament history (e.g., on Saul, Balaam, David) but on all believers: "I will pour my spirit upon your *offspring*," said the Lord to Isaiah (44:3); "I will pour out my spirit on *all mankind*," to Joel (2:28-29); "a spirit from on high is lavished upon us," again to Isaiah (32:15); and "my spirit is present among you," to Haggai (2:5). A conviction is found in rabbinic literature that the Lord's Spirit had been withdrawn after the last of the prophets and was promised again for the end time.[47]

It is remarkable that this expectation bore a unique relationship to Servant of the Lord and to the messiah. Of "the shoot [which] shall grow from the stock of Jesse," it is said that "The Spirit of the Lord shall rest upon him" (Isa. 11:1-2). The same chapter speaks clearly of the end-time character of this expectation. It emerges again in the Servant Songs of Isaiah: "Here is my servant, whom I uphold . . . I have bestowed my spirit upon him" (Isa. 42:1). This also emerges in Isa. 61:1 read in the light of Luke 4:18ff.: "The spirit of the Lord God is upon me because the Lord has anointed me; he has sent me to bring good news to the humble." Two things emerge therefore from this Old Testament expectation: that the general outpouring of the Holy Spirit is an eschatological expectation, and that there is a connection between this outpouring of the Spirit and the coming of the messiah.

A. A. van Ruler displays rare insight into the many-faceted relationship between Christ and the Holy Spirit.[48] The Holy Spirit works through Jesus in a particular way during his earthly ministry,

---

47. R. Bultmann, *Theology of the New Testament* (1951, 1955) I, 41; E. Sjöberg, *TDNT* VI, 384f.

48. Van Ruler, *De Vervulling van de Wet*, 165-199. See also H. Berkhof, *The Doctrine of the Holy Spirit* (1976), 17ff.

in which Jesus bears and is filled with him. The Holy Spirit takes the initiative at Jesus' birth, baptism, and temptation (Matt. 1:20; 3:16; 4:1; Luke 4:14). By the Spirit Jesus drives out demons (Matt. 12:28); in the Spirit he rejoices (Luke 10:21); through the Spirit he offers himself to God (Heb. 9:14); the Spirit is involved in his resurrection (Rom. 1:4; 1 Pet. 3:18); in the Spirit he preaches to the imprisoned souls (1 Pet. 3:19); and through the Spirit he commands his disciples after his resurrection (Acts 1:2). With justice van Ruler asserts that it is the Spirit that gives (in the Dutch, *poneer*) Jesus. Jesus is the messiah (the "anointed") because he is anointed with the Holy Spirit (Acts 10:38). Thus it is entirely correct to regard the person and ministry of Jesus as the beginning of the Holy Spirit's work among men and women. Christ's coming is the work of the Spirit for Christ is the bearer of the Spirit (Isa. 11:2; 16:1; Matt. 3:16; 12:18; Luke 4:18; Acts 10:38); the Spirit has come in Christ. And *that* is the relationship between the Holy Spirit and Jesus Christ during his earthly ministry.

But the emphasis changes with Jesus' ascent to heaven, especially in the subsequent outpouring and work of the Holy Spirit. Then—particularly in the writings of John and Paul—we notice a certain priority which Christ is accorded over the Holy Spirit. Christ receives, confers, and sends the Holy Spirit (Luke 24:49; John 14:26; 15:26; 16:7; 20:22; Acts 2:33, etc.). "The Holy Spirit, whom the Father will send in my name, will teach you everything" (John 14:26). And this is because "He will not speak on his own authority. . . . He will draw from what is mine" and tell it to the disciples, for "no one can say 'Jesus is Lord!' except under the influence of the Holy Spirit" (John 16:13-14; 1 Cor. 12:3).

Berkhof states correctly that the relationship between Christ and the Spirit during this period can be expressed as Christ's work constituting the content of the Spirit's work. There may even be a sense in which the Spirit's work is not original but rather applies Christ's work. But Berkhof criticizes the Reformers for stressing only this aspect of the relationship and, in consequence, being insufficiently cognizant that the Spirit's outpouring was one of the great *new* acts of God for our salvation. He finds the significance of present-day Pentecostalism in its attempt to recover this forgotten fact—though, according to him, it ends up at the opposite extreme, dissociating the Spirit from Christ and his work. I am not so sure that this verdict is fair.

But how are we to formulate the relationship between Christ and the Spirit, particularly during this interim? Van Ruler regards the relationship as mobile, multiform, even contradictory as measured by formal logic. Berkhof expresses it as an identification between the exalted Christ and the Holy Spirit, but one which is not total. He is convinced that this identification is to be found in all strands of the New Testament tradition. He points to 1 John 3:24; he links John 14:18 with Matt. 28:20; and he points out that Christ is he who addresses the seven churches in Revelation 2 and 3, though his message to each ends with the words "hear what the Spirit says to the churches" (cf. 1 Cor. 6:17; Rom. 8:9-11). Berkhof further asserts that Paul uses "in Christ" and "in the Spirit" interchangeably.

Because this subject is so important to this study, we must probe it more deeply. Let us begin with the matter of Christ's location between his ascension and second coming. It is striking that the evangelists all stress Christ's continuation of his work during this interim. Some mention the ascension, others do not; but all underscore Christ's activity—on earth—during the interim. So the ascension does not mean that Christ went away and now is absent.

Matthew does not refer to the ascension and ends with Jesus' promise, "And be assured I am with you always, to the end of time" (28:20). John refers to the ascension (20:17) but goes on at once to tell of Jesus' work among his disciples (20:19-31; 21). Evidently the conclusion of Mark is not part of his original gospel, but it ends in almost the same way as Matthew: "and the Lord worked with them." Luke, the evangelist who most emphasizes the ascension (24:44-53; Acts 1:9-11, 22; 2:33; 3:21), also recounts in the greatest detail that Jesus continues his work on earth (Acts 2:47; 9:5ff.; 16:14).

This means that whether or not the ascension is described in detail or even mentioned, the evangelists' united witness is that Jesus continues his work on earth. However the ascension is understood, one thing is perfectly clear: Christ has not gone away, and his work on earth has not been interrupted. He continues it without a break.

So Christ's presence during the interim must be taken seriously. The God-with-us of Matt. 1:23 means that Jesus will never depart. That is why Matthew could end his Gospel with "be assured, I am with you always, to the end of time" (28:20). The meaning of John 1:14-16 (already considered), that Jesus completely identified himself with us, points also to this truth. The Gospels and Acts give no hint that Jesus' promise in Matt. 18:20 ("where two or three have met together in my name, I am there among them") might someday expire.

Paul's statements on Christ's real presence in the eucharist can be seen as a fulfillment of this promise. "When we bless the cup of blessing, is it not a means of sharing in the blood of Christ? When we break the bread, is it not a means of sharing in the body of Christ?" (1 Cor. 10:16). The *Belgic Confession* correctly affirms in Article 35 that, "In the mean time we err not when we say that what is eaten and drunk by us is the proper and natural body and the proper and natural blood of Christ." This does not imply that his body and blood can be detached from Christ's person, however; the Confession hastens to add, "This feast is a spiritual table, at which Christ communicates himself with all his benefits to us, and gives us there to enjoy both himself and the merits of his sufferings and death."

Naturally, Christ's real presence in the Lord's Supper is exceptionally important. But Berkouwer points out correctly that Christ is not present in the Lord's Supper alone, and so we ought not to view it as an interruption of a "desert life" which is the normal condition of the Church. Rather, celebration of the Lord's Supper is directly oriented toward *continuous* fellowship with the living Lord.[49] Indeed, Paul's prayer for the Ephesians is "that through faith, Christ may dwell in your hearts in love" (Eph. 3:17), and this may be regarded as fulfilling Christ's promise, "we [Father and Son] will come to him and make our dwelling with him" (John 14:23).

It follows that the ascension did not inaugurate a period of mourning. It was not the beginning of the time of which Jesus said, "the time will come when the bridegroom will be taken away from them, and on that day they will fast" (Mark 2:20). That "day" came between the crucifixion and the resurrection. But Luke reports that immediately after Jesus' ascension "they returned to Jerusalem with great joy and spent all their time in the temple, praising God" (Luke 24:52ff.).

Jesus himself spoke of the advantages which would accrue to the disciples from his ascension (John 16:7). When he spoke of the fleeting sorrow his departure would cause, he also promised the joy to follow—"no one shall rob [them] of [their] joy" (vv. 20-22). Their reunion with him was not the second advent but his presence in the interim.

So the ascension poses no problem to Christ's presence during the interim. This fact by itself sufficiently explains how the New Testament can speak of the interim in the radically eschatological terms pre-

49. G. C. Berkouwer, *The Sacraments* (1969), 241.

viously indicated. The *Eschatos* is really present—no less now than at his first or second coming.[50]

How then can Christ be present on earth at this time? And what is the relationship between him and the Holy Spirit? Jesus speaks of being away for a little while between his crucifixion and resurrection (John 14; 16). Then, after his ascension, he is to return to his disciples in the Holy Spirit. Thus he promises them the Holy Spirit and, directly afterwards, that they will not be left orphans, as *he* will come to them (14:16-18; 16:13-16). From John 14 it further appears that the world will not be able to see him, though his disciples will (v. 19).

From this follow two consequences. First, there is a direct link between Jesus' return to his disciples and the coming of the Holy Spirit. So his ascension cannot be seen as a farewell, as if he were departing, but rather as his transition to another mode of being wherein the world can see him no more. This mode of being is directly related to the Holy Spirit's coming.

Second, any clear description of the relationship between Jesus' continuing work on earth and the Holy Spirit's coming is lacking, though some data in Paul's writings help us. 2 Cor. 3:17-18 is very important: "The Lord . . . is the Spirit"; "where the Spirit of the Lord is, there is liberty"; and "such is the influence of the Lord, who is Spirit." Appeal is made by some, including Berkhof, to this text in attempts to base on it a complete (or incomplete) identity between Christ and the Holy Spirit.[51] Berkhof suggests that the identity is incomplete because it is only the exalted Christ who is the Spirit, so that we cannot baldly announce that "Holy Spirit" is just another name for the exalted Christ. Two things are said about this relationship in 2 Cor. 3:17. There is identity ("the Lord is the Spirit"), and there is distinction ("the Spirit of the Lord"). And this became a problem for the Church, which reached a solution for it only at the council of Nicea in A.D. 325.

The Spirit is the manner in which Jesus is present in the Church, in which the Lord and the Spirit are working together, because the Spirit carries out Christ's work. This functional identity between Christ and the Spirit (i.e., that it is Christ who works on earth through the Spirit) is confirmed by Paul, particularly in those passages where there

---

50. Since we are not now involved in a wide-ranging discussion of the ascension, we will not go into the particular problems of the connection between ascension, resurrection, and exaltation.

51. Berkhof, *The Doctrine of the Holy Spirit*, 28. Berkhof's *Christian Faith* (1986[2]) reflects a change in his views on the relationship between Christ and the Spirit.

is alternation between Christ and the Spirit. For example, the faithful are told that they are both "in Christ" (Rom. 8:1) and "in the Spirit" (v. 9); both that Christ indwells them (v. 10) and that his Spirit does (v. 11). They speak both in Christ (2 Cor. 2:17) and in the Holy Spirit (1 Cor. 12:3). The faithful are both dedicated to Christ (1 Cor. 1:2) and "consecrated by the Holy Spirit" (Rom. 15:16). They are justified both in the name of Christ and in the Spirit of their God (1 Cor. 6:11).

It is impossible to separate Christ and the Spirit from each other, treating them as independent agents both present in the faithful. There is a decisive bond between them: "Any one who does not have the spirit of Christ does not belong to him" (Rom. 8:9 RSV). Thus it is necessary to equate Christ's presence during the interim with his ind-welling of the Church through the Spirit.

This agrees with John's emphasis on the Spirit who glorifies Christ and calls him to mind, declaring what belongs to him. So it is not strange that the Holy Spirit is frequently called "the Spirit of Christ," or the "Spirit of the Lord," or "the Spirit of his Son" (Rom. 8:9; 2 Cor. 3:17; Gal. 4:6; Phil. 1:19; 1 Pet. 1:11). That the Spirit serves Christ is apparent in these texts and in John 14–16. Eph. 3:16-17 also indicates that there is a decisive connection between the Spirit who strengthens our inner selves and the Christ who dwells in our hearts.

These data enable us to state that the presence of Jesus is his presence in the Spirit. The Holy Spirit's work is not something parallel to or distinct from Christ's work. Even that aspect of the Holy Spirit's work which Berkhof so emphatically terms his "original work" is really that which Jesus does through him during the interim. (In contrast to Berkhof, the Reformers and Barth insist on an unoriginal work of the Spirit, contending that he only witnesses to Christ—i.e., that he applies subjectively in our lives what Christ merited objectively on the cross.)

As examples of this "independent" work of the Holy Spirit, Berkhof cites conversion, sanctification, speaking in other tongues, prophecy, miracles, mission, and the edification and leading of the Church. The Spirit also appoints leaders, organizes, enlightens, inspires, and cares for the congregation. He aids the saints and strengthens them in weakness.[52]

But many of the things which Berkhof considers the Spirit's original work are attributed directly to Christ: conversion (Acts 9:3ff.),

52. Berkhof, *The Doctrine of the Holy Spirit,* 23.

sanctification (1 Cor. 1:30; Col. 1:21-22), miracles (Acts 3:6, 16), mission (Matt. 28:18-20; Mark 16:20; Rom. 1:5), edification (Eph. 3:16; 4:15-16; Col. 2:6-10), offices (Eph. 4:11), aid (Rom. 8:34), and strengthening (Heb. 4:15). It is therefore unwarranted to distinguish between the Holy Spirit's "original" and "unoriginal" work. The whole range of the Spirit's activities is what Christ does through him, whether as a continuation of that already begun during Christ's earthly ministry or as something new. Whatever the Spirit does, he does as the Spirit of Christ. So Christ does it—in and through him.

And Barth is entirely correct, unlike Berkhof, in upholding the dependent nature of the Holy Spirit's work by asserting, e.g., "that those who accept the witness of the Holy Spirit cannot tarry with Him as such. There can be no abstract receiving and possessing of the Holy Spirit. There can be no self-moved and self-resting life in the Spirit, no self-sufficient spiritual status. The witness of the Holy Spirit does not have itself either as its origin or goal. It has no content of its own. . . . Jesus Christ is its power and light, its content, its origin and goal."[53]

The relationship between Christ and the Holy Spirit during the interim may be summarized thus: Christ is present in and works through the Holy Spirit in such a way that the presence and work of the Spirit is the presence and work of Christ. Naturally the same cannot be said for their relationship during Jesus' earthly ministry. As mentioned earlier, during that time one might rather speak of the Holy Spirit's presence and work in and through Jesus.

Now it is possible to say a word or two about the difference between this presence of Christ and his second coming.[54] In the nature of things, there are various problems involved here. If already Christ is *really* with us through the Holy Spirit, how can he come again? This question also confronted us in connection with the ascension. In that case as in this, the simplest solution seems referring to the manner in which he is present. During his earthly ministry he was on earth in the form of his humiliation. At present he is with us in and through the Holy Spirit. When he comes again, it will be in glory.

Now I can explain why I have not joined with Barth in taking the comings (parousias) of Jesus as the basis for the structure of eschatology. This is because the New Testament does not deal explicitly with

53. Barth, IV/2, 130-131.
54. Berkouwer, *The Sacraments,* 236f.; *idem., The Return of Christ,* 142f.

his *coming* in the Holy Spirit, favoring rather the concept of his *presence* and work through the Holy Spirit.

Barth himself offers small exegetical foundation for his teaching of Christ's coming in the Holy Spirit. This does not mean that the idea contradicts the New Testament witness (see John 14–16), only that the outpouring of the Spirit is not termed a *coming* of Christ, and so the idea does not loom very large in the New Testament. The relationship between Christ and the Holy Spirit as the presence and work of Christ through the Spirit is, however, prominent. This is why the structure of eschatology ought rather to be built around the three modes in which Jesus attains God's goal in creation than around his three— or four—comings.

The Holy Spirit as Eschatological Gift

This relationship between Christ and the Holy Spirit leads us to expect that the Spirit himself must have an eschatological character. Since Christ is the *eschatos,* and since it is through the Holy Spirit that he attains God's goal in us, we might expect that the Spirit himself would be described in eschatological terms.

In fact the Old Testament does look forward to the outpouring of the Spirit in the end time (Joel 2:28). It is noteworthy that Peter quotes this verse at Pentecost—but with an addition. Joel 2:28 reads, "*Thereafter* the day shall come when I will pour out my Spirit on all mankind." Peter's quotation of the prophecy reads, "This will happen *in the last days:* I will pour out upon everyone a portion of my Spirit" (Acts 2:17). Though no doubt exists that Joel meant his words to be a promise for the end time, it is striking that Peter deliberately adds "in the last days," thereby stressing that the Holy Spirit is an eschatological gift.

Two concepts which Paul uses when referring to the Holy Spirit underscore the Spirit's eschatological nature: "pledge" and "firstfruits." Paul uses the idea of pledge (Gk. *arrabōn*) three times in referring to the Holy Spirit (2 Cor. 1:22; 5:5; Eph. 1:14). The TEV gives a most satisfactory paraphrase of this concept: "God who gave us the Holy Spirit in our hearts *as the guarantee of all that he has for us*."

In New Testament times the concept of "pledge" had with it something of the meaning of "deposit"—but with significant additions. A deposit placed an obligation on a purchaser. Nowadays a purchaser forfeits only his deposit if he pays no more. But then he was obliged by law to pay the whole if he had paid a part. He could not withdraw. Paul says that God has given us his Spirit as such a guarantee or deposit. This means that God has bound himself to give us everything he spoke of, in due course. By giving us the Holy Spirit, God has guaranteed us complete salvation. The Spirit's eschatological character is that he is the guarantee we already have of the completion of salvation.

Yet another facet of "pledge" emphasizes the Spirit's eschatological character. A deposit or pledge was considered part of the whole amount to be paid. In receiving a pledge, therefore, one already had received a part of the whole price. So we hold not only the guarantee of someday receiving complete salvation; we have part of it now. We fix our eyes on the future not only because of our present lack but also because of our present possession—a foretaste which makes us eager for complete salvation.

Thus we can accept Berkhof's viewpoint, which rejects both a completed and a onesidedly futuristic eschatology in favor of an eschatology in the process of being realized. We could just as well say that full eschatological reality requires all three: a realized eschatology ("for us"), an eschatology being realized ("in us"), and an eschatology yet-to-be-realized ("with us").

The concept of "firstfruits," applied once to the Holy Spirit and twice to Christ (Rom. 8:23; 1 Cor. 15:20-23), poses problems for the translator. Older translations (KJV and RSV) have "the firstfruits of the Spirit," leaving an impression either that the Spirit is only partially received or that only some part of him is received. In contrast, later translations (NEB, NAB, TEV, and GN) have "the Spirit . . . as firstfruits of the harvest" or something similar.

A. A. van Ruler offers convincing evidence that the genitive absolute construction should be rendered as "we who have received *the Spirit as the first gift*."[55] He draws attention to two Old Testament "firstfruits," that at Passover when harvest began, and that at Pentecost when harvest ended. When Jesus is called "firstfruits," this refers to the firstfruits sacrifice at Passover; when the Holy Spirit is called "firstfruits," this refers to the end of harvest at Pentecost.

In the Holy Spirit, then, we receive the first gift of the full salvation promised us by God. But we are concerned here with the Old Testament firstfruits feast of Pentecost—at the end of harvest. The harvest (full salvation) has therefore already been gathered and stored in heaven

55. Van Ruler, 147-150. See especially the three arguments on p. 148.

(1 Pet. 1:4). Put another way, the *eschaton* has already been achieved, and we have received our first installment, the Spirit. He is therefore an eschatological gift in the fullest sense. And this agrees with the idea that Jesus realizes the *eschaton* in us through the Holy Spirit.

We note in passing that, as was true in the first mode, the nature of this gift points up the *eschaton's* need to be realized in yet another way. The Spirit is a thoroughly eschatological gift—but only the first part, a guarantee that the balance has still to be paid.

In Chapter 1 we established the eschatological character of the interim. In the preceding two subsections of this chapter we concluded that Jesus, the *eschatos,* is himself present and at work in and through the Holy Spirit during the interim, and that the Holy Spirit is himself an eschatological gift. It is clear that the interim is fully eschatological; so is the work done by Jesus in and through the Holy Spirit during this time.[56] This is eschatology in its second form: the goal of God attained *in* us and *in* the world, a mode which began with Jesus' earthly ministry. Now we can move on to an exposition of the content of Jesus' work in and through the Spirit during this eschatological interim.[57]

The Kingdom of God—Again

It is sometimes alleged that, unlike the Synoptics, Acts and the Epistles relegate the kingdom of God to the background. This leads some to conclude that the whole content of the gospel underwent similar change. They suppose that Acts and the Epistles replace Jesus' an-

56. In *Pentecost and Missions* (1961), H. Boer states that G. Vos remarked that the work of the Holy Spirit in the believer has so captured attention that the Spirit's eschatological meaning remained in the background. Boer accounts for this by saying that eschatology is usually limited to Christ's return and matters linked directly with it. "This approach to eschatology was never able to do justice to the many references in the New Testament that the last days are *now,* and to the work of the Spirit in and his significance for the eschatologically qualified New Testament present."

57. That the interim is eschatological time, i.e. already the end time—because the *eschaton* and *telos* are realized in it as well—ought not to be confused with Bultmann's doctrine that in the time in which we live, "every hour is the last hour" (W. Schmithals, *An Introduction to the Theology of Rudolf Bultmann* [1968], 310). That this time is already the last hour does not mean that it is always (timelessly, for good and all, without prospect of change or termination) the last hour. In fact, according to Christ's promise, after this mode (*in* us) comes the final mode (*with* us). Only then will it always (and not "already") be the last hour.

nouncement of the approaching end and kingdom with proclamations that the Church and salvation can be enjoyed right now—more succinctly, that the Church has supplanted the kingdom.

As far as terminology is concerned, this is true. The "kingdom" is mentioned less than twenty times in the non-Synoptic New Testament. (In the Synoptics, it is the central concept in Jesus' preaching.) But when one looks into the matter more closely, it is seen that the content and meaning of the "kingdom" is at the heart of apostolic preaching. A different formula is introduced, however: "Jesus [Christ] is Lord." Stauffer has pointed out that "Lord" *(kyrios)* is used in Psalm 110 for "king." This Psalm is frequently cited with reference to Jesus (Mark 12:35ff.; Acts 2:30ff.), so that "Lord Jesus" or "Jesus is Lord" speak of Christ as king.[58]

"Lord" is applied to Jesus from another source as well. The Old Testament name for God, Yahweh, is rendered *kyrios* in the Greek Old Testament. But the New Testament rarely applies *kyrios* to the Father, usually calling him *theos*. *Kyrios* instead becomes the usual name for Christ. Especially important is that Old Testament quotations referring to Yahweh are applied to Jesus as Lord *(kyrios)* in the New.[59] It appears indisputable that New Testament writers meant to apply God's name (Yahweh) to Jesus.[60] Apart from the question of Christ's divinity, it is clear that at least the functions of Yahweh are ascribed to him.[61]

And this fact is extremely important. As we saw earlier, the king-

58. E. Stauffer, *New Testament Theology* (1955), 114. W. Foerster has shown in *TDNT* III, 1054f. that *kyrios* usually applied to the *ruler* in the days of Caesars. He later explains that, during the formative period of the LXX, *kyrios* "denoted the one who had lawful power of disposal" (p. 1082).

59. T. F. Glasson, *The Second Advent* (1947[2]), 159ff. A. E. J. Rawlinson, *The New Testament Doctrine of the Christ* (1949), 77ff. P. Feine, *Theologie des Neuen Testaments* (1919[3]), 175. Feine cites among others the following: 1 Cor. 1:31; 2 Cor. 10:17; and Gal. 6:14 from Jer. 9:24; 1 Cor. 2:16 from Isa. 40:13; 1 Cor. 10:22 from Deut. 32:21; 2 Cor. 3:16 from Exod. 34:34; Eph. 4:8 from Ps. 68:19; Phil. 2:10-11 from Isa. 45:23; 2 Thess. 1:9 from Isa. 2:10, 19, 21; and 2 Thess. 1:12 from Isa. 66:5.

60. O. Weber, *Foundations of Dogmatics* (1981, 1983) I, 362; W. Foerster, *TDNT* III, 1088; Barth, III/2, 450. Bultmann's remark (I, 124), "It is highly improbable that the title "Kyrios" as applied to Jesus is derived from the LXX," is not relevant. In fact there is much more at issue than a mere title. The *functions* of Yahweh are applied to Jesus, as will emerge in the course of the argument.

61. Stauffer, 115, mentions the day of Yahweh, which becomes the day of the Lord (Jesus Christ) and the Name of Yahweh which becomes the Name of the Lord (Jesus Christ). He speaks here of *interpretatio christologica*.

dom of God is not a territory over which God rules—neither in the Old Testament, nor in the rabbinic literature, nor in Jesus' preaching. The kingdom means "the Lord is king" or "the Lord reigns." When in Jesus' deeds the kingdom is realized, he is the Lord who rules, who comes to make his lordship known, who breaks the power of demons.

This leads us to conclude that the confession "Jesus is Lord" meant precisely the same thing to the apostles that "kingdom of God" did in the Synoptics: that Jesus is the Lord God who reigns, he who exercises God's power over the world. "He is the Lord of all" (Acts 10:36; Rom. 10:12), indeed, "every power and authority in the universe is subject to him as head" (Col. 2:10; Eph. 1:21-22).

Realizing the centrality of this confession to the apostles' preaching, we cannot justify saying that the content and the meaning of the "kingdom" is relegated to the background by their proclamation. The opposite is true: as of John's and Jesus' preaching, it is the core. Indeed, theirs is the credit for replacing the abstract concept "kingdom of God" with a formula nearer the original Old Testament concept: Jesus is Lord, i.e., the ruler or king of Psalm 110.

By his presence and work in the Holy Spirit, therefore, Jesus continues to realize the *eschaton* in this world: to herald the Lord's dominion and to confirm it; to make of us his loyal subjects by bringing us to the peace which he has made, that we might accept and experience it; and, by healing the sick, raising the dead, and otherwise bringing a demonized nature under control, to reorder chaos. It is interesting how closely the apostles' and early Church's activities followed the pattern of Jesus' earthly ministry. This should convince us that the kingdom of God (of which Jesus' miracles were signs) is still arriving during the interim.

Having seen that the confession "Jesus is Lord" was the heart of apostolic preaching, by which was meant that the kingdom of God has come, we can assume that the apostles' gospel will, upon examination, turn out to be thoroughly eschatological. That assumption we shall now test.

The Eschatological Character of the Gospel Proclamation

This topic could have been discussed with Jesus' earthly ministry. He preached the same gospel as the apostles did later, using the term "kingdom of God" while they used the formula "Jesus [Christ] is Lord."

We will the more readily appreciate that the gospel proclamation is eschatological if we take the Old Testament background into account. In Isaiah 52 and 61, particularly, there are references to "the herald . . . who brings good news" (52:7; 61:1-2). Among Jesus' Jewish contemporaries there was strong expectation that a messenger of peace would come—indeed, would come at the end of days and introduce the messianic age. With his coming, the kingdom would dawn, as the core of his message would be, "Your God reigns!"

When Jesus began his work, he identified himself deliberately with this expected herald of good news. He applied Isaiah 61 to himself in Luke 4:21. In his preaching, the great moment of salvation dawned: the poor had the gospel preached to them (Matt. 11:4-6). The eight beatitudes must also be viewed in this light. Indeed, H. Boer considers them a sign of the end.[62]

This gospel or "good news" stresses the forgiveness of sins. Indeed, Ridderbos calls this the heart of the gospel.[63] And because we cannot examine every facet of Jesus' preaching, we have elected to deal with this one. In emphasizing the forgiveness of sins, Jesus associates himself directly with the Old Testament. Such Scriptures as Pss. 32:2-4; 51; 103:3, 8-10; 130:3-4, 8; Isa. 53; and Prov. 28:13 show the continuity between the Old Testament and this aspect of Jesus' preaching.

This message was not strange to Jesus' contemporaries. Forgiveness of sins was central to John's preaching of the kingdom. At his baptism people confessed their sins (Matt. 3:6); and his baptism is even referred to as "baptism of repentance for the forgiveness of sins" (Mark 1:4).

The *message* that sins are forgiven was not a point at issue between Jesus and the scribes. They disagreed over the *manner* in which sins are forgiven. The scribes also knew of the love of God even for the sinner; but from this they deduced that his love for the righteous must be even greater. Were it possible for a sinner to be saved (and by their doctrines of merit and reward this could certainly happen, if he broke with his sins and observed the law), how much more must this be true for the righteous!

---

62. Boer, 99, calls their proclamation "the sign of the end," referring to Matt. 24:14 among other texts.

63. H. Ridderbos, 213-232: "salvation whose heart and sum is *the remission of sins*" (213-214). Much of the material in the following pages is derived from this section.

We see how fundamental was the difference between Jesus and the scribes when we look at such texts as Luke 18:9-14, the parable of the Pharisee and tax collector. Here the tax collector went home justified, the Pharisee did not. Within the Jewish framework of salvation, to preach this was scandalous. If the sinner were saved, how could the righteous not be? The scribes had no framework for understanding such a verdict because they did not know of God's free grace and because—unlike Jesus—they did not admit the radical corruption of the human being or acknowledge that all were lost.

The distinction drawn by Jesus between sinners and the righteous (as between the sick and the healthy) is not, of course, a concession to Jewish belief that people were able by nature to keep God's law and so earn merit with him. Rather, it is the ironic use of a distinction which Jesus often encountered, while acknowledging its *relative* value.

A further important distinction between Jesus and the Pharisees—and John—is that Jesus not only proclaimed God's forgiveness but himself forgave sins. This provoked the scribes' and Pharisees' exclamation, "This is blasphemy! Who but God alone can forgive sins?" (Mark 2:7). Their point is entirely correct: God alone can forgive sins. But they failed to perceive that this, precisely, was why Jesus could forgive sins—because he was God. That of which the Jews accused him (and that he never denied their accusation speaks volumes!), that he made himself equal with God (John 5:18), is his due; it is no more than the truth.

At issue here is far more than the Old Testament message of forgiveness. Here is the forgiver! Here we have the year of jubilee (the "year of the Lord's favor") in human form; here captives are set free; here the brokenhearted are healed; here the blind see; here the ears of the deaf are opened; here cripples walk; here the gospel comes to the poor (Luke 4:18-21; Matt. 11:1-6). Salvation, redemption, and forgiveness of sins are gifts from his hand.

In fact, in Jesus' method of forgiving sins we find an eschatological reality. He forgives, and at the same time he heals as a sign of the reality of his forgiveness (Mark 2:1-12). He is the God who is able to restore our broken relationship with him and bring us back, body and soul—the entire person—to be his free, happy, and faithful sharers in the covenant.

He illustrates this by welcoming to intimate fellowship—table companionship—publicans and sinners. He overcomes sin not only by eradicating the separation between "the righteous" and "sinners" but also by forgiving sins and abolishing alienation between God and sinners. He creates a new community by welcoming them into his fellowship. He attains the *eschaton* in us by effective forgiveness of sins even during his earthly ministry. The prophets and the Old Testament faithful looked forward to this forgiveness. Zechariah sees it fulfilled in Jesus (Luke 1:68, 70, 77ff.).

The Structure of the Gospel Proclamation—Mission

To gain a wider perspective on the eschatological nature of gospel proclamation, we will now examine the general structure of proclamation itself and thereafter the fruit of and resistance to proclamation. It may be as well to begin our investigation by giving its results. Proclamation (or mission) is the Holy Spirit's work; the Spirit causes the Church to proclaim the gospel throughout the world, bringing people to faith and so attaining God's goal in their lives and in the world. There are three important points here, and we will deal with them consecutively: the Church as the proclamation's agent, the good news as the proclamation's content, and faith as the proclamation's purpose. It is evident that this proclamation is concerned with the attainment of God's goal, i.e., with humanity becoming God's people as he is their God. So worldwide proclamation of the gospel is correctly seen as a sign of Christ's second coming (Matt. 24:14).

The agent of proclamation—the Church. The Church exists to proclaim the gospel. The Spirit leads believers to speak. There is a direct relationship between the work of the Spirit and believers who speak. The sign of his outpouring is tongues, and its result is that they begin to speak (Acts 2). Throughout Acts we read that when the Spirit fills people they speak, witness, and proclaim. Before he came, Peter could not even speak before a servant girl (Matt. 26:69ff.). Filled with the Spirit, he could not refrain from speaking even before the Jewish Council. H. Boer concludes "that there is a surprising and unanimous testimony in the New Testament to the relationship between the Spirit . . . and the witness of the Church. . . . All underscore that the root activity of the Spirit in the Church is to effect witness to Christ."[64]

The Church must proclaim the gospel in order for the world to believe, to live in obedience, and so to achieve God's purpose. The Church is called out from the world to be sent back into it, to proclaim

64. Boer, 112; cf. Berkhof, *The Doctrine of the Holy Spirit,* 36.

salvation to it. If this be true, the Reformers—especially Calvin—favored a rather selfish model of the Church: a mother caring for the faithful, whose enemy was the world. In contrast it should be pointed out that we live in the period wherein Christ achieves God's goal for creation in us and in the world, through the Holy Spirit.

As the Spirit's instrument, the Church is directed toward the world, not against it. The Church has many other responsibilities, too, among them building up itself and caring for young and old. But all edification should be undertaken for the essential task of being that instrument through which Christ reaches God's goal in the world. Barth points out that the Bible contains stories not so much of conversion as of calling. According to him, the purpose of Christian living is not personal holiness but gospel witness.

In the *Fragment,* Barth reiterates that either the Church is a missionary Church sent out into the world—or it is no Church at all, that the Christian is not a member of the community simply to share its comforts but also to share responsibility for executing the missionary command which constitutes it the Church. This command is aimed at every Christian. Baptism is our consecration or ordination to take part in the mission committed to the whole Church. All the baptized are by their baptism ordained and consecrated missionaries.[65]

Bearing directly on this is the inseparability of Jesus' promise to be with us always and his missionary command. Between his claim that all power is given to him and his promise to be with us always, there stands his missionary command. Whoever wishes to claim and rely on these two promises can do so only through obedience to the Great Commission. Mission is the meaning of the interim. Through mission Christ (through the Holy Spirit) attains God's goal in humankind and in the world. This is why the Holy Spirit makes of the Church a missionary, one who proclaims the gospel.

The content of proclamation—the gospel. In his farewell discourse, Jesus emphasizes that the Spirit will glorify him (John 14:26; 16:13-14). Acts 1:8 tells us that the Spirit will give the disciples power to bear witness for Christ. Paul summarizes his entire proclamation in one word: Christ (Col. 1:28). Reading through a single chapter like Ephesians 1 shows clearly how central Christ is to the gospel.

Proclaiming Christ included proclaiming certain facts about his life, e.g., that he fulfills Old Testament prophecy (Acts 2:16ff.; 3:18-26; 4:11, 28; Rom. 1:1-3), that he died (Acts 2:23; 3:14-15; 4:10; 10:39;

65. Barth, IV/4, 200-201.

2 Cor. 2:2; Rom. 6:3ff.), that he rose again (Acts 2:24; 3:15; 4:10; 10:40; Rom. 1:4; 6:4), that he was exalted (Acts 2:33; Eph. 2:6; Phil. 2:9; 1 Tim. 3:16), and that he will come again (Acts 3:19-21; 10:42; 1 Thess. 4:13ff.; 5:1ff.; 2 Thess. 1:7ff.; 2:1-12; 2 Tim. 4:1). The earliest sermons in Acts proclaim these facts about Christ and then, somewhat independently of them, add the call to repent (cf. Acts 2:14-36 with 2:38; 3:12-16 with 3:17-21). Later, however, Paul in particular directly relates our salvation more closely to what Christ did. He died for our sins. Still later he proclaims that we somehow died with him and rose to new life with him. More and more, our salvation is related directly to the historical facts of Jesus' life.

Further, we must give attention to the traditional distinction between proclamation by word and proclamation by deed. As in the earthly ministry of Christ so in the proclamation of the Church, these two go hand-in-hand. There is remarkable agreement between the signs shown during the interim and miracles wrought during Jesus' earthly work. Thus we read twice in Acts of a cripple being healed (3:1-11; 14:8-11) and of Aeneas, bedridden for eight years with paralysis (9:33-34). As in the Synoptics, many exorcisms are reported (5:16; 8:7; 16:16ff.; 19:12). Further, the dead are raised (9:36-41; 20:9-12), and all manner of sick people are healed (5:12-16; 8:6-7; 14:3; 19:11, 12; 28:8, 9).

But at the same time, there is a remarkable difference between the Gospels and Acts. After one of the prophets in Antioch "was inspired to stand up and predict a severe and worldwide famine" (Acts 11:28), the Christians there did not employ supernatural means to provide enough food "for the relief of their fellow-Christians in Judea"; they contributed something out of their own means (vv. 29-30; cf. 1 Cor. 16:1-4; Acts 6:1ff.). Dorcas is brought back from the dead, but Stephen is not (Acts 8:2). Paul leaves Trophimus sick in Miletus. When a storm threatens their lives, Paul does not calm the sea, but God does preserve them in the midst of the tempest (Acts 27). So in Acts the course of events is even more natural.

So although the structure of Jesus' work is retained (proclamation by words and by deeds including miracles), miracles are not so prominent here as in the Gospels. In a number of instances the more natural course is followed. But the general rule remains: the gospel proclaimed during the interim is concerned with the whole person and must therefore involve both word and deed.

A number of related issues are important. The first is the continuation of those miracles by which Jesus caused the kingdom to come, both in his earthly ministry and according to Acts. In the past it was too glibly taught by some that the "age of miracles is past," and that miracles occurred in the first century to effect a rapid and thorough establishment of the Church.[66]

G. C. Berkouwer has gone into this in depth and shown what was the legitimate motive for miracles: they were aimed at founding and extending the Church throughout the world.[67] He levels severe criticism at overzealous attempts "in faith" to exert power which cannot with certainty be identified with the triumphant revelation of God's kingdom.

He also, on the other hand, repudiates the restriction of miracles to the first centuries. We find nothing in Scripture to suggest a specific age of miracles and a specific age without them. The numerous signs which followed Pentecost should make us cautious about setting boundaries to God's wonderful deeds during our enlightened age. There is nothing in the New Testament to prevent God from making use of miracles and signs today in order to extend and establish the Church. He who genuinely believes that miracles no longer happen must ask himself if he still takes God's power seriously—or has secretly capitulated to determinism. Berkouwer asks whether or not the impotence of our times is related to the feebleness of our faith.

Two principles emerge clearly. First, there is no decisive New Testament witness against the continuation of miracles. It is therefore wrong in principle to deny their possibility or to neglect asking the Lord for them. Yet it is clear from Acts and the rest of the New Testament witness after Pentecost that things may take a more natural course. This does not suggest that Jesus' working through the Spirit has been discontinued; simply that he is working in more ways than miracles only. So far as miracles and the gifts of the Spirit are concerned, we must recognize that the Spirit distributes his gifts separately to each individual "as he wills" (1 Cor. 12:11), and that we cannot demand miracles as if they were God's only way of dealing with our problems. We must respect the Lord's freedom to give the Church those gifts and miracles which he sees fit.

The other matter to be discussed in regard to the content of the proclamation is the relationship between the vertical and the hori-

66. It is not improbable that this attitude goes back to Calvin, who, in his comment on Mark 16:17, regards it as more likely that the gifts are temporary than that God wishes them to continue. However, Calvin speaks with many qualifications and a good deal of reticence on this matter (J. Calvin, *A Harmony of the Gospels* III [1972], 254).

67. Berkouwer, *Providence,* chapter 7, especially 224f.

zontal dimensions of the gospel. The vertical dimension is our relationship with God, including our spiritual lives, forgiveness of sin, and eternal salvation or damnation. The horizontal dimension is physical needs, human relationships, social justice, and a humane social order.

In *Here Am I,* I went to some lengths to show that the horizontal dimension implied in the vertical and that the two are simply head and tail of the same coin. Indeed, the will of God is precisely that there should be justice and righteousness in society.[68]

In eschatological terms, this means that God wants justice and peace among all human beings because his purpose for creation is to dwell among them, they living as his people in his presence. He created us as physical beings with specific relationships. Therefore he is concerned about our life on earth and our relationships with each other. The horizontal dimension, peace and justice in society, is no afterthought, an extra to be tacked onto the gospel or left off at whim.

To love God and neighbor are commandments which stand equal to each other. To treat others as you would like them to treat you can be regarded as the whole message of the Bible (Matt. 7:12). And Paul sums up the entirety of the law in one command: love your neighbor as yourself (Rom. 13:8-9; Gal. 5:14). It is remarkable that Jesus could depict judgment in a parable whose decisive point is the behavior of people toward their underprivileged fellows (Matt. 25:31ff.).

There can be no doubt that the proclamation of justice and righteousness in society is essential to the gospel—as mandatory as is our relationship with God. Paul is not playing with words when he makes the whole gospel stand or fall with the resurrection of the body, nor is John by closing the Bible with a glimpse of human harmony on the new earth. The Church's message includes more than only a just society on an unrenewed earth; but the Church may never stop striving to see justice and righteousness prevail within this broken reality.

The goal of the proclamation—faith. The goal of the proclamation can be summed up as faith. As we proceed, it will become clear that much is contained in this one word. Jesus began his preaching with a call to faith (Mark 1:15); John sees the purpose of his Gospel and first Epistle as faith (John 20:30-31; 1 John 5:13); and Paul sees the purpose of his apostolate as leading people to faith (Rom. 1:5).

We did not discuss personal faith in Chapter 3, when we spoke about the goal being realized "for us." There we saw that Christ

68. A. König, *Here Am I* (1982); see subject index s.v. social righteousness.

achieved God's goal for us without our faith—indeed, before we were even able to believe. Enmity was annihilated, peace restored, the new humanity created, the world redeemed, access to the Father obtained— all through Christ alone, without our faith (Rom. 5:6-11, 15-19; 1 Cor. 1:30; 2 Cor. 5:18-19; Eph. 2:15-18; Col. 1:20; 2:13-15).

But when the *eschaton* is attained in the second mode (i.e., in us), the call to faith is "added" as an essential and decisive element to the proclamation. We place "added" in quotation marks, for the moment, because it is not yet clear how anything could be added to the completeness of our salvation, justification, righteousness, peace, and access to the Father obtained by Jesus. Nevertheless, it is unmistakable that there is indeed an addition, and that it is of decisive importance. Throughout Acts, the call to faith and repentance echoes like a refrain (Acts 2:38; 3:19-20; 10:43; 13:39, 48; 16:31; 17:30-34; 18:8; 19:18).

Paul agrees with this emphasis on faith. He who expresses himself so radically on the fullness of the *eschaton* attained by Christ for us, though without us (Eph. 2:15-18; Col. 1:20; Rom. 5:6-11), adds faith to the message as if it were a self-evident component and no addition at all. "God designed him [Christ] to be the means of expiating sin by his sacrificial death, effective through faith" (Rom. 3:25).

It is noteworthy that this affirmation follows v. 24, in which Paul states that we are justified without meriting it through the liberating act of Christ. This means that the liberation is real, yet we receive it through faith. So too in Ephesians, without mentioning faith, Paul writes of the peace and access which we have in Christ (2:14ff.) but also asserts that we are saved by faith (2:8). The "without us" aspect sounds nowhere more radical than in Rom. 5:6-10, 15-19; yet at the start of the same chapter we read, "we have been justified by faith" (5:1). So it is not at all strange that Brunner says the self-manifestation, self-revelation, and self-communication of God attain their goal when a person comes to faith.[69]

Before the proclamation's goal can be broadly outlined, it is necessary to show that this "addition" of faith is no addition at all, and that because of the nature of faith there is agreement in Reformation theology on the emptiness of faith.[70] This does not mean that

---

69. E. Brunner, *Dogmatics* (1950-1962) III, 171.
70. Berkouwer has pointed this out about (among others) Gogarten, Brunner, Barth, and Calvin (G. C. Berkouwer, *Faith and Justification* [1954], 172f.). See also Barth, IV/1, 631.

faith is unimportant, but rather that its importance—even indispensability—lies in that it is nothing on its own, is not autonomous, is no human contribution, but must receive its content and its meaning from the other side: in fact from God in Christ through the Spirit. In faith we confess God as the subject and ourselves as object of salvation. Salvation means that Christ has fully attained God's goal *for* us. And when a person believes this, God's goal is attained *in* that person.

Proclamation has as its goal the bringing of people to this knowledge and trust. How radically this faith involves our whole life is shown by the New Testament's equation of faith with obedience.[71] So it is clear that, because of the nature of faith, no tension can exist between "Christ alone" and the "addition" of faith. Faith lives solely from Christ, and is filled by what he has done. Stated in eschatological terms, Christ's attainment of the goal *for* us (but without us) and his attainment of the goal *in* us are not concurrent.

Yet it is this very emptiness of faith in itself which leads to its decisive character. Because it is directed solely to Christ and his work for us, faith is necessary—and its lack excludes one from salvation. Without faith, God's goal in us is not reached. Precisely because faith is neither a human accomplishment nor a human contribution, but rather a confession that everything has been done for us by Christ, we have no Christ if we have no faith. This is why Scripture speaks so strongly about the necessity, value, and power of faith. Faith receives value only from its object. And because of faith's necessity, we are bound to speak of the mortal peril of unbelief (Rom. 9:30-33; 11:20-23; Heb. 3:18-19; 4:1-11).[72]

71. Brunner, III, 162f. Here Brunner reflects Bultmann's comments on faith in *TDNT* VI, 203f. Cf. among others John 3:36; Rom. 1:5. Bultmann brings these facts to the fore by comparing Rom. 1:8 and 1 Thess. 1:8 with Rom. 15:18; 16:19 or 2 Cor. 10:5ff. with 10:15. He refers also to Rom. 10:3, 16; 2 Cor. 9:13; and Rom. 1:5. See also Barth, IV/1, 620f. Further attention should be paid to the striking connection between faith and obedience in Hebrews 3 and 4.

72. It is not correct to claim that faith is unimportant to Barth; if the difference between the Church and the world—according to Barth—is that the former knows the atonement has taken place while the latter does not, this is not simply a question of theoretical knowledge. This "knowing" must be viewed in its biblical sense, i.e., that knowledge (Heb. *yāḏaʿ*) is knowledge-as-community, as G. Vos says in *Biblical Theology* (1948), 280. John carries over this meaning into the New Testament, e.g., in John 17:3, "This is eternal life: to know you who alone are truly God and Jesus Christ whom you have sent." In place of the "mere" difference between knowing and not knowing, Barth speaks of "the decisive dif-

To believe involves one's entire life: justification, sanctification, and a life of service to God. It includes involvement in God's will for society. Therefore, the importance of proclamation by deed—the gospel's horizontal dimension—has also been mentioned here. If we designate faith the goal of proclamation, we must also point out that the gospel cannot be restricted to our personal relationship with God. Faith includes an attitude and way of life which touch every facet of individual life and of society as a whole.

We conclude with a repetition of those results of our investigation which we presupposed at the beginning: The Holy Spirit causes the church to proclaim the gospel throughout the world in order to arouse faith in people and, by so doing, to reach God's goal in them and in the world. One of the specific forms in which this goal becomes visible is the Church.

The Fruit of the Gospel Proclamation— The Church

During the interim, this proclamation results in a division that was not visible in Christ's realization of the *eschaton* for us. It can be seen in Paul's distinction between "spiritual" and "natural" persons (1 Cor. 2:14-15), insiders and outsiders (5:12), saints and pagans (2 Cor. 2:15), believers and unbelievers (2 Cor. 4:4; Eph. 1:1), etc. Here we confront the Church over against the world and believers over against unbelievers.

Paul often refers to the believers as "us" or "you." This same apostle who speaks so universally about reconciliation and the peace made for all people and things can, in the same breath, deny the achieved goal to all but the faithful: "you . . . are members of God's household" (Eph. 2:19; cf. "you" and "us" in vv. 1-10). These same terms, "us" and "you," for believers over against unbelievers occur in many other places, e.g., Gal. 1:4; Col. 1:13. In the latter, the apostle makes this distinction only a few verses before his universalist pronouncement that "everything is reconciled by Christ's blood"(Col. 1:20).

This distinction of "us" and "you" is no mere literary device and is not used automatically because Paul is addressing a specific group

ference" (*Church Dogmatics* IV/1, 77, 103-104). We will not now go into the problems which, despite this, crop up in Barth's dogmatics—particularly on the subject of universal salvation.

rather than the whole world. What is at issue between "us" and "you" on one side and "them" on the other, those inside and those outside, is faith. Faith "is able" to do this because it is directed toward the merits of Christ. So to say that faith separates is to say that Christ separates. This is why the division is valid and final; it runs through to the third and last mode in which the *eschaton* is realized, at Christ's second coming—and it is echoed in the final judgment (2 Thess. 1:6-10). Yet because the human being is the subject of faith, we cannot hold Christ responsible for some being lost.

The biblical authors, we note, view seriously the realization of the *eschaton* in the interim. No longer is it realized without us, i.e., without our faith, responsibility, or acceptance of enmity's end and the covenant's restoration. This means that it goes unrealized in those who will not accept the cessation of hostility, who will not begin anew by dying to their old lives and being raised to new ones in Christ.

We must now investigate more closely those groups who stand opposed to one another because of this division, i.e., they who believe the gospel and are gathered into the Church (they in whom Christ achieves his goal in the interim) and they who do not and stand opposed to the Church (having their culminating point in the Antichrist). The former are the fruit of the proclamation, the latter its opponents.

The characterization of the Church as "the people of God" has grown very popular in recent decades, not only among Protestants but, especially since Vatican II, among Catholics as well. The concept lends itself very well to a dynamic view of the Church. And within the framework of this book, of course, it is also well suited to reflecting the eschatological meaning of the Church. Indeed, God's goal in creation is simply that humanity should become his people—and the Church is the group known as the people of God. It is not strange that this was the most favored name among early Christians, forming a link with Israel of old yet emphasizing the Church's newness (cf. Matt. 1:21; 2:6; 4:6; Luke 1:17, 77; Acts 15:14; Rom. 9:25; 11:1; 15:10; 2 Cor. 6:16; Titus 2:14; Heb. 4:9; 8:10; 10:30; 1 Pet. 2:9-10; Rev. 18:4; 21:3).

As we have indicated, this description of the Church is particularly reflective of God's goal for creation that he should be our God and we his people. The alienation between God and humanity resulted from our unfaithfulness. Therefore reconciliation is directed toward us and our sin. Christ's sacrifice was not intended to make God change his mind and persuade him to accept us. Indeed, it was God who loved us so much that he gave his only Son (John 3:16). God reconciled us through Christ, thereby himself providing an expiation to take away the sin of the world. We are the objects of reconciliation, because we became God's enemies.

So it is that "people of God" assumes its eschatological significance. God has always been our God. But we have broken the covenant and become children of Satan (John 8:44). If we now become God's people through faith in Christ, this means that we participate in the realized goal of God—he becomes our God and we his people. In Christ, this has been accomplished without us. While we were yet enemies of God, Christ created by the cross "one new humanity," the people of God, including both Jew and Gentile. Reconciled humanity was thus *in him* already the faithful people of God without reference to the faith of any individual (Eph. 2:15-16). But now individuals have to come to faith to be members of this new humanity or people of God.

The question arises whether or not this term "people of God" had any eschatological significance where it was applied to Israel in the Old Testament. But this suggestion was dismissed in our previous chapter. Eschatology is built upon the *eschatos,* Jesus Christ, the successful end. Israel failed to be the people of God. What is the history of Israel, viewed as a whole and from the human perspective, but an account of faithlessness, failure, degeneracy, and decay?

Hans Küng shows that being the people of God always meant the threat of judgment for Israel, precisely because Israel could never turn the title into fact. Therefore, the future entered more and more into the preaching of the prophets: God would make Israel truly his people by doing something new. Thus it became part of prophetic expectation that Israel should become the people of God (Jer. 24:7; 31:31-34; 32:37-40; Ezek. 11:19-20; 14:11; 36:28; 37:23; Hos. 1:9).[73] That this expectation was directed specifically to the end time can be seen from Isa. 61:6; Jer. 9:24ff.; Hos. 1:10; Joel 2:28-32.

That "the nations" loom large in this eschatological expectation reminds us that God's goal was, through Israel, also directed more broadly; that by Israel's failure, God's intention for the nations also went unrealized; and that in the future the nations would be included in the new people of God. Dahl correctly states that what is at issue in

---

73. H. Küng, *The Church* (1967), 118; N. A. Dahl, *Das Volk Gottes* (1941), 38. The latter gives more texts and refers to G. von Rad, *TDNT* III, 358, who writes: "This means, however, that in the post-exilic period Israel increasingly becomes the object of a hope that God will perform an eschatological act of salvation."

Old Testament expectations of Israel's restoration as God's people is not that restoration only, but a new form of Israel on an earth made new.[74]

So it is incorrect to view the Church as the new people of God, if that is taken to mean that it is merely a prolongation of Israel. The Church is the fulfillment of an expectation in which the original purpose of God for Israel (and through Israel for all humanity) comes into its own. This is why national boundaries for the New Testament people of God are decisively and finally broken down. This does not mean that such boundaries were either absolute or legitimate in the Old Testament. Despite Israel's failure to be a light to the nations, mention is often made of Gentiles who, to worship the Lord, attached themselves to Israel. Israel's exclusivist, nationalist definitions were not legitimate because God wished to bless all peoples in Abraham (Gen. 12:3). Israel's status as God's people in no sense diminished God's ownership of the whole earth (Exod. 19:5).

Yet we find a legitimate *relative* national exclusiveness for the people of God in that individuals from other nations who wished to serve the Lord had (with few exceptions) to become Israelites, and all nations had to be attracted to Jerusalem in order to see the glory of the true God (Isa. 2:2). How relative this national character of the covenant was, however, is apparent from the facts that "not all descendants of Israel are truly Israel" (Rom. 9:6) and that the people of Israel can continue to exist without being the people of God.

After Christ, the good news goes out to all peoples, nations, and languages; there is no longer any division between Jew and Greek (or Gentile) in the Church, because Christ "has made the two one," i.e., the one eschatological people of God (Eph. 2:11-18). In this way all people are to be considered potentially part of the people of God. And thus God's purpose is achieved: to bless all earth's peoples through Abraham's seed (Gal. 3:13-16), to be the God of all humanity (Rev. 20:3), and to assemble them and bless them.

Now the "secret of Christ" is made known, "that through the gospel the Gentiles are heirs together with the Jews, part of the same body, sharing together in the promise made in Christ Jesus" (Eph. 3:4-6; cf. Rom. 11:25; Eph. 1:9ff.; Col. 1:26ff.; 4:3ff.;1 Tim. 3:16). No matter how scandalous this was for the Jews (from which we perceive how radically they misunderstood God's intentions), God reached his goal of being God to all earth's peoples in this way. So the *eschaton*

74. Dahl, 41.

is attained in us during the interim. It is the fruit of the proclamation. Barth is right to consider the Church "the eschatological fact *par excellence*."[75]

The Church as the people of God fully answers God's original intention to create a being other than God that might share in God's happiness. This is why, when the *eschaton* is realized in its third form, there is a reference back to the title "people of God" and to the covenant as creation's goal. "Now at last God has his dwelling with mankind! He will dwell among them and they will be his people, and he himself will be with them" (Rev. 21:3).

We should note that the reason God's goal is truly realized in the Church—as it was not in Israel—is not that we have been more faithful or exercised our calling more effectively than the people of Israel; rather, Christ has come and—without our aid—realized the covenant for us and has created the new humanity independently of our faith (Eph. 2:15). The Church existed in Christ before any individuals came to faith. He is the *eschatos*, who reaches the *eschaton* before our decision of faith, thus guaranteeing that where Israel failed the Church succeeds. That the gates of hell will not prevail against the Church, while Israel is rejected (Matt. 16:18; Rom. 11:15), is, from a salvation-historical viewpoint, owing to no virtue of the Church but to Christ. And this is exactly what opens a new perspective for Israel.

Israel's Future

Jesus Christ has reached the goal for all people (universally in a salvation-historical sense), "the Jew first and also the Greek." Greeks (Gentiles) are what is added, the wild olive shoot grafted into the domesticated olive tree (Israel), as is pictured in Rom. 11:17-24. It is not Jews who are aliens in the Church but we—converted Gentiles!

The biblical perspective is distorted, however, when it is suggested that the incorporation of Gentiles is somehow alien or unexpected to the Old Testament. That it was alien to the Old Testament was Israel's view because it misunderstood and denied its vocation. We have already considered the original universalism of the Old Testament (Gen. 1–11), which was not exchanged for a particularism with Israel's election. Rather it assumed a new form of universalism when Israel was called to be a blessing for all peoples—a salvific end not

75. Barth, IV/3/1, 321.

achieved because of Israel's failure. Gentiles are therefore "aliens" in the Church only in that it is through *Israel's* God, in *Israel's* covenant, and through *Israel's* messiah that they have access to salvation. In actual fact this is nothing less than the execution of God's original plan of salvation.

Similarly, it is wrong to neglect missions to the Jews on the grounds that Israel is actually the historical monument to God's love and faithfulness, that they are the one and only extra-biblical proof of God, that they can learn nothing from us which they do not already know—and that we might rather learn from them.[76] The Jews of today have no special religious advantages over those of Jesus' time. Those who rejected the messiah in that day ceased to be part of the people of God, by this deed showing that at that decisive point they misunderstood even the Old Testament and therefore had indeed something to learn from Jesus and his disciples. This still holds true for Jews who today persist in rejecting him. They do not understand the revelation they have received. It is still true that "there is no other name given to mankind through which we may be saved" (Acts 4:12), and that "he who puts his faith in the Son has hold of eternal life, but he who disobeys the Son shall not see that life; God's wrath rests upon him" (John 3:36).

The Church must announce this message to the Jews—and to everyone else—as the one and only word to which we must cling in life and in death. In essence there is no difference between the salvation-status of the unbelieving Jew and the unbelieving Gentile. "There is no difference between Jew and Greek, because the same Lord is Lord of all, and is rich enough for the need of all who invoke him . . . everyone who invokes the name of the Lord will be saved" (Rom. 10:12-13). This inclusive statement has as well an exclusive meaning: he who does not invoke Jesus' name shall not be saved. If this is the gospel message and if mission means proclaiming the gospel, then the Church has a mission to Jews. This does not mean that the relationship between the Church and Jews is the same as that between the Church and non-Christian Gentiles. But it does mean that the relationship between the Church and Jews is not the same as that between different Christian denominations,[77] because the Jews (possessing revelation but rejecting messiah) are lost.

76. These are some of the arguments advanced by Barth (IV/3/2, 876f.) against missions to the Jews.
77. A. de Kuiper, *Israel tussen Zending en Oecumene* (1964), 189.

This shows clearly what the Jews' future is: it is a fresh opportunity offered by the gospel to be saved through faith in the messiah or, expressed in terms of this study, to attain God's goal for them—as for the Gentiles—during the interim.[78] The proclamation calls Israel to faith because "if they do not continue faithless, they will be grafted in; for it is in God's power to graft them in again" (Rom. 11:23).

To probe the nature of the Jews' future more deeply, it is necessary to study Paul's treatment in Romans 9–11 of the topic of whether or not they are still God's chosen people. To answer this question we need first to clarify what the question really asks. Israel was not chosen to be God's people because God had lost interest in the other nations. When he chose Abraham, he said, "through you I will bless all the nations" (Gen. 12:3 TEV). God did not choose Israel in order to treat it as a favorite, but to make it the instrument of his love for the whole world (Exod. 19:5; Rom. 2:11).

When through disobedience Israel failed to be a light to the nations, God turned its disobedience and hardness of heart to his use by reaching the Gentiles through that disobedience. In fact, Rom. 11:12-15 teaches that the fall of Israel means the enrichment of the Gentile world and that its rejection brings reconciliation to humanity. This means that both despite and through Israel's rejection of its messiah and his good news, God has caused the gospel to be proclaimed to the Gentiles (cf. Acts 13:44-48; 18:5-8).

Israel's future appears dark. The Jews have not attained the purpose of their election. Romans 11 speaks of their falling away, their rejection, and their hardening (vv. 7, 12, 15). Yet Paul affirms that "God has not rejected the people which he acknowledged of old as his own" (v. 2). Beginning at v. 11 he unfolds the secret of God's future for the Jews. Evidently God's faithfulness is stronger than Israel's faithlessness. It appears that though Israel rejected the messiah, God has not repudiated Israel.

In his mercy he reverses roles. In Genesis 12, Israel is chosen to be a blessing to all peoples and, in this sense, to be the chosen people. Israel failed. According to Romans 11 the gospel is now proclaimed to the Gentiles in order to provoke Israel to jealousy. In other words, the Gentiles, having come to faith, must now give back the blessing of

---

78. From this point considerable use is made of Berkouwer's view of the future of Israel in *The Return of Christ* (chapter 11), which generally agrees with H. Ridderbos's exposition of Rom. 9–11 in *Aan de Romeinen* (1959). In *Israel in die Krisis* (1967), P. A. Verhoef agrees along broad lines with this.

the gospel to Israel (Rom. 11:11-14). We could say that believing Gentiles are now the chosen people through whom the Jews are to be reached. The idea behind this "provocation to jealousy" (v. 14) is for the Jews to see Gentiles coming to faith in *their* messiah and thereby reaping all the rich promises originally made to *them* (9:4-5).

Three important points emerge from these considerations. First, it is remarkable that Paul expects Israel will easily be aroused to jealousy and so come to faith. Indeed, if wild olive branches are successfully ingrafted to the cultivated tree, how much more easily should cultivated branches be ingrafted to their native tree (Rom. 11:17-24). After all, unlike the Gentile world, Israel is not unacquainted with the true God. This is the legitimate distinction between an Israel which has overtly rejected the messiah and unconverted Gentiles who have not—a difference which, missions to the Jews notwithstanding, must be allowed its full weight.

Second, Paul does not expect one Jew here and another there to grow jealous and be ingrafted. Rather he expects that a large number of Israelites—indeed, Israel seen as a whole—will come to repentance. This is evident from his use of "some" (Rom. 11:14; cf. his use of the same word in 3:3 and 11:17: in both instances, "some" means a large number or nearly everyone). This is Paul's expectation for Israel's salvation, and it is only reasonable; they, after all, are the natural branches. "How much more readily will they, the natural olive branches, be grafted into their native stock?" (11:24).

Third, Paul expected this mass conversion of Jews in his own time, not in the remote future. This is clear from his hope that he himself will make his nation jealous and so save them. It also surfaces in his use of "so" in v. 26, "and so all Israel will be saved" (RSV).

"So" is frequently mistranslated "then" (NAB) or "when" (NEB) and thus seems to refer to a miraculous future conversion of Jews at the end time.[79] This implies a picture of the "end time" which overlooks the fact that it began with the birth of Jesus and that there *is* no

---

79. F. Flückiger, *Der Ursprung des christlichen Dogmas* (1955), 138; H. Berkhof, *Christ, the Meaning of History* (1966), 145-146. Berkhof, who adheres to a "last generation" conversion of the Jews living at the end, has no explanation for the "and so" (RSV); he attempts to interpret it as "later in time." The same misunderstanding exists in regard to Luke 21:24. This "until" does last to the end, for nothing is said about what happens "afterwards." Similarly, the obstinacy which has come over some Jews persists to the end; yet it does not exclude "all Israel" from being saved, because the Bible thinks in salvation-historical terms, not individually.

separate end time isolated from the period between the first and second comings of Christ. Further, if only the generation of Israelites happening to live in such an "end time" underwent miraculous conversion, this would bar the rest of the Jews from salvation. What of the Jews who have lived and died during the past two thousand years? The apostle did not refer only to the last generation of Jews but to "all Israel."

Considering the use of "so" in v. 26, we can paraphrase like this: the whole of Israel is saved *in the following way:* "a hardening has come upon part of Israel, until the full number of the Gentiles come in" (v. 25, RSV). This situation lasts until the second coming: as a consequence of Israel's stubbornness the gospel is proclaimed to the Gentiles to make the Jews jealous, and this is the way "all Israel" is brought to salvation.

The expression *"until* the Gentiles have been admitted in full strength" does not mean "and then after that Israel will be saved," but rather "until the full number of Gentiles come in, Israel will continue to be made jealous and be saved." Paul is not looking for the Jews' conversion in the distant future, a miracle from heaven. It is toward their conversion here and now that Gentile Christians ought to be working. This is even clearer in Rom. 11:30-31, "Just as formerly you [Gentiles] were disobedient to God, but now have received mercy in the time of [the Jews'] disobedience, so now, when you receive mercy they have proved disobedient, but only in order that they too may receive mercy." This in no way implies a remote, future conversion.

In Romans 9-11 Paul is not writing a fragmentary, incidental, and abrupt history of the Jews in advance. What is more, he expects vastly more for the Jews than an apocalyptic miracle which will rescue only the last generation. Berkouwer rightly if rhetorically asks of Berkhof: Is this what excites Paul to rejoicing, that a fraction of the people of Israel then living will be included at Christ's coming? Is this what is meant by "all Israel"? Is this the fulfillment of the unsearchable gifts of God's grace?[80]

In contrast to apocalyptic end time expectations stands Paul's radical missionary approach—Paul, burning with zeal for Israel, hoping to arouse his own people to jealousy. The passion, dynamism, and tension characteristic of Paul suggest anything but an abstract forecast of what will occur but once in a dim and distant future. Paul is active and

---

80. Berkouwer, *The Return of Christ*, 345f. Ridderbos asks almost the same question in connection with Rom. 11:26 (*Aan de Romeinen*, ad loc.).

prayerful, busy with the Israel of his own day (Rom. 9:1-3; 10:1-2; 11:11-14). The words "will be saved" in 11:26 are not soothsaying history in advance. If they were, they would be utterly unlike Paul. They are rather a prayerful, serving involvement with the Israel of his own day, an attempt to move them through the open gate (11:23). Ridderbos correctly states that the idea of a conversion of "all Israel" sometime in the future, based on a miracle rather than on gospel proclamation, is a remarkable excrescence on theological thought, one which in no way fits the course of salvation history taught by Romans 9–11.

Apart from Romans 9–11, little is written in the New Testament about the future of the Jews. We will discuss a few important texts.

Acts 3:19-20. "Repent then and turn to God, so that your sins may be wiped out. Then the Lord may grant you a time of recovery and send you the messiah he has already appointed, that is, Jesus." Peter addressed these words to Jews who had flocked to the temple. To these who had earned God's judgment by their rejection of Christ (2:23), Peter's message throws open a wonderful perspective on the future. If they repent, their sins will be forgiven and a time of recovery will be granted by the Lord. "A time of recovery" refers to Christ's second coming, which is also described in the clause which follows. So Israel's future consists of repentance, faith in Jesus, and acceptance as God's children. On this point Peter and Paul agree. There is no indication here of any special position for the Jews as a nation or of any marvelous, national conversion in the future.

Luke 21:24. "They will fall at the sword's point; they will be carried captive into all countries, and Jerusalem will be trampled down by foreigners until their day has run its course." The last words are most important. Some are of opinion that they mean Jerusalem will once more be the capital of Israel as the people of God, after the day of the Gentiles has run its course. Making such a claim, however, they fall into the same error discussed in our exposition of Rom. 11:25. Both texts include the concept of "until," but neither implies that of "thereafter." In both cases, statements are made only about what will happen up to a certain point, not what will follow. Luke 21:24 states only that Jerusalem will be trampled down by the nations until a certain moment. That moment is the day when the Gentiles' time has run its course, an expression which points toward the return of Christ. Nothing about a future restoration of the Jews is suggested. Even now, as Israel occupies Jerusalem, it remains every bit one of "the nations," because it is one with them in unbelief. So Jerusalem continues to be "trampled on by the nations" to this day.

Matthew 10:23. "When you are persecuted in one town, take refuge in another; I tell you this: before you have gone through all the towns of Israel, the Son of man will have come." This unusually difficult text has troubled exegetes across the centuries. What we can deduce from it is that the gospel must be proclaimed to Israel until Christ's return; with this the statements of Peter and Paul are in full agreement. And beyond this we cannot go with certainty.

Matthew 19:28. In this text we read that at the end the twelve disciples will sit on thrones, "judging the twelve tribes of Israel." But there is not much to be deduced from this text. The idea of the twelve tribes is also applied to the Church in the New Testament (Jas. 1:1), but even if this passage refers to Israel in a literal sense, it tells us nothing about Israel's earthly future. It might as easily refer to the twelve Old Testament tribes.

Matthew 23:39. "And I tell you, you shall never see me until the time when you say, 'Blessings on him who comes in the name of the Lord.'" There have been attempts to deduce from this passage that the Jews as a people will come to repentance in the future and then utter these words. Now, it is clear that Paul also prayed and worked for the conversion of his own people. And it is true that many Jews were converted during his time and afterward. Yet we must remember that it is not only converted Jews who cry out, "Blessings on him!" The crowds who shouted this in Matt. 21:9 a few days later shouted, "Crucify him!" (27:22). Beyond this, "until the time when you say" expresses no more in the original than a possibility. Therefore this text is really no more than the announcement by Jesus to a number of scribes and Pharisees that they *might* recognize and honor him in future.

In addition to these texts, others are sometimes applied to Israel, e.g., Matt. 24:32-33 and Mark 13:30. The former cannot be applied to Israel. The budding tree is not Israel, merely a parable teaching the disciples to fix their eyes on heaven when they see certain signs being fulfilled. This is why Luke says, "Look at the fig tree, or any other tree" (21:29). The fig tree therefore has no special significance; in fact, the text becomes absurd if its symbolism is pushed to extremes. For one thing, it is arbitrary to allege that the budding of the fig tree indicates Israel's return to Palestine. But were this for the moment to be accepted, then the budding of the other trees in the Lukan form of the passage must represent the return of other peoples to their lands of origin! Mark 13:30 offers a good many problems, but it is at any rate not concerned with the return of Israel to Palestine or anything like it.

This short survey leads us to but one conclusion about the Jews' future in the New Testament. The message expressed most fully by Paul is that, despite Israel's rejection and merited judgment, God continues to hold open the doors of his mercy so that the Jews can again be ingrafted through faith in Jesus. The New Testament knows nothing about a miraculous end-time conversion or any future role for them as a separate elect people.

There are, however, some who believe that the Old Testament prophesies a return of the Jews to Palestine not fulfilled by Israel's return from the Babylonian exile. They point out, first, that the prophecies speak of a return from many lands, while in 539 B.C. Israel returned from Babylon only; second, that some of the prophecies date from after the return from Babylon, and therefore must also be fulfilled at some time after the return.

We do indeed find a whole range of statements concerning disobedient Israel and God's judgment, and these sometimes speak of Jewish exile. The same prophets make statements about a Jewish return to Palestine, but only after repentance. That repentance is decisive means that present-day Israel cannot be the fulfillment of prophecy. Individual Jews have come to faith in Christ, but this has happened in every age since the apostles and is exactly the future held out for Israel by the New Testament (e.g., Acts 3:19, 20). Modern Israel is an ordinary secular state, just one more of the "nations" which will trample Jerusalem under foot (Luke 21:24).

Meanwhile there remains the question whether there are indeed Old Testament prophecies which tell of a return from exile and which were not fulfilled in the return from Babylon. Two groups of prophecies require our attention.

The first are those written, according to some, after the return from Babylon in 539 B.C., particularly Zech. 8:1-9. But a reading of Zech. 8 makes it clear that nothing is said of another return in the distant future, only of a completion of the return from Babylon. The return had begun, and by the time Zechariah prophesied, the temple foundations were already laid, but ordinary social life was still impossible. Of course this was a great disappointment to those who returned, especially when compared with Deutero-Isaiah's prophecies of a glorious return. Then Zechariah received this prophecy that the return was by no means complete, that scores of Jews would still return, that conditions in Jerusalem would improve to where even old men and women "leaning on a stick" could sit again in the streets, and the city would be full of children, utterly safe. This and similar prophecies focused on the completion of the return, not on a future return.

Long after the return from exile began, thousands of Jews still lived in exile. Fifty years after Zechariah there were still enough Jews in the provinces around Babylon to kill 75,000 of their enemies (Esther 9:16). And seventy-five years after Zechariah, Nehemiah was still in Susa—far to the east of Babylon—praying for the return of the remaining Israelites (Neh. 1:5-11). So, long after the return began prophecies of its completion were to be expected.

Another group of prophecies refers to an exile among and a return from "the nations," "many lands," "the four winds of heaven," "the four corners of the earth," etc. (Ezek. 11:16-17; 12:14; 17:21; Isa. 11:12). As Judah was exiled only to Babylon and returned only from there, some believe that this return from among the nations must still be in the future. But such an explanation is baseless. Scripture speaks of the exile to Babylon in these terms: "I scattered them among the nations, and they were dispersed among different countries. . . . When they came among those nations . . ." (Ezek. 36:19-20; cf. 20:34; Jer. 30:11; 31:10; Ps. 44:12). This notion, that prophecy requires Jews to return from all the directions of the wind, mistakes the character of prophecy and its manner of fulfillment (dealt with in the next chapter).

There is therefore no scriptural reason for regarding that which happens to the Israelites of our day as a fulfillment of prophecy. Among New Testament writers, Paul devoted the most attention to the Jews' future. He teaches that Israel was unfaithful to its calling; that God's faithfulness is greater than Israel's faithlessness; and that he reaches the Gentiles despite—even through—Israel's disobedience. He chooses the Gentiles as his people, and for the same purpose of service as that for which he chose Israel, holding out this opportunity to all Jews—not just to the last generation of them.

At the same time, Paul warns the "new Israel" to beware of being broken off like Israel (Rom. 11:21). This is no apocalyptic threat. It is a very real warning for the Church to pay heed to every step of its journey through history as it pursues the calling of its election, which is to provoke Israel to jealousy.

This means that, as it is for the Gentiles, so it is for Israel: the *eschaton* reached *for* Israel by Christ must now be attained *in* Israel (Eph. 2:11-18) by its coming to faith in the messiah. Just as God's goal is not attained in Gentiles unless they come to faith, so Jews remain outside and cannot be grafted in again unless they come to faith. And this is not because God is unwilling or unable to do otherwise ("for it is in God's power to graft them in again"), but because God wills to graft them in only by way of their faith. Thus—and only thus—is God's purpose achieved during the interim in Jew and Gentile alike.

Opposition to the Proclamation—Antichrist

As we have already affirmed, limiting terms are never applied to Christ's achievement of the goal *for* us. The universality (in a salvation-historical sense) of reconciliation is proclaimed with emphasis. We first notice that some people do not participate in the goal which Christ has reached when we consider the second mode, i.e., *in* us. Here, where we must come to faith, a division appears between those who believe and those who do not. The final judgment will merely reveal this decision for which human beings carry responsibility.

Neutrality toward Jesus Christ is impossible. All are called to believe in him, which means to believe that through him their sins are atoned for and that they have been made participants in the new humanity which he created by his death and resurrection. Everyone who does not come to faith remains "outside"; the *eschaton* is not realized in that person. But no one can remain neutral. Those who do not decide for Christ decide against him and against the *eschaton* which he realized for them (2 Pet. 2:1) because "He who is not with me is against me, and he who does not gather with me scatters" (Matt. 12:30; Luke 11:23).

Unbelief is a perilous matter. It means being radically opposed to Christ, even if one is not in open, active, and aggressive rebellion against God. The mere fact that a person is not with and for Jesus means that he or she is positively against Christ (thus anti-Christ), as one of Christ's enemies, ravaging Christ's flock. This is why we discuss the Antichrist under the general heading of opposition to proclamation.

Every form of negative reaction to the gospel is in essence an expression of Antichrist. This does not mean that every form of disbelief must automatically be regarded as a manifestation of *the* Antichrist. But it does mean that there is some connection (as we shall see from the corporate nature of the Antichrist) and that the Antichrist is merely the nadir and concentration of unbelief and sin.

Indeed it is generally acknowledged that the Antichrist is "bound" to and "dependent" upon Christ because he is a reaction to Christ's ministry. For this reason van Niftrik declares that the Antichrist can attain full stature only in a world where the gospel is proclaimed and believed.[81]

This perspective also makes it clear why New Testament writers can preach so vividly about the Antichrist. Just as it was obvious to Paul that Israel's conversion is no remote, theoretical miracle, so it was obvious to the New Testament writers that the Antichrist is no distant figure who will appear but once at some isolated end time. Just as the missionary Paul prayed and labored for Israel's conversion, so John warned his congregation passionately against the Antichrist—and described him in no uncertain terms (1 John 2:18-22; 4:3; 2 John 7).[82] Similarly, when Paul admonishes the Thessalonians about "the enemy," "that wicked man who shall be revealed," he does not imply that this rebel is to be expected only in the dim and distant future (2 Thess. 2:3, 6). Indeed, "already the secret power of wickedness is at work, secret only for the present, until the Restrainer disappears from the scene. And then he will be revealed" (vv. 7-8). Paul is not concerned with the remote future. He does not put off the premature "already" of the congregation (v. 2) to distant times but with an expectation that is "at hand." The congregation's mistake lay not in the closeness of their expectation but in believing that it was "already" taking place. We learn from 2 Thessalonians and 1 John, then, that the Antichrist is *actual,* not a far-off and theoretical expectation for the future. And this fits perfectly with our discovery that the Bible knows no end time which, in the apostles' days, was still remote.

It is consequently clear that whether the Antichrist should be seen as an individual or a collective force must be answered in favor of the second alternative, supposing for the moment that this question ought even to be asked.[83] That the Antichrist is collective is clear from

81. G. C. van Niftrik says in *De Vooruitgang der Mensheid* (1966), 196, that one could say that the light of Christ, the sun of the gospel, in fact evokes the shape of the Antichrist. The *Anti*-Christ presupposes Christ. He is the pseudo-Christ. A. E. Brooke, *The Johannine Epistles* (ICC; 1912) says (at 1 John 2:18): "Their [viz., the Antichrists'] appearance was the natural outcome of the growth of Christianity." See also Berkhof, *Christ: The Meaning of History,* 114f.; Stauffer, 213.

82. Berkouwer, *The Return of Christ,* 260-268. In this section we have also made extensive use of pp. 37-72 of Berkouwer, as we did when discussing the future of Israel. In *Die Letzten Dinge* (1957[7]), 283, 285, P. Althaus has strongly emphasized the actuality of the Antichrist. See also van Niftrik, 190f., 196.

83. In *Paul* (1975), 514-516, H. Ridderbos has pointed out that the Bible frequently thinks in a collective manner about individuals (e.g., Adam and Christ), and the striking manner in which the "analogy" between Christ and the Antichrist is treated prompts the conclusion that "As Christ is a person, but at the same time

1 John 2:18ff. The word "Antichrist" occurs in Scripture only in 1 John 2:18-23 (in vv. 18 and 22); 4:1-5 (in v. 3); and 2 John 7. Two matters are clear at once from these texts: John sees the Antichrist as a *present* reality and as a *plural* reality.

The faithful have already heard that the Antichrist is coming. This appears to have been a fixed part of apostolic preaching, since Paul can say that he has preached about this man of sin (2 Thess. 2:5). John now announces that this expectation is fulfilled: many anti-Christs are already abroad, and this means that the faithful must know that the last hour has arrived.

No reason exists for reading into this text any notion of "forerunners" heralding an Antichrist who would himself appear only much later, i.e., at "the end." Neither John nor any other New Testament writer knows of any such separate and delimitable end, and there is nowhere any talk of forerunners to the Antichrist. John writes "in the last hour" and affirms that the Antichrist has come in the many Antichrists. In fact the idea of forerunners to an ultimate Antichrist directly contradicts what John says, because he sees the many Antichrists who have already appeared as proof that the last hour has struck.

In 1 John 2:22 John identifies the Antichrist with false teachers in the congregation who deny the Father and the Son. In 4:1-3 he calls these straying teachers "false prophets" and repeats that they are the anti-Christ of whose coming the congregation has been warned, that now they "have gone out into the world." The translation, "the spirit of the Antichrist," represented in many versions, has in it nothing of the idea of forerunners, though it might create this impression. The NEB is to be preferred: "This is what is meant by 'Antichrist'. . . ." That Antichrist has already appeared is also clear from 2 John 7: "Many deceivers have gone out into the world. . . . These are the persons described as the Antichrist." So the Antichrist was a present reality in John's day, and John knew who the Antichrist was.

Still H. Ridderbos tries to make a case for forerunners, despite all this evidence to the contrary.[84] He deduces this from the structure

---

one with all who believe in him and are under his sovereignty, so the antichrist is not only a godless individual, but a concentration of godlessness that already goes forth before him and which joins all who follow him at his appearance into a unity with him" (516).

84. Ridderbos, *Paul*, 517. The notion of forerunners is widespread. It is the way in which John's emphasis on the present used to be avoided because of Paul's futurist stress. See Stauffer, 214 and note 704; K. Dijk *Het einde der Eeuwen* (1953), 149.

of Johannine preaching, in which future events are presented as current without denying their future reality. But Ridderbos has to begin from an Antichrist that has not as yet appeared, which is precisely opposite to what John clearly says.

When John sets future events in the present (e.g., the resurrection) it is clear from his style that he acknowledges the yet-to-be character of his subject. All three references to the Antichrist involve a present reality, however, and John emphasizes that the expectation of the coming Antichrist has been fulfilled. His appearance in the form of the many Antichrists proves that this is the last hour. The idea of forerunners is an attempt at harmonizing, but it does violence to John's obvious intention and must be dismissed. For John, the Antichrist is a present reality. This is why his message about the Antichrist is so pressing.

The question now is how we should understand Paul's equally clear statement that the man of sin has not yet appeared and cannot yet be revealed. To answer this, we must investigate the Restrainer (or restraining hand) mentioned in 2 Thess. 2:6-7. This is the person or power which restrains the Antichrist so that he cannot yet appear.

Throughout history there have been proposals about who or what this might be. The Restrainer is referred to in both the masculine gender (v. 7) and the neuter (v. 6). So Christian thought has always centered around something which could be both masculine and neuter. Some have seen the Roman Empire as the neuter and its Caesar as the masculine.[85] Some have considered a supernatural alternative: God, the Holy Spirit, a benign or demonic supernatural being, or even Satan.[86] Others have suggested the Gentile mission (neuter), epitomized by Paul himself (masculine).[87] Yet others have suggested the delayed second coming, part of God's salvation-historical plan.[88]

For the purposes of this study, we need not explore the matter

85. J. Ernst, *Die eschatologischen Gegenspieler in den Schriften des Neuen Testaments* (1967), 49ff.; J. E. Frame, *The Epistle to the Thessalonians* (ICC; 1912), ad loc.; Cullmann, *Christ and Time*, 164.

86. Frame, ad loc., provides a good exposition of this, as does Ernst, 53f. In *Paul*, 525f., Ridderbos is in sympathy with this explanation: "a supernatural power or a ruler ordained by God (in Rev. 20 'a strong angel')," which nevertheless can include "the progress of the gospel."

87. Cullmann, *Christ and Time*, 165f.; J. Munck, *Paul and the Salvation of Mankind* (1959), 36-42.

88. Ernst, 55ff., defends this position. On p. 57 he presents an extensive survey of all the attempted explanations which we have named.

further. Most exegetes agree that certainty on this point is unattainable. What is of utmost importance is Paul's statement that, because of the Restrainer's presence, the wicked one has not yet been revealed. This does not mean that Paul expects that revelation only in the far-off future. Although the evil one is not yet revealed, the faithful must keep alert for the last confrontation which might occur at any moment.

The difference between Paul and John therefore does not lie in the fact that the former has a remote and the later an immediate expectation of the Antichrist. Both are alert for the Antichrist, whom Paul expects to appear any moment and who John declares has already appeared.

At this point Berkouwer and van Niftrik both stop short. According to Berkouwer, one faces an impossible task if the two are to be harmonized. To do so would be to misread the purpose of the revelation concerning the Antichrist. And van Niftrik concludes with the affirmation that the Antichrist is both already here and still to come.[89]

Of course it is not unthinkable to admit that on a given point one does not know or is unsure of an answer. But to do so on this point and then proceed like Berkouwer to assume that the Antichrist is a present reality is to expose oneself to the charge of interpreting Paul through John—or even of using John to silence Paul.

The real question is whether it is necessary to stop at this point. It is well known that 2 Thessalonians was written some forty years before the epistles of John. There is in principle not a single reason why the Restrainer could not have been removed during this interval, making it possible for Paul to say that the Antichrist had not yet been revealed and for John to say that he had.

Nor need this remain total conjecture. At least two of the interpretations of the Restrainer we have mentioned apply here. If the restraining hand was Roman authority and the Restrainer Caesar, both of which, before A.D. 60, had protected Paul and so aided the gospel proclamation, then it was also precisely in the period between A.D. 63 and 90 that this situation altered radically. Nero, Diocletian, and others turned their authority against the Christians, possibly accounting for the great difference between Romans 13 (government as God's minister) and Revelation 13 (government as the Antichrist personified; cf. Rev. 17, where the beast with seven heads is equated with the whore on seven hills—a clear allusion to Rome).

89. Berkouwer, *The Return of Christ*, 274; van Niftrik, 198.

Another interpretation of the Restrainer, that which identifies it with the mission of the Gentiles, also allows us to say that the Restrainer was removed between the time of Paul's Thessalonian epistles and that of the Johannine epistles. Not only did Paul die during this period but, before his death, he stated that the gospel had been proclaimed to the whole world (Rom. 15:19, 23; Col. 1:6, 23; 2 Tim. 4:17). If the gospel proclamation and Paul himself were the Restrainer, i.e., if the Antichrist could not appear before the gospel had been announced by Paul to "the whole world," then indeed the Restrainer was no longer present when the Johannine letters were written. By then Paul was dead, and the gospel had been proclaimed "to the whole world."

A third explanation, in which the Restrainer is understood to be supernatural power (male and neuter), might also fit the period concerned. The power could certainly have been removed in the interval between Paul's writings and John's. If this approach is correct, Paul's message in A.D. 50 (that the Antichrist had not yet appeared, though he was close by) and John's about A.D. 90 (that the Antichrist had already appeared) can both be taken seriously.

Of course we must take into account the phenomenon of repeated fulfillment, true of many prophecies. (This will be discussed extensively in the next chapter.) If this were true of prophecies concerning the Antichrist, that they could be fulfilled repeatedly and by every power which acts in radical opposition to Christ and his faithful, then surely removals of restraint could also occur repeatedly. At certain times, specific forces which made it impossible for the Antichrist to appear might be removed, enabling him to assume one form or another. The Antichrist was not only a present reality in John's day; across the centuries he has adopted many forms, and, tomorrow as today, he may do the same.

A second point made by John is that the Antichrist is a *plural* reality. This follows from what has already been said. When John speaks of the ultimate Antichrist, he speaks of a plural figure (1 John 2:18, 23 ["everyone"]; 4:1; 2 John 7). If we take John seriously, we will not find it strange that the Antichrist is a collective person who appears in many different persons and shapes. However, if we work one-sidedly from 2 Thessalonians 2 alone, we will probably arrive at the notion that the Antichrist must be exactly one person. There he is termed "that wicked man" and "the enemy." But we must remember that Paul was working with concepts and images taken from apocalyptic writings (Daniel in particular) and that those sources unmistakably mean these concepts to be taken collectively.

Indeed Revelation, also apocalyptic, takes even further this tendency to depict the Antichrist as a collective entity. Daniel, for example, sees four separate beasts, the fourth of which has ten horns, among which arises an eleventh, a figure of the Antichrist. But John (Rev. 13) sees the four beasts amalgamated into one terrible monster and identifies this monster so *constituted* as the Antichrist. Daniel's four beasts were four successive kingdoms which spanned a great period of time. So, according to Revelation, this entire hostile force, which has stretched across the centuries, is the Antichrist. This monster rages for twenty-four months, a symbolic number for the period between Christ's ascension and his second coming.

The idea that the Antichrist assumes various forms in various prophecies agrees with this. According to the Johannine epistles, the Antichrist is revealed in a number of false teachers, who sow serious heresies and falsehoods. Once they were part of the congregation but in the end broke their ties with it. This suggests that the Antichrist emerges from the Church. But according to Revelation 13, the Antichrist is the civil power which persecutes the Church. And according to 2 Thessalonians 2, the Antichrist acts inside the Church, arrogating divine powers and prerogatives to itself. It is clear that no single individual could possess all these characteristics. Therefore these prophecies fit the model of a collective Antichrist who appears in different forms at different times, always to destroy the Church—now as a hostile state, now as a schismatic false teacher, and now as a false church leader.

So it is not in the least strange that in the course of its history the Church has often identified the Antichrist in different forms. Sometimes hindsight makes it evident that certain identifications were rather unfortunate, but in concrete situations the Church is nevertheless called to "test the spirits to see if they are of God, since so many deceivers and false prophets exist in the world "(1 John 4:1-3; 2 John 7).

Neither may the Church look for the Antichrist only outside its own membership. The Church must always take seriously the terrible possibility that it might itself be acting as the Antichrist.[90] And the fragmented parts of the Church must be particularly careful not to go about branding other parts of it as the great whore. It is more fitting that each search his or her own church.

90. Althaus, 284-285.

Chapter 5
CHRIST REALIZES THE GOAL WITH US

WHY IN YET A THIRD WAY?

This section must be read against the background of the first sections of Chapters 3 and 4. At the start of Chapter 3, especially, the whole structure of eschatology is outlined briefly. Jesus Christ, himself the last (the *eschatos*) and the end, attains God's goal in three ways: for us, in us, and with us. Each time the goal is really reached; yet inherent to the first two is a certain deficiency which requires a third mode. Christ does indeed achieve the goal for us, but this does not yet mean in us. That which he achieves for us (ending our hostility toward God and reconciling us to him) must yet be reached in us, through our acceptance in faith and our experience of this peace.

But as we do this only imperfectly, our new life remains imperfect. This incompleteness of the second mode exists also because, though the Spirit is indeed a fully eschatological gift, it is only the guarantee and first portion of the full harvest and heritage. It is not the fullness itself. So it is a function of the divine economy, not only of our imperfection, that the second mode be incomplete and call for a third. We repeat, however, that no mere "possibility" is created by the first two modes. Nor are different goals reached in the different modes. The *eschaton* realized in all three is the same, i.e., creation's original purpose: that God should be our God and we his people.

It is supremely meaningful that this goal should be attained in three ways, that the first two should bear some marks of incompleteness and point toward perfection in the third. If the first mode had not been accomplished without us, God's wrath would have fallen upon us and we would have perished eternally. Then the *eschaton* could not have been realized in any mode at all! This is true of the second mode, too, since God's intent was to make a being other than himself to behave freely and responsibly, sharing in his love and joy. Therefore God ordained this interim that humanity might actively cooperate in reaching the goal and participate in reaping the harvest, rather than (as the women at the crucifixion) merely standing by and looking on. When this is seen as the meaning of the interim (i.e., our participation in the harvest — kingdom, mission), naturally our responsibility and its inadequate discharge becomes an issue. And this adds to the imperfectness of the second mode—which of course should be laid to our account, not God's.

The third and final mode in which God reaches his goal is complete in every respect. We are actively drawn into it, and thus the (limited) inadequacies of the first are overcome—yet without our being summoned to assume responsibility for it, which caused a certain incompleteness as in the second. What is at issue here, Barth remarked, is that the goal is realized quite independent of any Christian activity and development. Again the mover is God: he himself, he alone, working in yet another mode and form. The New Testament does not anticipate a gradual development focused on Christ, but rather the coming of the Lord: *Maranatha* (1 Cor. 16:22).[1]

"With" in the title of this chapter has a more inclusive meaning than "in" in the previous chapter. "With" indicates those particular aspects for which we still wait: the coming of Christ, the resurrection, the judgment, and the new earth. Again, "with *us*" does not exclude the world, i.e. the whole creation. God's eschatological purpose for creation can never be restricted to people; it has cosmic, all-inclusive dimensions.

It is remarkable that only at this late stage, and for the first time, will we really concentrate on the future. It may seem strange that so large a part of eschatology has to do with the past and the present, i.e., with Jesus' first coming, earthly ministry, and work through the Holy Spirit. Yet that is what the New Testament teaches. The last days and end time began at his incarnation; it is in the last days that the Holy Spirit is poured out. Nevertheless, we cannot forget the future, supposing that everything has already been accomplished or pretending that God's purpose has been fulfilled in every way. Of course the future is *emphatically* a part of eschatology. Certainly Christians are persons poised for the future, even though Christ has already accomplished God's purpose for them and is even now achieving it in them.

Two familiar expressions must be used at this point: "already" and "not yet." Much of eschatological reality has *already* been fulfilled and is being experienced by us: our enmity with God, other humans,

1. K. Barth, *Church Dogmatics* (1955-1969) III/2, 486f. Barth makes some exceptionally valuable remarks about the meaning of the interim (IV/3/1, 1-33).

and ourselves is ended (Eph. 2:16), and the great, eschatological peace has *already* been concluded. Through faith we *already* take part in this peace; we are the children and heirs of God; we are *already* in receipt of the Spirit, our eschatological gift; our full heritage is guaranteed by him; the kingdom of God (his eschatological lordship) has come *already* and is still coming; Jesus is Lord *already*, to whom all power in heaven and on earth is given; *already* we have been awakened to new life in Christ; with him we have ascended into heaven (Eph. 2:5-6), and our life is hid with Christ in God (Col. 3:3).

What, then, remains for the future? Is any third mode necessary? Yes; in fact, our eyes gaze expectantly toward the future—*despite* and *because of* what has been fulfilled already.

Despite everything we have already received and experience, our hopes for the future remain because the Spirit is not the full inheritance, only its guarantee; not the full harvest, only its firstfruits. Though we have peace with God already, we do *not yet* experience it in full measure. We still live frequently as his enemies—or at least, as his disobedient children. And though the evil powers have indeed been conquered, they have *not yet* been abolished. This results in so much misery and suffering in the world, so much sin and misfortune, and so much fear of death and the devil. So long as sin, death, and their strongholds in society go unabolished, we cannot help but yearn for the future—*despite* our present privileges. But also, *because* we have already received and experience so much, we long for the future. In fact, if we longed for it only *despite* the past and present, we could hardly speak of them as eschatology. But it is precisely the eschatological character of Christ's first coming and his work through the Holy Spirit which makes us await his second. *Because* complete peace has been won for us but we do not yet experience it fully, we look to the future. *Because* the Holy Spirit is the earnest of our full inheritance, we look forward eagerly to gaining the inheritance. And knowing the blessedness granted by our Lord to his children on this old earth, how much greater must it be on the new!

PROPHECIES AND THEIR FULFILLMENT

Discussing the shape of future eschatology presents exceptional problems. Up to this point we have dealt with history, i.e., with events which have already taken place or are now taking place. Because Old Testament prophecies of Jesus' incarnation and the Holy Spirit's outpouring are already fulfilled, we have not paid much attention to prophecy and the manner of its fulfillment, concentrating instead on the actual history of Christ and the coming of the Spirit. But in discussing the future, we have no alternative to depending on prophecies and promises. Suddenly we face the vital question of how prophecy is fulfilled.

To begin, we must state that the fulfillment of biblical prophecies and promises differs radically from predictions or forecasts which happen to work out. Two specific differences are of prime importance.

First, promises are fulfilled repeatedly; predictions or forecasts come true only once. The forecast that New York City would receive four inches of rain on April 10 could only "come true" if it happens precisely as predicted. And, if it did, this particular forecast would have achieved its purpose; no one would expect anything further of it. Vindicated or otherwise, a prediction loses all interest once its period of significance has passed. Of course there are predictions of this type in the Bible, especially in the Old Testament. That in 1 Kgs. 11:29-39 comes true in 12:15-20; that in 1 Kgs. 13:1-2 is realized in 2 Kgs. 23:15-20; that in 1 Kgs. 14:1-16 finds fulfillment in 14:18 and 15:19; that in 1 Kgs. 16:1-4 comes true in vv. 11-12; that in 1 Kgs. 21:17-24 finds reality in 2 Kgs. 9–10; that in 1 Kgs. 22:17 comes true in vv. 29-37.

But these predictions have a limited value, exerting no particular influence on salvation history. Distinct from these are prophecies and promises which are repeatedly fulfilled and which decisively influence the unfolding of salvation history. In salvation history, a whole series of "new" things develop along the lines laid down by repeatedly fulfilled promises.

The promise of the exodus is fulfilled, for the first time, when God leads his people out of Egypt. When they are exiled in Babylon, centuries later, Deutero-Isaiah prophesies a new and more glorious exodus than the first, in which the nation will return to their land (Isa. 43:16ff.; 48:20-21; 49:8-13). The exodus prophecy achieves a third fulfillment when the infant Jesus returns from Egypt (Matt. 2:15). In fact, Matthew uses a word for this fulfillment that means that the promise is again fulfilled or fulfilled completely (Matt. 13:14).[2]

2. In *The Use of the Old Testament in St. Matthew's Gospel* (1967), 213, R. H. Gundry says of the fulfillment of Isa. 6:9-10 in Matt. 13:14 that "The I.F. [introductory formula] introduces Isa. 6:9-10 in Mt. 13:14 and uses *anapleroun*, 'to fulfill completely' or perhaps even 'to fulfill again.' Thereby is displayed a consciousness that the Old Testament text had a meaning for Isaiah's day and a further meaning for New Testament times." G. Delling, *TDNT* VI, 306 explains

J. Ridderbos points out that Old Testament prophecies about Zion are only partially fulfilled by Old Testament Zion; they achieve far richer fulfillment in the New Testament Church and, in the end, will receive the crown of ultimate fulfillment in the new Jerusalem on the new earth.[3]

Amos's prophecy concerning the day of the Lord (5:18-20) finds repeated fulfillment: in the fall of Jerusalem (586 B.C.; Ezek. 13:5; Lam. 1:12; 2:1, 22), in the ministry of John the Baptist (Mark 1:2, cf. Mal. 3:1-2), in Jesus' earthly ministry (Luke 4:16-21; cf. Isa. 61:1-2), in the outpouring of the Spirit (Acts 2:16-21; cf. Joel 2:28-32), and in Jesus' second advent (2 Pet. 3:12; Rev. 16:14). And all this is quite apart from the the first day of the week, the day of the Lord, fulfilling this prophecy week by week (Rev. 1:10).

Then there is the well-known promise of Emmanuel (Isa. 7:14), fulfilled in the time of Ahaz (vv. 15-16) and again in Jesus' birth (Matt. 1:22-23). There is the promise of Zech. 12:10, fulfilled in the crucifixion (John 19:37) and to be so again at Christ's second coming (Matt. 24:30; Rev. 1:17).

Malachi 3:1-2 is fulfilled in the ministry of John the Baptist (Mark 1:2) and will be again on the day of judgment (Rev. 6:17). Joel 2:28-32 is fulfilled at Pentecost (Acts 2:16-21) and will be once more at judgment day (Rev. 9:1ff.). Isa. 49:8 is fulfilled in the return from Babylon as well as in the preaching of the gospel (2 Cor. 6:2).

We could also point to the new David, the new Jerusalem, and the new covenant. David was himself a fulfillment of God's promise of a king, and this promise is fulfilled also in Christ, David's Son, and will be ultimately fulfilled again at Christ's return.[4] The land of Canaan was promised first in Gen. 17:8. This promise was fulfilled when Israel took possession after the exodus from Egypt; but the same promise is extended in Eph. 6:3 to include the whole earth—and, finally, the new earth (Matt. 5:5; Rev. 21–22).[5]

---

anaploroun as "fully actualized" and refers to Zahn's commentary on Matthew. F. W. Grosheide, *Het Heilig Evangelie volgens Matteus* (Commentaar op het Nieuwe Testament; 1922), ad loc., uses the term "supplementary," in the sense that the entire prophecy was not fulfilled in Isaiah's time; it happens in a "larger measure" in the experience of Jesus. So these exegetes are aware that a promise does not finish being fulfilled in one fulfillment. See also J. Moltmann, *Theology of Hope* (1967), 106-120.

3. J. Ridderbos, *De Psalmen* (1955-1958) II, 359.
4. R. Rendtorff, *God's History* (1969), 67ff.
5. G. C. Berkouwer, *The Return of Christ* (1972), 213.

Predictions do not work out that way. They come true once or they do not; either way, they are at an end. But the prophecies of salvation history are fulfilled repeatedly. And they maintain their energy and character as promises, pointing us decisively to the future. The very fact that the whole Old Testament has continued to operate in the Church *since* Christ's coming is itself indicative of the radical difference between Bible prophecies fulfilled and predictions that come true.[6] It seems that prophecies cannot be fulfilled completely in this imperfect world.[7] Again and again fulfillment is incomplete, so that the preliminary fulfillment becomes a promise of a yet more glorious fulfillment.[8]

There is a second important difference between prophecy and predictions. Predictions come true in a literal and exact way, so that it is possible to say beforehand exactly what should happen. Predicting is a form of history-in-advance. Some people regard the book of Revelation as just such a set of predictions, telling us beforehand just what will happen in our day.

Prophecy and promises do not work like that. They are fulfilled in a freer manner. No one can deduce from prophecy exactly what shape events will take. In fact, it is not even possible to recognize prophecy's fulfillment without faith in Christ. That is why the Jews could not see Old Testament promises fulfilled in Jesus, even though he fulfilled the entire complex of Old Testament promises. Whoever does not accept Jesus in faith is simply unable to recognize him as the promised messiah.

This free fulfillment of prophecy becomes clearer when one consider a few examples of prophecies fulfilled in the New Testament. Two good examples are Joel 2:28-30, which, according to Peter, is ful-

6. G. C. Berkouwer, in *The Person of Christ* (1954), chapter 7, has dealt extensively with the continuing significance of the Old Testament after Christ and the difference between biblical promises which are fulfilled and mere predictions which come true. In this chapter he also correctly criticizes van Ruler's rejection of progressive revelation, because it implies an intellectualistic notion of what revelation is. He takes the position that progressive revelation indeed leaves room for the biblical idea of the acts of God in meeting his people.

7. T. C. Vriezen, *An Outline of Old Testament Theology* (1958), 100, quotes H. W. Obbink: "Fulfilment does not mean that the promise comes to an end and is replaced by the very thing that was promised, but it means that now the promise itself becomes completely unambiguous, and consequently effective."

8. G. von Rad, *Old Testament Theology* (1962, 1965) II, 117f.; P. Heinisch, *Theology of the Old Testament* (1950), 340f.; J. A. Alexander, *Commentary on the Prophecies of Isaiah* (1953), at Isa. 7:14; G. C. Berkouwer, *The Work of Christ* (1965), 113-117.

filled on the day of Pentecost (Acts 2:16ff.), and Amos 9:11-12, fulfilled in Acts 15:15-17. It is impossible to determine from Joel 2:28-
32 the actual events of the Holy Spirit's outpouring in Acts 2. Anyone
who wishes not to believe that Acts 2 fulfills Joel 2 can come up with
numerous formal rebuttals or unfulfilled particulars, such as the
moon's failure to turn to blood or that we are not told in Acts 2 that it
was specifically young men who dreamed dreams and old ones who
saw visions. In fact nothing in the New Testament says that there was
more dreaming after the Holy Spirit's outpouring than before.

In fact—and this is rather more important—anyone who took
Joel 2:28-32 by itself would predict a totally different Pentecost from
the one that happened. In fact, John does read Joel 2 in a different light
entirely, finding there not the day of Pentecost but the day of judgment
(Rev. 9:1ff.). Without faith it would be impossible to see in Acts 2 the
fulfillment of Joel 2. Were Joel 2 a forecast which required literal fulfillment, it could never been said to have come to pass in Acts 2.[9]

The fulfillment of Amos 9:11-12 in Acts 15:15-17 poses even
graver problems, if one takes it as a prediction. Indeed, Amos 9:11-12
promises the nation of Israel that it will regain its former glory and rule
over Edom and its environs once again. Yet, according to Acts 15,
Christian missions to the Gentiles fulfills this prophecy. This should
show how perilous it is to expect that Old Testament prophecies about
Israel's future must literally come true. God reserves the prerogative
of giving us a fundamental surprise, when he fulfills his promises.

In fact, if he did not, we would be moving toward a rather arid
and uninteresting future. Predictions cannot escape the confines of the
known; all they can offer is repetition of what we have already experienced. Anything really and *essentially* new can never be predicted.
So it is that, were the prophecy of the New Jerusalem (Rev. 21) to be
literally fulfilled, it would lose all appeal. In fact, save for the height
of this city, skillful contractors could build it right now.

But prophecies explode our poverty of experience. They are
vague signposts, hazy, dotted lines, offering hints of the essentially
new and unimaginable (and thus unpredictable) future which God has

---

9. F. P. Möller, in *Die Diskussie oor die Charismata soos wat dit in die
Pinksterbeweging geleer en beoefen Word* (1975), 208-209, refers critically to
this viewpoint and example. The problem with his criticism, however, is that those
things specifically quoted by Peter are not fulfilled on the day of Pentecost. The
question then is why Peter should quote it. If Möller is correct, Peter ought not
to have included Joel 2:30-31 in his quotation.

promised. Because our past and present are confined to this unrenewed earth, to the sin-stained world of our experience, God can give us only glimpses of the future. That which he has promised cannot be described, either in whole or in detail, with available concepts. One need only think of the concept of "glorification": Paul labors in vain to say what glorified life will be like (1 Cor. 15).

So one indispensable aspect of the future—and one without which it would lose its power to attract—is that prophecy remains open and that God is free to take us by surprise. If Joel 2 and Amos 9 were literal predictions, of what use to a needy world would blood, fire, and smoke be, compared with the Spirit who brought tongues of fire to overcome the world with good news? Of what possible use would a restored Israel ruling over Edom be? Should not all the world be grateful for the Gentile mission which has brought whole peoples into the dominion of Israel's God rather than under the domination of Israel's state? The openness of prophecy and its surprising fulfillments fit admirably with the idea of the God of the promises, who places neither himself nor his promises at our disposal. He alone rules over his promises and so over history.[10]

This does not imply a future of impenetrable obscurity, still less that kind of openness which arouses nervous hesitancy or provokes uncertainty and fear. We know this God of promise surely, for we have discovered his trustworthiness in past deeds. Therefore we know in which direction history will move: God will become all in all, dwelling at last with us as our God; we, his loyal people, will live daily in his service and intimate fellowship. So we know a great deal about the future, in broad outline, and can approach it with confidence, while expecting to encounter many surprises along the way. We know that the fulfillments of his promises will far exceed anything that our fragmentary language and limited imagery can express. "Now to him who is able to do *immeasurably more than all we can ask or imagine* . . ." (Eph. 3:20).

It follows from the unique character of biblical promises and their free, repeated fulfillments that we must write with considerable caution when dealing with the eschatology of the future. This modest

10. Von Rad, II, 384: "It was also revealed, however, that what the New Testament designates as fulfilment cannot be understood as a straightforward and literal realisation of the promise, but as a fulfilment which, even from the beginning, far surpasses it." J. Moltmann, *Theology of Hope* (1967), 106: "Hence every reality in which a fulfillment is already taking place now becomes the confirmation, exposition, and liberation of a greater hope."

and cautious approach must not be equated with the idea that, since the end is outside history, we can have absolutely no idea of its nature.[11] Bultmann has made much of this thought and especially of Luther's famous comment on Romans 8, "What Christians know is *that* they hope, but they do not know *what* they hope." Bultmann claims that modern people, their minds formed by natural science, can no longer accept the thought of Christ coming on the clouds of heaven.[12] The end, at first expected to come speedily, has not come at all. This continuance of history has destroyed eschatological expectations. For Bultmann there remains but a personal, individual future after death. Of even this he believes we can form no clear idea, but says that the believer may nevertheless approach it comforted (though entering darkness) while trusting in God. As far as the world's future is concerned, Bultmann maintains that we live perpetually in the end, i.e., in the eschatological moment in which Jesus meets us in the proclamation.

Moltmann points out the price which must be paid for this solution. First, it becomes unclear just what distinguishes the Christian faith from idealistic or Marxist philosophy, since there is no reason to attach this standpoint exclusively to Jesus of Nazareth. It makes of the earthly, historical Jesus no more than at best the beginning or presupposition of Christian faith. Second, it spiritualizes the future and renders it subjective, whereas the Christian faith is in essence a resurrection faith—not merely belief that Jesus rose, but belief that the resurrection of the dead began with his resurrection.[13] A. A. van Ruler, for one, has reacted vigorously against such spiritualizing and, by appealing to apocalyptic ideas, emphasizes that our future expectation involves the whole created order.[14]

When we plead against detailed maps of the future, this should in no way be seen as a denial of Christ's return or of the new earth. It

11. Cf. O. Weber, *Foundations of Dogmatics* (1981, 1983) II, 679f.

12. W. Schmithals, *An Introduction to the Theology of Rudolf Bultmann* (1968), 304.

13. J. Moltmann, *Hope and Planning* (1971), 170-171. In *Theology of Hope,* 166, Moltmann writes, "The confession to the person of Jesus as the Lord and the confession to the work of God who raised him from the dead belong inseparably together." He refers here to Rom. 10:9, where these two matters are permanently united: "If on your lips is the confession 'Jesus is Lord,' and in your heart the faith that God raised him from the dead, then you will find salvation."

14. A. A. van Ruler, "Grenzen van de Eschatologisering," *Vox Theologica* 37 (1967), 181.

amounts to nothing more than allowing God to surprise us in the fulfillment of his promises and thereby far surpass our highest thoughts about his intentions. In the final analysis, it is a protest against the idea that prophecy is history written in advance.

Surely this is one of the most common errors in interpreting Revelation: to regard it as the history of our own day written in advance. In fact, every generation has had people who tried to read the events of their days in Revelation. Napoleon, World War I, Hitler, World War II, Stalin, and the European Economic Community have all served as candidates for predictions based on minute details of Ezekiel, Daniel, and Revelation. And they who indulge in such diversions seem not at all perturbed by the incredulity to which they expose the gospel by the failure of their interpretations. Revelation, however, has nothing to do with forecasting the events of the late twentieth century. It was written to encourage and comfort persecuted believers at the end of the first century. It has meaning for us only because prophecy is fulfilled repeatedly. Not because *we* live in the end time, but because we live in the same end time as that in which the early Christians lived, is it pertinent to us.[15]

We sum up by reaffirming that prophecy and promises are fulfilled more than once, and that in a manner which far surpasses anything which one could deduce from reading them. This is the attractive power of the future. It is the power of the God who is of course not unknown (if he were, we should truly have grounds for fearing the future) but who does new things which transcend all that we can imagine or represent by the images at our disposal—and so also more than prophets have been able to express.

THE SIGNS OF THE TIMES

We must give some attention to the "signs of the times," viewing them in light of the foregoing section. In fact some important signs (the gospel proclamation and mission, Israel, Antichrist, and millennium) were examined in the previous chapter. There Christ's work during the interim was under consideration. As was made clear there, these signs are not prophecies whose validity is restricted to an isolated or

15. W. Hendriksen, *More than Conquerors* (1949⁵), 14; Berkouwer, *The Return of Christ*, 277ff.

localized end time which, for the New Testament authors, lay in a dim or distant future. On the contrary, they are signs of Christ's imminent return which have accompanied the Church in its course through history and have summoned it to unceasing vigilance. That these signs were dealt with in connection with the interim period, rather than in the present chapter about the second advent, is based on an important principle, that the interim is part of the *biblical* end time, which is the period since Christ's birth and the outpouring of the Holy Spirit.

It is remarkable that the traditional approach to signs in certain Reformed circles and elsewhere has actually misunderstood and distorted the purpose and meaning of the signs and with them the central message of the second advent. The central message of Christ's return is, "Stay awake, be ready *every* moment" (Matt. 24:42, 44; 25:13; Mark 13:23, 33-37; Luke 21:34, 36; 1 Cor. 15:52; 1 Thess. 5:2-3, 8). The moment signs are viewed as history in advance, informing the reader of what will take place in a specific future end time, they lose their message for the Church of the past nineteen centuries. In that case, the Church of those centuries could never have preached that the end was near, since the Antichrist had not yet appeared, Israel had not yet returned to Palestine, and the gospel had not been preached to all nations. The central message of the second advent would have been rendered inoperable for those centuries.

Notwithstanding outspoken and repeated New Testament warnings against all calculation of the second advent, since its day and hour are unknown (Matt. 24:36, 42, 44, 50; 25:13; 1 Thess. 5:2ff.; 2 Pet. 3:10ff.) this mistaken approach to the topic has consistently stimulated calculations concerning the time of Christ's return. How right Berkouwer is, when he asserts "that the signs of the times cannot be interpreted futuristically, that such an interpretation mistakes the gravity of eschatological preaching, which is relevant for all times, and that it is impossible to distinguish on the basis of the New Testament between the last days and an end-time in which the signs will take place."[16]

The signs of the times are pointedly announced by Jesus. He was not addressing the twentieth century Church over the heads of the first disciples and nineteen centuries of Church history; he spoke to his disciples as such. He opens his prophetic discourse on the signs of the

16. Berkouwer, *The Return of Christ*, 245.

times with the urgent warning, "Take care that no one mislead *you*" (Matt. 24:4). This means that his original audience, the first disciples, would themselves experience the fulfillment of the signs. He was not referring to a distant generation two thousand years beyond them in history. His whole prophetic discourse is aimed at "you," his hearers (vv. 6, 9, 15, 20, 23, 26, 32). Throughout the sermon, in all three Synoptic accounts of it, Jesus is engaged with his disciples and the signs they would see. Matt. 24:33 is an example: "in the same way, when *you* see all these things, *you* may know that the end is near, at the very door."

The message about signs was therefore not directed to remote generations. It was an urgent word to the Church of there and then, irrespective of which century a particular congregation happened to live in. In fact, any view of the signs which makes it impossible to preach Christ's near return is a distortion.[17] If in a golden age of tranquillity and prosperity the signs are not preached but are postponed for a time of catastrophy and disaster, the biblical message of the signs will have been misunderstood. One consequence of this would be that the message of the Church would lose its credibility, since the world could only think that the Church merely exploits times of distress, shrinks back abashed when peaceful times return, and then waits for more catastrophes. Whether such calculation is done with detail or approximation makes no difference. Both have led unbelievers to reject the message of the Church. In contrast, we are struck by the consistent, pointed, and pressing prophetic utterances of Jesus and the New Testament letters about the signs of the second advent.

The congregation at Thessalonica, for example, seems unable to relate the death of some of their members to expectations of Christ's imminent return. Paul does not solve their problem by proclaiming a far-off coming of the Lord, but simply by assuring them that Christians who have died will be raised when Christ returns and so lose nothing (1 Thess. 4:15). It is important—and consistent with Jesus' use of "you"—that Paul does not speak of "those" who will be alive at the second coming but of "we." In truth, he reckoned with the possibility that the Lord could come before he died. (Notice also the use of "we" in 1 Cor. 15:51; on the other hand, Paul took account equally of the

17. O. Cullmann, *Christ and Time* (1964), 166-167: "It belongs rather to the nature of the sign that to the very end *it appears in every generation* that belongs to the present intermediate period in the final phase of redemption history."

possibility that he could die before the second coming—as witness the "we" of 1 Thess. 5:10.) And when it appears that the Thessalonians have the mistaken notion that the day of the Lord has already arrived (2 Thess. 2:1-2), once again the apostle does not solve their problem by referring to a far-off return but continues to speak of things which will shortly take place (v. 7).

The same is true of Revelation. This much-abused book is thought by many Christians to predict events which will occur only many centuries later. In fact it is filled with an urgent message for the Christians who lived when it was written. They had to be ready, for it spoke of things that "must shortly happen" (1:1) because "the hour of fulfillment is near" (1:3) and because Christ is "coming soon" (3:11). Three times in Revelation 22 Jesus says, "I am coming soon." This is another instance, not of distant things, but of signs which lay before the door, since the Judge was at the door (Jas. 5:9).

It is noteworthy how many times in the New Testament documents there is even talk of signs already fulfilled. The Antichrist to whom John pointed has been discussed. Jews who came to faith and then were reincorporated—who so excited Paul's missionary fervor—are examples of things already fulfilled. We should also refer to the "great famine" (a sign, according to Matt. 24:7 and Mark 13:8) which afflicted the "whole world" in the reign of Emperor Claudius (Acts 11:28), to repeated persecutions (also signs, according to Matt. 24:9 and 1 Cor. 7:26) which were visited upon the early Christians (Rev. 1:9; 2:9-10; 3:10), and supremely to the worldwide Gentile mission, which some regard as the most important sign that Christ's coming was at hand.[18] "And this gospel . . . will be proclaimed throughout the earth as a testimony to all nations; and then the end will come" (Matt. 24:14; Mark 13:10). Taken at face value, this might be construed as implying that Christ's coming has never been near in the past nineteen centuries, since it is only now that the gospel is preached throughout the world. But to interpret it in that way would involve forgetting Paul's clear statements that the gospel had already reached everyone under heaven in his day (Col. 1:6, 23), that he had completed the proclamation, and that all the Gentiles had heard it (2 Tim. 4:17). Jesus did not mean something different from Paul when he used the phrases "throughout the earth" and "all nations," so this sign, too, was

---

18. H. Boer, *Pentecost and Missions* (1961), 99, calls proclamation "the sign of the end." D. Bosch, *Die Heidenmission in die Zukunftsschau Jesu* (1959), 167, states that mission *"ist das von Gott errichtete Zeichen der Endzeit."*

fulfilled in the apostles' lifetime and the end could then already have come.

In the light of all this, it is clear that Jesus could have come at any moment in the past nineteen centuries and no sign would have been unfulfilled. Whoever denies this does not honor the ban placed by the New Testament on all calculations of the end and misconstrues the real meaning of the signs which, in every generation, bring us the message to be prepared because "you do not know when the moment comes" (Mark 13:33). It is a grave misunderstanding of the signs of the times and of the nearness of the Lord's return to interpret Israel's return to Palestine as a sign that the second coming is about to take place or to expect the prophecy of Antichrist to be fulfilled in one personal Antichrist. This undermines the message which the Church has had to preach during every one of the past nineteen centuries, which is that Christ's second coming is near and may happen at any time. Such a doctrine as the "rapture" is open to the same criticism. It enfeebles the Bible's message about the second coming's nearness, since the natural reaction of the unregenerate is to wait and see, because after the "rapture" there will still be time to repent—even if it will, in the opinion of some, be more difficult.[19] One cannot possibly conclude from the New Testament that the signs are intended to be fulfilled in a very last end history immediately before Christ's coming. They are rather a summons to believers to be ready at all times. It would be senseless to send special signs to inform the faithful when, in the distant future, the end will draw near—if the end were already near in the apostles' time. Christ's second advent has been near ever since the apostles' time, because the last days began with the first coming of Christ. Consequently, there is no sense in calculating when his return will be imminent. What are meaningful and necessary are signs which serve as continual reminders that his return is always near. This is the function of the signs of the times.

THE IMMINENT RETURN OF CHRIST

The function of the signs of the times is, then, to stimulate people to moment-by-moment readiness and vigilance, and not at all to en-

19. E.g., C. Larkin, *Dispensational Truth* (1920[2]), 11f.

courage calculations of how near that moment might be. This function is of a piece with the New Testament message that the return is near. All New Testament traditions agree on this point. Jesus himself put this into words when he told his followers, "When all this begins to happen, stand upright and hold your heads high, because your liberation is near" (Luke 21:28; cf. v. 30; Matt. 24:33; Mark 13:29: "The end is near, at the very door"). Paul writes that "it is far on in the night; day is near" (Rom. 13:12; cf. 16:20) and "the time we live in will not last long" (1 Cor. 7:29; cf. Phil. 4:5). According to 1 Thess. 4:17, Paul clearly reckons with the possibility that the Lord will return during his lifetime (1 Cor. 15:51 makes a similar assumption), and yet he also entertains the possibility of dying before that time (1 Thess. 5:10). The writer of Hebrews knows that "soon, very soon . . . he who is to come will come, he will not delay" (Heb. 10:37). According to Jas. 5:8-9, the Lord's return is near and the Judge stands at the door. Peter says, "the end of all things is upon us" (1 Pet. 4:7). John's Revelation lays heavy emphasis on the fact that Christ will come swiftly (Rev. 1:1, 3; 3:11; 22:7, 12, 20).

From the outset it is essential to note that this message about the nearness of Christ's coming has its roots in the Old Testament. G. von Rad has demonstrated that the idea of history developed in Israel. Before the writing of Daniel, however, Israel had no vision of universal or world history; history consisted only of God's dealings with Israel. When this concept of history was projected into the future, then expectation of the future began to take shape. It began as the conviction that God would soon deal with the Israelites. (This belief developed particularly after the prophets Amos and Hosea.) God is on his way to the future with the people of Israel. He is always nearby. This gives eschatology an immediacy and relevance to the present. According to von Rad, the distinguishing feature of the prophets' message is this immediacy, this imminent expectation. To this characteristic, New Testament eschatology remains loyal.[20]

From its moment of birth, therefore, Israel's hope was that very soon God would intervene. This was closely connected with the idea of his spatial nearness. Since God—as God of the covenant—was near to his people spatially, they expected that his deeds were also at hand and that he would soon perform them. Time and space are closely related here, and neither can be omitted from the imminent expectation

20. Von Rad, II, 99ff. Cf. Vriezen, 370.

in eschatology.[21] The kernel of Old Testament future expectation is thus that the Lord's coming was near (e.g., Isa. 13:6; Ezek. 30:3; Joel 1:15; 2:1; 3:14; Obad. 15; Zeph. 1:14).[22]

Sometimes God's intervention did not take place soon. This poses a problem already in the Old Testament, long before the New. Though some regarded the return from Babylon as the fulfillment of the day of the Lord, others awaited some other fulfillment. When this was delayed, they became rebellious and said that God no longer loved them.[23] This was the situation in which Malachi insisted that the Lord did indeed love them, and that his day would come "suddenly" (Mal. 3:1ff.; 4:1ff.).

Similar circumstances prevailed in Ezekiel's time. Certain people alleged that the prophets always threatened them but their

21. Unfortunately, von Rad does not go into the question of the relationship between spatial and temporal nearness in the Old Testament. The following I owe to my late Old Testament colleague, I. H. Eybers: The meaning of $q\bar{a}r\hat{o}\underline{b}$ is a good example of the way in which space and time (and consequently the nearness of Yahweh and the nearness of the expected future) are related and even united. The word is used for a nearby town (Gen. 19:20) and country (45:10; Exod. 13:17; 1 Kgs. 8:46), but also, in a temporal sense, of salvation (Ps. 85:10) and of the day of Yahweh (Zeph. 1:4).

One finds the same relationship in $q\bar{e}s$. It usually means the end of a time (Gen. 6:13) and, sometimes with '$\bar{e}\underline{t}$ an indication of the end time (e.g. Dan. 8:17, 19; 12:4, 6, 9, 13). In the Qumrân texts it even indicates a period of time (1QS 7:4). But it is also used in a spatial sense (2 Kgs. 19:23; Ps. 119:96; Isa. 37:24) as the antithesis of "very wide." The related form, $qese\underline{t}$, means an edge or boundary (Gen. 23:9), and $q\bar{a}sas$ means to cut off (Deut. 25:12). In '$\hat{o}l\bar{a}m$ we encounter the same connection between space and time. It means a long time off or a long time ago, and in Ugaritic it means durability. According to L. Koehler and W. Baumgartner, *Lexicon in Veteris Testamenti Libros* (1958²), s.v., the same stem indicates "creation" and "world" in Moabitic, Phoenician, Biblical Hebrew, Aramaic, and Arabic. In Syriac, Mandean, and Arabic, it can even mean "people." The same is true of such prepositions as $lipn\hat{e}$ (Gen. 23:12; 27:7) and '$ahar$ (Gen. 15:1; 37:7) which, like the English "ahead" and "behind," may be used in a temporal or spatial sense. It is especially clear in the case of $qedem$ which, in a spatial sense, may even mean "the East" (Gen. 2:8; 29:1), but also has a temporal meaning and can, e.g., refer to ancient times (Mic. 5:1, and especially, with $y\hat{o}m$, 7:20).

22. Vriezen, 370. John the Baptist and Jesus both proclaimed that the kingdom of God was *near*, which is entirely understandable in view of this. Vriezen also points to the harmony between the vision which the prophets had of the Gentile mission and the end which is close—something which, according to him, was always the case, even in the New Testament and in Church history (p. 362).

23. *Ibid.*, 365.

prophecies were never fulfilled (Ezek. 12:21-22). Ezekiel does not repudiate immediacy and espouse some remote expectation. He simply affirms the Lord's message, "The time is near" (v. 23). Malachi and Ezekiel are thus like the writer of 2 Pet. 3:3-14, who also responds to incredulity about the coming day of the Lord with assurance that it will come, but also saying that there is a connection between God's patience and that which mockers think is delay.[24] Thus, already in the Old Testament, the immediacy of the expectation had to be safeguarded against the disbelief of those for whom the day of the Lord seemed too long postponed.

There are, therefore, two cardinal principles for correct treatment of the New Testament's concept of immediacy. One is that there is repeated fulfillment of promises. The other is that eschatological imminence does not necessarily coincide with believers' feelings of how near that day should be.

The New Testament tension between expectation of an imminent second advent and apparent delay of the parousia has determined much of eschatological thought in our century. It was decisive both for Schweitzer's "consistent" eschatology and Bultmann's "existential" eschatology. It played leading roles in Barth's earlier and later visions. It may be regarded as one of the problems against which Dodd had to delimit his realized eschatology. For salvation-historical approaches it has remained a persistent difficulty. On the other hand, it is noteworthy that this issue seldom appears on the agenda in recent eschatologies such as, e.g., Moltmann's and Pannenberg's.

The imminent expectation *(Naherwartung)* is an unmistakable element of every tradition in the New Testament. To this we have already drawn attention. Over the span of the centuries—and particularly in our own lifetime—there have been various attempts to explain this expectation in the light of the nearly two thousand years which have passed since the New Testament period. Some have dismissed it as an insignificant by-product in the preaching of the New Testament, as in, for example, nineteenth-century liberal theology which proclaimed the

---

24. In *The Return of Christ* (76f.), Berkouwer gives many other examples of "delays" in God's Old Testament promises. Indeed, there is a close relation between Hab. 2:3 and 2 Pet. 3:8-9. A. Strobel, *Untersuchungen zum eschatologischen Verzögerungsproblem* (1961), 88ff., offers much additional material in support of the idea that the New Testament vision of the parousia, imminent return, and "delay" stands in a close relationship to Old Testament eschatology. P. A. Verhoef, *Die Dag van die Here* (1956), 86ff., has written in some detail *Naherwartung* in the Old Testament.

essence of Jesus' message to be his timeless gospel of love. Others, such as Cullmann, Küng, and Gollwitzer, who have little or nothing in common with this liberalism, have nonetheless adopted similar views on eschatology.[25] They let go of the immediacy of the expectation while they acknowledge the fact of Christ's coming again as an essential aspect of his proclamation. Yet others abandon the expectation of his return altogether as unacceptable to modern people, conditioned by natural science. For Schweitzer, e.g., the immediacy of the end was so essential a feature of Jesus' preaching that, as he did not come soon after his death, one cannot expect him now to come at all. In this way all eschatology is amputated, and Schweitzer reinterprets eschatology in ethical terms, as the will to a moral perfection of the world.

To clarify the relationship between imminent expectation and the nineteen hundred years which have elapsed, we must observe that, beside some clear pronouncements that the second coming is near, other New Testament statements seem to suggest a remote expectation *(Fernerwartung)*.[26] This is true of the idle servant who says in his heart: "My master is delayed" (Matt. 24:48 RSV; Luke 12:45-46).[27] Ten virgins fall asleep because "the bridegroom was late in coming" (Matt. 25:5). In this last, there is undeniably an implication that the bridegroom stayed away longer than expected. The parable of the talents is closely related to this theme. According to Luke 19:12, a man of noble birth "went on a long journey abroad." In Matt. 25:19, he returned "a long time afterwards." Luke states the purpose of this parable to be admonition to those who entertain mistaken notions of the nearby expectation as "they thought the kingdom of God might dawn at any moment" (Luke 19:11). Luke (20:9) reiterates the idea in his parable of the vinegrowers. "A man planted a vineyard, leased it to tenants, and went abroad for a long time." It is as well to note the same theme in Paul's letters. When he finds the Thessalonians believing that the day of Christ has already dawned, he replies

25. H. Ridderbos, *The Coming of the Kingdom* (1960), 444, on the views of nineteenth-century scholars; Cullmann, 87f., 149f.; H. Küng, *The Church* (1967), 59f. H. Symanowski, in *Post Bultmann Locutum,* I, 22-25, deals with Gollwitzer's viewpoint.

26. H. Berkhof, *Christ, the Meaning of History* (1966), 72f. F. Flückiger, *Der Ursprung des christlichen Dogmas* (1955), 114f.

27. Berkhof, 72. This example can in fact be used against the *Fernerwartung,* because the Lord comes "on a day that he does not expect"—i.e., before he expects it! Berkhof, *et al.,* are therefore unfair in referring to this statement. Jesus in fact used it to combat an illegitimate and dangerous *Fernerwartung.*

with a firm "not yet." Here, he too challenges a misconceived imminent expectation. In 2 Pet. 3:3ff., we encounter people who think that
the second coming ought to have taken place already, and who must
therefore be reminded of God's great patience. Finally, we must listen
to the deceivers, referred to in Luke, who say "The day is upon us"
and to whose teaching we must respond, "but the end does not follow immediately" (Luke 21:8-9).

It is, however, not a foregone conclusion that these examples
refer to a remote expectation. In fact, they are not critical of imminent
expectations *per se,* but rather of a faulty version of such an expectation and especially of attempts to calculate the time of the Lord's return. Neither the Thessalonian epistles nor 2 Peter offer a remote expectation to combat the faulty expectation of an immediate
(calculated) return. The writers' perspective always remains one of imminence (in 2 Thess. 2:7 "already" and "only"; in 2 Pet. 3:12ff. "look
eagerly for" and "hasten"). Furthermore, Matthew's and Luke's parables on this topic must be viewed in light of the direct statements
about the imminent return which we quoted earlier. (In any case, parables cannot be pressed to have meaning in every detail.) The journey
to a "far" country and the return after a "long" time only have the meanings ascribed to them by direct statement, i.e., emphasizing that the
kingdom will not appear *"immediately"* (Luke 19:11) and that "the
end does not follow *immediately"* (21:9). What is at issue here, once
again, is a faulty expectation, based—as is so common—on the insid-
ious temptation to calculate! Luke is not playing off a remote expectation against an immediate expectation. In fact, it is impossible to
speak of an expectation which is at once imminent and remote. These
forms of expectation are mutually exclusive.[28]

If we are to grasp the biblical vision of the imminent return, it is
decisively important to take the ban on all calculation with the utmost
seriousness. We elaborated on this point in the previous section. The
message of the imminent return is "be alert, be wakeful, for you do not
know when the moment comes" (Mark 13:33). "The day of the Lord
will come . . . unexpected as a thief" (2 Pet. 3:10; see also 1 Thess.
5:2ff.). "The Son of man will come when you least expect him" (Matt.
24:44). This is a ban on every form of calculation. The imminence of
his return serves as a call to vigilance, not as neutral information from

---

28. G. Sauter, *Zukunft und Verheissung* (1965), 86, note 10. Sauter says
correctly that *Fernerwartung* is *ein Wort, das gegen sich selbst spricht,"* i.e., a
contradiction.

which we can calculate the time of his return. Every form of calculation misreads this message—and that holds true for Cullmann's and Berkhof's conclusion that Jesus had only a few decades in mind. All that the New Testament ever combats is a *calculated* imminent expectation, not an imminent expectation as such. It is the believers' task to understand the immediacy of their expectation in terms of being alert every moment, whether the bridegroom delays (Matt. 25:5) or comes "at evening or midnight, cock-crow or early dawn" (Mark 13:35).

This is why there was no talk of a crisis in the Church when, after several decades or even a half-century, the second coming had not yet occurred.[29] They did not misunderstand this message of ceaseless alertness as merely neutral information, designed to aid in precise or approximate calculations. Every misconception of this type was firmly dealt with (Luke 19:11ff.; 21:8ff.; 2 Thess. 2; 2 Pet. 3). It was not the Church's business to work out how soon Jesus would return, how long ago the ascension had taken place, how long the time stretched out, or to make any other such estimate. They heeded the message that the second advent was near and consequently did not enter into problems because of its apparent delay. Berkouwer has shown that the early Church grasped the meaning of the interim (God's patience and the Church's mission), applied itself wholeheartedly to its task, and experienced no crisis over the Lord's delay.[30]

Both Berkhof and Flückiger draw attention to the greatest difference between Jesus and the apocalyptists of his era, which lay in

29. Various writers have pointed out that nowhere in the New Testament can signs be found of the "crisis" into which the second coming's "delay" is supposed to have plunged the Church. One can read about this "crisis" in the works of such exponents of "consistent eschatology" as Schweitzer, Werner, Grässer, and Buri, and of most critical theologians (among them Bultmann). See also H. J. Schoeps, *Paul: The Theology of the Apostle in the Light of Jewish Religious History* (1961), 118-125.

Cullmann, 83-89, has taken great pains to demonstrate that there is no such crisis in the New Testament. Naturally he does not deny the delay of the parousia; but the crisis which was supposed to have resulted from this did not occur, because the first believers' center of gravity lay in the past, in Jesus' cross and resurrection, while a wrong date (*irrtummliche Datumsangabe*) for the future was too unimportant to plunge them into a crisis. This idea of a date shows the extent to which Cullmann regards the nearness of the coming as neutral information, rather than a message (p. 76).

Berkouwer, *The Return of Christ,* 67f., 76f., 81, shows clearly that there is no talk of a crisis in the New Testament. All that is said is that the Lord tarries.

30. Berkouwer, *The Return of Christ,* 122f., 129f., 132f.

the latters' contentment with an immediate end to the world, only their little band being saved. Jesus, on the other hand, reached out in compassion to the crowds, to the tax collectors, and (after his resurrection) to all nations.[31]

Wherever the imminence of the second advent functions properly in its biblical context as a call to unceasing vigilance and service, there God's people cease from their calculations and are no longer confused. The compassion of God, who desires all to be saved, remains the most profound and satisfying answer to the question of why the Lord has not yet returned (2 Pet. 3:9ff.). That with the Lord one day is as a thousand years and a thousand years are as a day cuts off all calculations at their roots (v. 8).[32]

The very concept of delay implies that some calculation has been made, which itself indicates a misunderstanding of the imminence of the second coming. That is why it is preferable not to use the term "delay" at all. It is impossible to express the biblical message with this term, in any case, because it is erected on another foundation altogether.

Two important Old Testament principles of future expectation were formulated earlier in our discussion. They should now be related to the New Testament expectation of Christ's return. (1) As a result of its origin, i.e., because it concerns the deeds of God who is near to his people, future expectation is directed to the near future. This remarkable association of spatial and temporal aspects commands our attention. It is because God's people believe God to be spatially near to them that they expect his future interventions to occur very soon. (2) The unique character of the fulfillment of biblical promises also commands our attention. They are fulfilled repeatedly in history, without their potential being exhausted or their character lost.

---

31. Berkhof, 77; Flückiger, 121-137.
32. A. L. Moore, *The Parousia in the New Testament* (1966), 207-214, asserts that there is no need to reinterpret or demythologize our hope. Our hope is meaningful because the time in which we live (the interim) has its meaning and foundation in the long-suffering patience of God. For this reason, all calculations are illegitimate. The early Church "steadfastly rejected such a delimitation because . . . they reckoned with the grace motif and realised that the time for repentance and faith could not be limited by men and that the provision of God's mercy could not be measured nor forecast." Moore sees the interim from the perspective of God's mercy and describes it under four headings: (1) the time for repenting and believing, (2) the time of the Church, (3) the time for Christian mission, and (4) the time of the Holy Spirit.

The first of these principles makes it easy to grasp why the New Testament speaks continually of a near second coming. Ever since their origins in the Old Testament, expectations are focused on the immediate future, since God is close to his people. This focus is already functioning in Jesus' proclamation that the kingdom of God is at hand. In fact, we have seen that Jesus himself is the kingdom. In his person the reign (or kingdom) of God is present. As he expelled demons, the kingdom arrived. Because he stands among the crowds, the kingdom of God "is among them." Thus, his announcement that the kingdom is near (Mark 1:15) is tied up with the fact that he is spatially close to them. Where he is, there, in a spatial sense, is the kingdom. In the same way, both time and space function in expectations of the nearness of the second coming. Since Jesus' ascension in no way implies that he has gone far away but rather that he will forever be very close (spatially) to his disciples, they expect his return in the near future. They reason along precisely the same lines as people did in the Old Testament. The nearness of the second advent is thus directly related to Christ's presence in the interim period.

Moreover, this imminent expectation is not of merely secondary importance. One cannot distinguish between the *fact* of Jesus' coming as the actual message and the *nearness* of his coming as a contingent and dispensable element, only loosely attached to the actual message—as Cullmann, for one, suggests. As in the Old Testament, the concept of imminence is inextricably bound up with expectation of the future. The earliest congregations quite simply expected Christ to come *soon*.

The second principle makes clear the repeated coming of the kingdom of God. It is an Old Testament promise which Jesus reiterates at the start of his earthly ministry and which is repeatedly fulfilled as he drives out demons (Matt. 12:28) or mingles with the crowds (Luke 17:21). Yet it always retains the character of a promise (Mark 9:1). Thus it is fulfilled repeatedly in different situations, so that it is indeed possible to regard Mark 9:1 as fulfilled in the transfiguration, in the resurrection, and in the outpouring of the Holy Spirit. Yet the promise of the coming kingdom remains in force throughout the New Testament as a promise to be fulfilled at the second advent. So it is that the Church, standing within the kingdom that has already come, still prays "Thy kingdom come" (Matt. 6:10). Indeed the return of Jesus is nothing other than the final fulfillment of the promise of the coming of the kingdom of God, when God will be all in all (1 Cor. 15:28).

Despite everything which we have thus far asserted concerning the nearness of Christ's return, which after nineteen hundred years has still not taken place, we cannot deny that neither Jesus nor the apostles took this period into account. There was certainly no hint in their preaching that they expected nineteen centuries to elapse before the Lord would renew the earth. In this sense it is true that we live in an unexpected, unforeseen time. This fact makes attempts at pinning down prophecy and predictions to our own time all the more incredible. Yet God's freedom and his way of surprising us by how he fulfills prophecy allows us to cling to his promises and remain constantly ready for the return of the Lord Jesus.

THE MANNER OF HIS COMING

If we remain loyal to the principle enunciated earlier, that prophecy is not to be taken literally but is an indistinct outline of what God intends in the future, it follows that we must proceed with great caution when dealing with those prophecies which speak of the manner of Christ's return. It is irresponsible to attempt to work out in advance from these texts how exactly he will return. In truth, the second coming of Christ is itself a repetition of the fulfillment of the prophecy of the coming of the messiah, a prophecy fulfilled in his incarnation and in the coming of the Holy Spirit and due for fulfillment again in his return.

It may be possible to deduce four characteristics of his second coming from the prophecies which deal with the subject. We may expect it to be *visible, sudden, cosmic,* and *glorious.* But these characteristics remain no more than possible boundaries within which we may expect his return.

There is a fairly general expectation in the New Testament that Christ's coming will be *visible.* In Rev. 1:7 we read, "Every eye shall see him." The Synoptic gospels also mention that "All people of the world will make lamentation, and they will see the Son of man coming on the clouds of heaven" (Matt. 24:30; also Mark 13:26; Luke 21:27). Luke also implies this in Acts 1:11, where men in white raiment inform the disciples (who have just witnessed Jesus' physical departure) that "this Jesus, who has been taken away from you up to heaven, will come in the same way you have seen him go." John mentions the same theme: "We know that when it [what we will become] has been disclosed we will be like him, because we will see him as he is" (1 John 3:2). Such concepts as "appear" are frequently used of

Jesus' return (e.g., 1 Cor. 4:5; 2 Cor. 5:10; Col. 3:4; 2 Thess. 2:8; 1 Tim. 6:14; 2 Tim. 4:1, 8; Titus 2:13; 1 Pet. 5:4; 1 John 2:28). Since the same authors apply the same terms to the first coming of Jesus (John 1:31; 2:11; Col. 1:26; 1 Tim. 3:16; Heb. 9:26; 1 Pet. 1:20; 1 John 3:5) as to the second, one is led to conclude that he will return visibly. K. Dijk is therefore correct in interpreting the "sign" which will appear in heaven (Matt. 24:30) as Jesus himself.[33] The idea that Christ will appear visibly agrees with Paul's statement that now, before Christ's return, "faith is our guide, we do not see him" (2 Cor. 5:7).

Despite all this, large groups of Christians deny the visible return of Christ or hold that it is to be preceded by an invisible return. In the last century, various calculations of Jesus' return included 1836 (Bengel), 1843 or '44 (William Miller, the Adventists), 1835, '38, '64, and '66 (England's Irvingites, who had to keep moving their date), 1873 or '74 (Adventists again), and 1876 (Barbour). By the end of the century, there had been such a multitude of wrong predictions that a new way out had to be found—Christ's coming would be invisible! It was this doctrine that the Jehovah's Witnesses appropriated; following in the steps of Russell, they announced that Christ came invisibly in 1914. Their calculations are based on numbers found in Daniel 6 and 12. But since Christ has been with us invisibly through the Holy Spirit ever since Pentecost (Matt. 28:20), in what sense could he possibly be said to have returned invisibly? Another line of thought to which we must attend is the doctrine that the faithful will be taken away secretly by an invisible coming of Christ called the "rapture." This alleges that when Christ comes invisibly, he takes away the faithful (in some variations the "sanctified," those who are exceptionally holy, on the basis of Matt. 5:8; Heb. 12:14; and 1 John 3:2) and that this is the first second coming of Christ. This will be followed by the great persecution and, thereafter, by his second second coming.

There are many variations to this doctrine, making it difficult to present a single, coherent picture. Nevertheless it is generally claimed that the New Testament teaches two different second comings. The first is invisible and for the sake of Christ's holy ones. The second is visible and will be *with* his holy ones. Matt. 24:40; Luke 17:34; John 14:3; 1 Thess. 4:15-17; and Heb. 9:28 are among the texts quoted as describing Christ's first return, the rapture. The second return is thought to be portrayed in such verses as Matt. 24:30; Luke 17:24;

33. K. Dijk, *Over de laastste dingen. De toekomst van Christus* (1953), 65f.

1 Thess. 3:13; 2 Thess. 1:7-8; and Rev. 1:7. This position makes it easier, of course, to maintain the visible coming of Christ. While the Jehovah's Witnesses spiritualize all references to a visible return, advo-
cates of the "rapture" assign the visibility to the so-called second (or
actual) return of Christ. During the invisible rapture, Christ comes only
for the believers.

This notion of the rapture presents insurmountable difficulties.
Important texts in Matthew 24 are referred to in support of it, but this
chapter in the Gospel mentions what is thought to be the second return
of Christ (vv. 29-31) before it mentions the so-called rapture (vv. 40-
41). Now, this might be possible in principle, but in this case it is obvious from vv. 29-44 that one and the same event is dealt with: Christ's
single return. In v. 29, Christ begins this section by referring to his second coming. In v. 30, he assures us that all will see the Son of man
coming on the clouds of heaven. At his coming "he will send out his
angels, and they will gather his chosen from the four winds" (v. 31).
If there has been a rapture before this coming, how is it possible that
the chosen will still be on the earth at his final return (cf. 1 Thess. 3:13)?
Jesus deals with exactly the same matter in v. 36. "The day and the
hour" refer to the return mentioned in previous verses. In vv. 37-38,
still discussing the same coming, he approaches it from another angle,
calling it the coming of the Son of man. He then proceeds (v. 39) to
say, "there will be two men in the field; one will be taken, the other
left." Matters are made even clearer by the fact that this portion of
Scripture closes (vv. 42-44) with precisely the same idea with which
it opened (v. 36). This makes it impossible to extract a few verses from
the middle and claim that they deal with another coming—above all,
if subsequent verses (24:45–25:13) continue the treatment of a visible
separation which will take place at the judgment.

The same situation is found in Luke 17. Here also what is thought
to be the rapture is mentioned only after the second coming. We learn
of the latter in vv. 24ff., of the former only in v. 34. Verse 30 affirms
that the Son of man will be revealed "on that day." The proponents of
two second comings must consequently accept that v. 30 does not
speak about the secret rapture—which, in their view, must of course
be hidden. Yet it is clear that vv. 30-34 are talking about the same event.

Luke 21 presents Luke's record of the prophetic discourse of
Jesus. In vv. 25-27 Jesus speaks of the visible second coming ("they
will see the Son of man coming," v. 27) and urges his disciples —and
so all the faithful—to be comforted when these things (vv. 25-26) happen. So there will be disciples on earth at the visible second coming

of Christ. Here, as in other passages, there is no allowance for an invisible return to remove the faithful from the earth before the "final" return.

There are yet further arguments which some advance in favor of two second comings. Scripture speaks sometimes of Christ coming *for* his children (1 Thess. 4:13ff.) but at other points of his coming *"with* all the saints" (3:13). But in reality, these statements speak of precisely the same event. According to the latter, Christ comes with all his saints (obviously the faithful departed); according to the former, "God will bring them (the departed) to life with Jesus." There are two reasons why we encounter "for" on some occasions and "with" on others. First, some of the faithful have died and are with the Lord (Phil. 1:23). They will accompany him when he comes. Others will remain alive, and he will be coming for them or to them. This can again be looked at from a different angle. Those who are dead will in a certain sense come *with* the Lord. But in another sense, he will also be coming *for* them, because—being in the grave—they will be raised to life. This is why we find both "with" (1 Thess. 4:14) and "for" (v. 16) in the space of two verses.

Many smaller points are also mentioned in favor of the "rapture" idea, e.g., that the Bible sometimes teaches that the Lord will descend to the earth and at other times says that the faithful will meet him in the air. But an awareness of the manner in which prophecies are fulfilled gives the basis for realizing that these apparent differences cannot be pressed to form a doctrine of two second comings.

Each part of Scripture must always be read in its context and in the light of its own background. If an apostle writing to a specific congregation in response to a specific problem touches on the second coming, he does so with an eye to the precise situation of that congregation and without any intent to present a comprehensive treatment of the subject. So if certain matters are not mentioned in each section (if, e.g., the resurrection of unbelievers is not mentioned in 1 Cor. 15), it is illegitimate to conclude that it will happen as a separate event. It is not mentioned at a particular point simply because it is not at issue. The Bible is not a systematic handbook which deals fully with each matter in turn.

As asserted earlier, we must speak of future events with diffidence and caution. God has not left us in the dark; but neither may we treat promises and prophecies as predictions which enable us to describe the full particulars of Christ's second coming in advance.

A second characteristic of his return is that Christ will come *sud-*

denly and *unexpectedly*. This is not a question of the nearness of his coming, but rather of the fact that it will evidently be a sudden event, not a gradual process. The idea is already present in Malachi, where the "sudden" arrival of the day of the Lord as a day of judgment is depicted (Mal. 3:1-3). In his prophetic discourse, Jesus uses the image of lightning (Matt. 24:27). The context in which this imagery is used is important. The discussion concerns false prophets who will work wonders in an effort to mislead the elect (vv. 23ff.). The false prophets will suggest that Christ will come in such a way that people will be able to find him in a specific place—possibly with the idea of only then repenting. In this regard, the image of lightning serves to affirm that he will come in such a way as to be seen everywhere simultaneously, and that the matter will be settled in a moment—with the possible implication that there will then be no time to repent. The picture of lightning certainly suggests an event without warning and therefore unexpected. During a thunderstorm, one must expect a bolt of lightning at any (and thus at every) moment. Unlike the thunderclap, for which we may be prepared, the lightning flash comes without warning. That is how we must expect the coming of Jesus. The Synoptic Gospels all depict this unexpected coming (Matt. 24:44, 50; Mark 13:35; Luke 21:34ff.). We must see in this a further indication that the signs of the times are not given to warn the faithful in advance about when he will come, but to call them to be ready at every moment for his sudden and unexpected coming.

The image of a thief is frequently employed for the same purpose (Matt. 24:43; Luke 12:39ff.; 1 Thess. 5:2; 2 Pet. 3:10; Rev. 3:1-3). It is precisely because a thief breaks in unexpectedly that he is so dangerous. The Son of man's coming is sudden, everywhere at the same time, without warning, and thus unexpected (Matt. 24:44). Even if he comes unexpectedly, we must be found expecting him.

An attempt is sometimes made to justify the idea that the signs of the times do, after all, give an approximate time when the second coming will take place and are meant to serve this purpose. This is done by taking the words "hour" and "day" very literally. This leads to the argument that the specific moment (hour and day) remain unknown, but that one may (and should) deduce in what period the event will take place. Thus we can calculate *more or less* when Christ will come. But this notion not only misunderstands the meaning of "hour" and "day" (and Mark 13:33 speaks more generally of the "time"); it also proceeds from the idea that Jesus could not have returned at any point during the past nineteen centuries and that the Bible knows of an era separate from that in which the apostles lived in which the coming of the Lord will be indicated by signs. We have already dismissed the idea that the New Testament contains any suggestion of a separate end time, which can be distinguished from that in which the first Christians lived.

A third characteristic, the *cosmic* significance of the Lord's return (only to be expected, in the light of the cosmic structure of the first two modes) is emphasized by certain cosmic phenomena which will precede or accompany his coming. (We will later pay particular attention to the resurrection of the body and the new heaven and earth, further indications of the cosmic character of the second coming.) Jesus' prophetic discourse mentions earthquakes (Matt. 24:7), the eclipse of sun and moon, the falling of stars, and the shaking of the heavenly powers (v. 29). In 2 Pet. 3:10ff., we read of the heavens vanishing with a great rushing sound and the elements disintegrating in flames. In Rev. 6:12-17 and 8:5, a considerable number of such cosmic phenomena are mentioned.

We must recall that we are here dealing with imagery. Unimaginable things are dealt with in thoroughly apocalyptic language. Stars certainly cannot fall to earth (even if people thought so in biblical times), since stars are many times larger than the earth. The other images are also concerned with such vast and all-embracing catastrophes that they are supernatural and supra-historical. But these images are related to the earthliness of the Old Testament and its expectation of the future.

The Old Testament knows no dualism between the blessing of the Lord and earthly prosperity (Deut. 26; 28). Although this does not limit the Lord's blessing exclusively to earthly prosperity, the Old Testament's future expectation is strongly directed to this world. Vivid earthly imagery is employed repeatedly to describe the future (e.g., Isa. 13:6-14; 24:16-23; Joel 2–3). It is clear from the way in which these promises are fulfilled that the images are not predictive history. And yet this does not imply that the cosmic meaning can be spiritualized. The outpouring of the Holy Spirit and the continuous coming of the kingdom of God in the interim (both fulfillments of Old Testament prophecies) have too strong a cosmic character. The New Testament is no less cosmic in character or directed toward the earth than the Old. In the Old Testament, the land of Canaan is promised to Israel, and in the New Testament it is the meek who inherit the earth. The New Testament believer does not have her or his prospects restricted to "the blessedness of my soul one day with God in heaven" but looks forward to everlasting fellowship with God in soul and body on the new earth (2 Pet. 3:13; Rev. 21–22). Therefore, without any attempt to deduce precisely how the coming of Christ will take place, we must realize that God will not abandon that which his hands have made, that the earth will really be involved in judgment and renewal at the second coming of Christ.

More than this should not be deduced from cosmic imagery. Some think that these events will give us some hint of when the coming of the Lord is at hand. That, they claim, will be when these cosmic disturbances will assume catastrophic dimensions. Apart from the fact that views of this type misunderstand the end time and purpose of the signs, there is no biblical warrant for suggesting that the signs must increase in intensity as Christ's return draws nearer. This widespread idea is to be encountered as early as the works of Kuyper, a Dutch theologian of the last century.[34] The signs are given to remind the Church that the Lord is near, and not to help us make any calculations.

A fourth characteristic of Christ's coming is that it will be *in glory.* Its convincing, indisputable character will silence all opposition. This is not the manner in which Christ came before. In his incarnation he was a sign rejected (Luke 2:34) because he came in humility (Phil. 2:5-8). He was mocked as a glutton and a winebibber, even as the prince of the devils (Matt. 10:25; 11:19-24). But at his second coming, "every knee will bow to him and every tongue confess him Lord" (Phil. 2:10-11; cf. Rev. 5:13). The powers of evil which, during the interim, have refused to accept their defeat and captivity, persisting in their destructive activity on earth, will finally be abolished (1 Cor. 15:24ff.), and the devil be cast into the lake of fire and brimstone (Rev. 20:10).

These factors lead to the frequent references to our Lord's "coming with great power and glory" (Matt. 24:30; Mark 13:26; Luke 21:27). Christ, for the present hidden in God, will then be revealed (Col. 3:3-4). Now, the faithful wait for "the happy fulfillment of our hope when the splendor of our great God and Savior Jesus Christ will appear" (Titus 2:13).

The glory in which Christ will come has everything to do with the glorification which awaits us (Col. 3:4; Rom. 8:18-23). Indeed, Christ will not come for his own sake; he will come rather to take us

---

34. A. Kuyper, "Locus de Consummatione Saeculi," *Dictaten Dogmatiek* (1910) V, 136ff. "The abnormal modality can exist in an extensive, intensive, or causative form. Such signs will indicate that the end is now at hand *(nu het einde komende is)*." The *nu* ("now"), like his whole presentation, shows clearly that Kuyper regards the end time as a separate time after the time of the apostles.

to himself, so that we can be where he is (John 14:3) and see his glory (17:24). This is how he reaches God's eternal goal for creation with us—to be God-with-us, in fellowship with us, to make us the people who share in his bliss and glory. What this means will be described in the following pages as "puzzling reflections in a mirror." But soon enough we shall know it face to face (1 Cor. 13:12).

DISCLOSURE AND FULFILLMENT

One extremely important question is whether any really new things await us in the future, things that will be *fulfilled* at Christ's return, or whether everything has already been attained and merely awaits his coming in order to be *disclosed*. Those who place major emphasis on Christ himself can easily take the extreme position of insisting that everything has already been accomplished by his crucifixion and resurrection and that this fulfilled reality can only be revealed more fully at his second coming. Others, who speak of eschatology as the last "things," may easily end up at the opposite extreme and affirm that nothing eschatological has taken place yet, that all eschatology is to be expected in a future which will consist only of new things occurring for the first time.

According to Asendorf and Bakker, the major emphasis of Luther's eschatology was that the second advent will be a disclosure of what is already a present but concealed reality, though it is evident that Luther also gave consideration to that which Christ would fulfill for the first time at his return.[35] Luther's motive was very important. Nothing can possibly exceed the importance of Christ's victory on the cross and in his resurrection. For this reason the end has already been reached, and that which is yet to take place is nothing more than a manifestation or unveiling of the meaning of the cross and resurrection. But Luther does not thereby devalue the future, suggesting that it is no more than disclosure. While on the one hand the decisive events were the crucifixion and resurrection, on the other Luther emphasizes

35. J. T. Bakker, *Eschatologische Prediking bij Luther* (1964), 50f., shows how Luther can say on the one hand that we should remember that the resurrection has already taken place *(iam factam)* but is not yet revealed *(nisi quod nondum revelatam)*, and on the other that though it sounds as if everything is already complete, it is still far from completion. See also U. Asendorf, *Eschatologie bei Luther* (1967), 14, 32f., 46, 125.

that Christ's cross and resurrection would have no real meaning without his second coming.[36] The future unveiling is no mere append-age without which the realities of cross and resurrection would retain their significance. Without future disclosure, the cross and resurrec-tion have no real meaning—now or later.

So the model of "concealment now, disclosure later" need not undermine the importance of future events. At its most profound, the motive can be to emphasize the immeasurable, decisive, and total sig-nificance of the word from the cross, "It is accomplished."

Barth evidently shared this motive.[37] Indeed, in Barth's view Christ's resurrection could have been his second coming; in a sense, that is what it was. According to Barth the content of the second com-ing is the same as that of the cross and resurrection: proclamation that he who was judged on Golgotha is the judge of the living and dead and that in him salvation and consummation have dawned. The only dif-ference is that everything has a provisional and passing form at Christ's resurrection, a sense of being the end in penultimate form. Yet even in this penultimate form, we are really dealing with the end. World his-tory has already closed, the resurrection of the dead has begun, eter-nal life has become a reality—but all are still contained in the resur-rection and life of the One. As Barth says, "All time might have terminated there."[38]

When Barth speaks in this sense of the exclusive, noetic, disclos-ing, and revelatory functions of the second coming, it is not difficult—especially within the basic focus of our study—to grasp his motive and appreciate it. The end, the goal, is not really a set of new things but a person, Jesus Christ, himself the *eschatos*. That which he reaches is the *eschaton*.[39] The cross is not one stage along the way, another

36. Asendorf, 125.

37. Barth, IV/3, 489. W. Kreck, in *Die Zufunkt des Gekommenen* (1961), 100, says that the fulfillment can be nothing more in principle than the revelation of that which is already real *in Jesus Christ*. According to Barth, this "in Jesus Christ" means "still enclosed in the life of this One" (IV/1, 734). He who denies that everything is already enclosed in his life and thus is real should indeed heed Barth's accusation, i.e., that "already" then has the character of a mere ideal (in the philosophical sense) and is therefore unreal (IV/3, 489).

38. Barth, IV/1, 734.

39. When J. Moltmann, in *Theology of Hope* (p. 229), sets "Person" and "the reality of the event" in opposition to each other in this respect, he risks mis-understanding both Barth and the reality that is Jesus himself. Because Jesus was born, crucified, and raised, the goal has been reached (it has really happened),

"item" onto which a list of other "things" is simply tacked. The cross and resurrection are the attainment of God's goal. Once it has been accomplished, there cannot be the expectation of something (or someone) essentially new and different. What follows can only (if "only" is not too weak a word) be a manifestation or unfolding of that which is already a reality in him. He remains always God-with-us and we-with-God. And he has come! Granted this, how can the future be anything other than an unveiling?

On the other hand, Barth also stresses the importance of the future. In doing this he characterizes the end already accomplished in the cross and resurrection as provisional, transitory, and particular. Once again we can grasp and appreciate his motive. Despite the fact that Christ is the end and achieved his goal in the crucifixion and resurrection, the Christian's hope is also fixed on the future because Christ will yet do decisive things.

The question remains, nevertheless, whether Barth has handled the matter satisfactorily. His idea that Christ's resurrection could have been the "last end" (in fact his final return) is particularly to be questioned—first, because it was indeed the "last end" if we remain loyal to the biblical concept of "end" (*telos* as "goal"), second, because the end had to come in yet another way after his resurrection.

In terms of the basic focus of this study, this means that Jesus is the end and that he realizes the end or *eschaton* in three ways. In all three he realizes the same goal, but each time in a different mode. The crucifixion and resurrection are certainly the end (for us), but this same end is also realized in us and with us. In essence there is thus nothing new to be expected; but the goal already accomplished has to be realized twice more, each time in the same full sense in which it was realized the first time.

No contrast between disclosure and fulfillment, therefore, is helpful at this point. As little as the goal is only *unveiled* in the second and third modes, so little is it fulfilled *for the first time* in the second or third mode in the sense that the first mode was no real fulfillment. In this sense, the future as unveiling is indeed to be stressed.

When we nevertheless want to underline the real actualization of the *eschaton* at Jesus' second coming, then we must call upon the term "fulfillment" as well. The manner in which the *eschaton* will then

---

and the same goal can only be realized again in another way. P. Schütz, *Das Mysterium der Geschichte* (1963), 193ff., also reflects something of this fact that *Christ* is the fulfillment.

be realized is not that in which it was realized in the first mode or the second. If we refused to speak of fulfillment here we would rob history of its reality, and it would be unclear how we could then even speak of the cross and resurrection of Jesus as actual, decisive fulfillments. We would have to be content with an unincarnate Word (ultimately just an idea, an unreality), and so would have to part company with Jesus of Nazareth! Anyone who desires to adhere to the reality of the first fulfillment on Golgotha will also have to accept that the same *eschaton* is not only *revealed* at the second advent but is also *realized* and *fulfilled*. In this sense we must agree with Hedinger, Cullmann, and Moltmann that the future also brings fulfillment.[40]

The radical manner in which one group of theologians clings to the revelatory function of the second coming, while another holds with equal tenacity to the fulfilling function, can be taken as a possible indication that both aspects will have to be put together before the full truth can be reflected. Christ's return will include both disclosure and fulfillment. It will include disclosure, because there is undisputably an element of concealment about the earthly ministry and resurrection of Jesus and about the interim period. Thus his second coming is indeed spoken of in the New Testament as a revealing. But since he really fulfills God's goal at his return in a third and final way, this third mode bears a no less real character than the first two, and we therefore must also speak wholeheartedly of the realization of the *eschaton* in the third mode and consequently of its fulfillment in an ontic sense.

The same question can be approached from another angle, simply by asking what aspects are being discussed. There are certainly aspects of eschatology which, fulfilled here and now, will be unveiled and made known at Christ's second coming. For example, he certainly does not become Lord at his return; at that point his lordship is simply revealed. The division between believers and unbelievers is another aspect which will not become a reality only when Christ comes again. Humanity is now already divided along these lines, but then it will be disclosed who really belongs on each side. So there are indeed certain aspects of eschatology which are already being realized, which await only manifestation on that day.

But when it comes to the resurrection and the new earth, the acceptance of God's children into his eternal bliss and peace, and their

40. U. Hedinger, *Hoffnung zwischen Kreuz und Reich* (1968), 176-182 *idem., Der Freiheitsbegriff in der kirchlichen Dogmatik Karl Barths* (1962), 147-158; O. Cullmann, *Salvation in History* (1967), 177; Moltmann, *Theology of Hope*, 227-229.

life in his presence, then we are dealing with things which have not yet happened and thus will be fulfilled only at Christ's second coming. We certainly have not yet risen from the dead, and the earth has not yet been made new. So the future also holds things that will be really new—but not, of course, isolated from Christ. In fact, the resurrection has already begun in him, and he will complete it by raising the dead. In him we already have a place before God's face, though not yet on the new earth.

So it is that we must speak of both unveiling and fulfilling. In the following three subsections, we shall confine our attention to matters which will be revealed or made known at Christ's second coming, and in the last two we shall consider really new things which he will accomplish or fulfill for the first time.

CHRIST'S COMING AS DISCLOSURE

The Disclosure of Christ's Lordship

According to the New Testament, Jesus is already king. All power has already been given to him, and he is already the head over all authority and power (Matt. 28:18; Col. 2:10). But this, after all, is true only in a hidden way, not yet visibly or indisputably. That is what we still await. But that will only be revealed at his second coming. Though the decisive hour has struck and victory has been won, it must still be disclosed. Various structures of his lordship indicate that, for the present, it is veiled. The way in which the powers are now subject to him (i.e., already really subjected, but in such a way that they persist in denying it and so still constitute a threat to the Church) indicates this. The image of the thousand years does not occur apart from the image of the little while (Rev. 20). The powers are bound and defeated, yet they must still be annihilated. The civil authority, intended to be a servant of the kingdom of God, often assumes the stance of Antichrist and denies the lordship of Christ. It even attempts to mimic him by signs and wonders (Rev. 13; cf. 2 Thess. 2:9ff.), enticing the whole world to run after it "in wondering admiration" (Rev. 13:3). This phrase calls to mind John 12:19, "why all the world has gone after [Jesus]," and the astonishment at and admiration for Jesus recorded by the Synoptists (especially Luke 2:18, 33; 4:22; 8:25; 9:43; 11:14, 38; 20:26). It is now still possible for the Antichrist and evil powers to create the impression that they are what Christ alone truly is. But when Christ appears—for at present he rules in a hidden way (Col. 3:3-4)—he will exterminate Antichrist by the breath of his mouth, reducing him to nothing (2 Thess. 2:8). The ease with which Christ will annihilate him is itself indicative of his total lordship. It is only because this lordship is temporarily hidden that the Antichrist and his powers have not been entirely destroyed— that the devil is still only bound, not yet cast into the lake of fire and brimstone.

And so it will be with those who negate or ignore Christ's present lordship. They too will tremble before him on that day. "Then the kings of the earth, magnates and marshals, the rich and the powerful, and all people, slave or free, hid themselves in caves and mountain crags; and they called out to the mountains and the crags, 'Fall on us and hide us from the face of the One who sits on the throne and from the vengeance of the Lamb.' For the great day of their vengeance has come, and who will be able to stand?" (Rev. 6:16-17). For the present, while he is still veiled from their eyes, they can be out in the open; but when he steps out from behind his concealment, the most terrifying of shelters (for mountains and crags crush, they do not hide!) are preferable to his revealed glory and dominion.

At present he is visible only to the eyes of faith (Acts 7:56; Heb. 11:1, 13, 27). But there are no limits to his power and lordship. "Full authority in heaven and on earth has been committed to me" (Matt. 28:18). "He has put all things in subjection under his feet" (1 Cor. 15:27). "Every power and authority in the universe is subject to him as Head" (Col. 2:10), but only in a specific, concealed manner, distinct from his lordship which will be revealed at the second advent, when "every created thing in heaven and on earth and under the earth and in the sea, all that is in them" will cry, "Praise, honor, glory, and might to him who sits on the throne, and to the Lamb for ever and ever!" (Rev. 5:13). Then Phil. 2:10 will be fulfilled, "at the name of Jesus every knee will bow—in heaven, on earth, and in the depths— and every tongue confess, 'Jesus Christ is Lord,' to the glory of God the Father."

It is evident that, after dealing with the kingdom of God in connection with both Jesus' earthly ministry and his work through the Holy Spirit, we should now discuss it for the third time. But since the fulfilling aspect of his return raises equally important issues concerning the kingdom, discussion of this will be postponed to the end of this chapter.

The Disclosure of God's Children

When the revelation of Christ's lordship occurs, we may expect the children of God also to be revealed. That which he did was not for himself but for the world, for those who through faith would be united with him. We have been crucified with him, and with him we have died and been buried (Rom. 6:3ff.). Similarly, we have been raised to life with him and are seated with him in the heavens (Eph. 2:6ff.), where, with him, our life is hidden in God (Col. 3:3). On the grounds of this "with him" (our corporate unity with him) it is anything but a surprise that the apostle assumes in terms of the second coming a decisive unity between Christ and his own. "When Christ, who is our life, is manifested, then you too will be manifested with him in glory" (Col. 3:4). "It is this revealing of the children of God for which all creation waits with eager expectation" (Rom. 8:19).

Romans 8 makes it clear that this is a joyful expectation. The revelation of Christ takes place with glory. All apparent uncertainty of his victory is dispelled—and with it the anxiety caused by the present activities of evil forces—as his visible dominion over all things becomes plain. That the manifestation of the children of God takes place in this same glory means that he openly adopts us as his children. What this involves is described in Rom. 8:23: God will "set our whole body free." This can be taken as referring to our physical bodies, and so to our resurrection, but surely it must also point to our present existence, our lives. This, then, does not imply that we are to be redeemed from our bodies, but that our bodies (i.e., our lives) will be saved from the power, influence, and consequence of sin. That is why v. 21 speaks of "creation itself being freed to share the glorious freedom of the children of God."

This glorious freedom must be seen as an expression of the goal that Christ reaches in a third and final manner: with us. While during the interim period it was realized in us, it was inseparably bound up with the necessity of *becoming* what we are in Christ. The new person is created in Christ (Eph. 2:15; 4:24); yet (in fact, for this very reason) we have to be clothed with this new person (Eph. 4:24; Col. 3:10-11; Gal. 4:19) and become like Christ (Eph. 4:32; 5:2, 25ff.; 1 John 3:3). Something of this new person must already be visible to the world (Gal. 4:19; Matt. 5:16) by our wholehearted obedience and free surrender to God's service. In this way we become the true covenant partners of God (Rom. 6:11-23). However, because of our imperfect response to this imperative, we do not attain to our full stature in this life, and the *eschaton* is attained *with* us only when Christ does so at his return.

When he comes, we will no longer be summoned to *become* perfect. We will simply *be* perfect. "We will be like him, for we will see him as he is" (1 John 3:2). For this we wait with longing sighs (Rom. 8:18-19, 29) because we have received the promise: "When Christ, who is our life, is manifested, then you too will be manifested with him in glory" (Col. 3:4).

Knowing that without any effort on our part we will be made perfect at Christ's second coming does not mean that we need not care how we behave at present. "Everyone who has this hope before him (Christ) purifies himself, as Christ is pure" (1 John 3:3). At the same time, this does offer a glorious consolation in this imperfect life, since we are assured that the purpose of God will be achieved without any call on us, and *therefore* attained in all perfection. On that day the paradox of the "already" and the "not yet" will be finally resolved, because there will be no other lord who can claim our obedience, trust, and zeal. "Then," says Paul, "comes the end, when . . . every kind of domination, authority, and power will have been abolished" (1 Cor. 15:24). Only that one God and one Lord, before whom every knee will bow and whom every tongue will confess (Phil. 2:10f.; Rev. 5:13), will reign. We will be his obedient and trustworthy people, and he our God.

The Disclosure of Judgment

Those who probe the Scriptures have always been struck that the New Testament announces with emphasis that believers are freed from judgment, yet it also says that they will appear at the judgment just as unbelievers will. In order to elucidate this matter, the concept of disclosure will again be helpful. The real (ontic) decision is taken in this life. "He who puts his faith in the Son has hold of eternal life" (John 3:36). "There is no condemnation for those who are united with Christ Jesus" (Rom. 8:1). What happens at the final judgment is no more than the disclosure or manifestation of this decision. At the present moment there is still a certain hiddenness about our decision. We cannot demonstrate that we have eternal life. Other people can doubt the claim. Truth to say, the incompleteness in our own life gives considerable grounds for such doubts. This is why an open adoption as children of God awaits us, a judgment in which the decision which has been made in this life will simply be made manifest—a judgment with a noetic significance.

Paul makes this clear in 1 Cor. 3:13 and 4:5, and John in John 5:29, that the decisive element is what believers have done in their earthly lives. This will only be made known at the judgment; the decisive events have already been played out in this life, in the interim period, and on these grounds the final noetic verdict is to be announced at the judgment. (In Chapter 4 we elaborated on the decisive character of faith, which by its very nature depends upon Christ's decision.)

The last judgment is therefore not decisive in the sense that any person's eternal future remains in the balance up to that moment, God then judging that person according to criteria which up to then remained obscure. Judgment is completed during the interim period, in the sense that faith in Christ or rejection of him is decisive. The believer knows already that he or she will not be lost (John 3:16), will not come up for judgment (3:18; 5:24), but has eternal life (3:36; 1 John 5:11-13). Similarly, to the disobedient it must be proclaimed that they will not see eternal life, but that God's wrath rests on them (John 3:36).

That this ontic decision is taken in this life and only a noetic verdict pronounced at judgment does not stem only from faith's decisive character but also from the fact that judgment is executed in the light of works performed. That works are the basis of judgment is presented in all the great New Testament traditions (John 5:28-29; Rom. 2:1-10; 2 Cor. 5:10; 2 Thess. 1:5-10; and supremely in Jesus' prophetic discourse, Matt. 24–25). In the parable of the talents this thought is fully developed, and we hear that it is those who have worked who enter the joy of their Lord (Matt. 25:25ff.). The one who buried his talent is repudiated. Detailed treatment is given to the subject in Matt. 25:31ff., where the kingdom is said to be inherited by those who gave food, water, shelter, and comfort to their Lord as he was present in suffering people. Those who failed to do these things enter the fires of perdition. The Bible knows no tension between justification by faith and judgment by works. That the object of our works is the Lord himself (represented in the least important of his brothers) shows at once the decisive unity of faith and works. Works are the result and vindication of faith (James 2:14ff.). This distinction between ontic and noetic judgment explains why, on the one hand, Christ says that he did not come to judge (John 3:17) and that he judges no one (8:15) and, on the other, declares that the Father has handed over all judgment to him (5:22, 27, 30; cf. Rom. 2:16). Paul said that God "has fixed a day on which he will have the world judged, and justly judged, by a man of his choosing" (Acts 17:31). The striking alternation between Father and the Son in the last judgment which emerges from these texts is also evident in Paul's writings. On the one hand he speaks of the tribunal of Christ (2 Cor. 5:10) and on the other of the tribunal of God (Rom. 14:10).

The chiliastic viewpoint, in which we are told of two distinct judgments, one exclusively for the faithful (Christ's judgment seat) and the other for unbelievers (God's great white throne), stems partly from the peculiar duplication of future events in chiliasm—a matter we disposed of when discussing the millennium and the return of Christ—and partly from unacceptable exegesis, according to which unbelievers do not appear before the tribunal of Christ, since Paul mentions only that believers will appear there. The possibility of two different judgments is excluded by John 5:28-29 and Matt. 25:31ff. Some chiliasts maintain that "the nations" of Matt. 25:31ff. are those who come to repentance only during the (future) millennium, after the faithful (the "bride") has been taken away in rapture to the wedding of the Lamb. In this way they suggest that Matt. 25:31ff. reports the judgment of a special group before the great white throne of God, not the judgment of the faithful before the tribunal of Christ. Apart from the fact that this entire avenue of thought fails to reflect the New Testament witness as a whole, it is rendered questionable by the fact that it is Jesus who judges in Matt. 25:31, while chiliasts say it should be God, sitting on his great white throne.

L. Mattern has pointed out that believers will be involved in the last judgment in two senses. First, whether or not a person was a Christian will be judged (Rom. 2:5ff.). Second, the manner in which he or she was a Christian will be judged (Rom. 14:10ff.; 1 Cor. 3:5ff.; 4:4ff.; 2 Cor. 5:10). Although Christ has saved us from judgment, we shall nevertheless be tested to see if we have indeed been saved and how we have responded to this salvation. The first of these tests ought to hold no tension, doubt, or uncertainty for the believer. The New Testament speaks in unmistakable terms of the assurance of faith. Nevertheless, this assurance of faith is not to be deduced logically from specific presuppositions. No certainty of faith exists outside the activity and tension of faith, outside obedience to the admonition to persevere. This is why the same Paul who knows in whom he has trusted (2 Tim. 1:12) still bruises his own body and masters it, "for fear that after preaching to others" he would find himself "rejected" (1 Cor. 9:27). This is not a repudiation of assurance of faith: there is no disharmony between certainty and striving, and the assurance of faith has everything to do with the command to "continue in your faith" (Col. 1:23).

It is evident that no conclusions about the "quality" of Christians' lives can be drawn from the mere fact that they have been freed from judgment. They may have built on that foundation with gold, silver, and fine stone, or with wood, hay, and straw. And when the work is tested, the Christians may well suffer loss—though they themselves are saved (1 Cor. 3:15). The fact that Scripture remains silent about further details of this "suffering [of] loss" prompts us to the greatest reserve concerning what kind of loss is involved. Mattern has pointed out that reward and salvation are not identical, and neither are punishment and damnation. Anyway, despite "suffering loss" the Christians themselves will be saved. At the same time, there is no indication that reward and loss have anything to do with a particular position in heaven or with "grades" of bliss.[41]

J. L. de Villiers also rejects the idea that the reward spoken of in 1 Cor. 3:14 might be salvation, affirming that it is evidently those privileges which trustworthy laborers enjoy—the Master's approbation for work well done and the joy of seeing how much blessing has crowned their efforts and how many people have come into the light of Christ through their preaching. The ultimate reward is that the work survives the purifying fires of judgment.[42]

Unbelievers are also discussed in connection with judgment—usually in parallel with believers. Thus in Matt. 25:31 Jesus speaks of sheep and goats and in John 5:29 of the resurrection to life and to doom. Paul also recognizes this distinction at the judgment (Rom. 2:5-10; 2 Thess. 1:5ff.; 2 Tim. 4:1). In Rev. 20:11ff., "the dead, great and small" (i.e., everybody) stand before God's throne.

The judgment must, in the case of unbelievers, again be seen as the disclosure of a decision already taken. "The unbeliever has already been judged, in that he has not given his allegiance to God's Son" (John 3:18). "He who disobeys the Son shall not see that life; God's wrath rests on him" (v. 36). "He who does not possess the Son of God does not have that life" (1 John 5:12). Similarly, in the parable of the sheep and the goats, the ontic decision which has been made is only later pronounced at the judgment noetically, "For when I was hungry, you gave me no food. . . ." So it is clear that for the lost, too, the decision is taken during the interim and reflects their attitude toward Jesus, not their works as such. This is clear from the fact that though on judgment day

41. L. Mattern, *Das Verständnis des Gerichtes bei Paulus* (1966), 123ff., 141ff.

42. J. L. de Villiers, *Die Loongedagte in die Nuwe Testament* (1957), 16f.

people will claim that they prophesied and cast out devils in his name, he will reject them, saying, "I never knew you: out of my sight, you and your wicked ways!" (Matt. 7:22-23). Therefore, works as such have no intrinsic value. What is at issue is that which results from a relationship with God in Christ, or, as the Westminster Confession puts it, "These good works, done in obedience to God's commandments, are the fruits and evidences of a true and lively faith. . . ." Christians' "ability to do good works is not at all of themselves, but wholly from the Spirit of Christ" (xvi. 2, 3).

This does not mean that unbelievers must wait until the end before hearing, out of the blue, that their works did not, after all, have the correct quality. They are lost because, when they heard the gospel, they did not pay attention and act accordingly (Matt. 7:24ff.). Non-Christian Gentiles have no excuse (Rom. 1:20), because in unrighteousness they suppressed the truth (v. 18). "Knowing God, they have refused to honor him as God or to render him thanks" (v. 21). God vents his fury and retribution (2:8) on those who have despised the richness of his mercy, patience, and tolerance (v. 4). It is "those who refuse to acknowledge God . . . and will not obey the gospel of our Lord Jesus" (2 Thess. 1:8)[43] who are subject to the vengeance exacted by Jesus. According to Rev. 20:15, the decision depends on whether an individual's name is written in the book of life. And Rev. 3:5 makes it plain that having one's name in that book has everything to do with obedience to Jesus Christ. The words addressed to the Gentiles in Rom. 11:22-23 are, "Observe the kindness and the severity of God: severity to those who fell away, divine kindness to you, if only you remain within its scope; otherwise you too will be cut off, whereas they [Israel], if they do not continue faithless, will be grafted in; for it is in God's power to graft them in again."

From the foregoing we see clearly that eternal judgment on the faithless is grounded not in God's reluctance to save them but in their attitude toward Jesus (Matt. 25:41-46). He has not even prepared for them a separate place of their own in eternity, since their damnation was not a part of his creative purpose. He simply sends them away to the place prepared "for the devil and his angels" (Matt. 25:41). In Matt. 25:34 we have the realization of God's goal in creation in its

43. There are ample exegetical grounds for accepting that mention is made here of only one group, who neither "know God" nor are "obedient to the gospel." This may be *parallelismus membrorum,* or the "and" may be intended to create a climax. See J. E. Frame, *The Epistles to the Thessalonians* (ICC; 1912), ad loc.

third form, i.e., with us. It is not simply that God has been busy pre-
paring this kingdom since the foundation of the world, but that he has
had it ready since the foundation of the world. On the other hand, there
is no indication in v. 41 that eternal fire is intended for the damned or
that it has been ready for them since the world's foundation. It is intended for the devil and his angels (the forces of evil). The discontinuity between vv. 34 and 41 is all the more remarkable when we consider the parallel constructions within the parable (cf. vv. 39ff. with
42ff.; also vv. 37ff. with v. 44; and v. 40 with v. 45). Damnation can
thus be regarded as no more than an "emergency measure" which, like
sin itself, does not fit into God's creative purpose for mankind. Indeed
he is "very patient with you, because it is not his will for any to be
lost, but for all to come to repentance" (2 Pet. 3:9).

In the light of this decisive inequality between those who are
saved and those who are lost, we are justified in introducing the topic
of hell at this point (where the noetic significance of the second advent
is under consideration) rather than later (when we shall turn to the ontic
aspect). We cannot speak of hell as we speak of heaven, as if it were
one of two streams rising from a common source and flowing down
opposite sides of a mountain. The sentence of final damnation is not a
realization of the *eschaton* or *telos,* God's original purpose in creation.
Hell is indeed an end, but only an end without an accomplished goal—
i.e., an end which has miscarried. Just as Christ does not realize God's
goal and so the *eschaton* during the interim period in unbelievers, so
also hell is no realization of the *eschaton* with them. What happens is
that the decisive character of unbelief produces a miscarriage. While
God is on the one hand the author of our eternal blessedness on the
basis of faith, which is in itself empty, but is directed toward its object,
living only by the merits of Christ, humans are on the other hand the
authors of their own damnation on the basis of unbelief, which is
oriented toward itself and its limitless reliance on its own capabilities
and merits (as in Luke 18:9ff.) to save itself.

But it is still God who pronounces the verdict. It is he who in
his grace and love determines to relieve us in this hopeless situation
and bring us back into fellowship by virtue of his Son's merits. But
he also determines to abandon the unbeliever, who refuses his help
and will not tread the path back to happiness opened by God in his
goodness. In this way God remains the king, the sovereign Lord, but
the lost have no one but themselves to blame for their condition. This
is in complete harmony with the New Testament preaching of damnation, according to which the damned are in every case themselves

responsible for their state, never able to "answer God back" (Rom. 9:20).

This division of responsibility can only be treated adequately if we do so at this juncture, counting judgment and hell as disclosing, noetic aspects of Christ's second coming. The new heaven and earth, by contrast, must be seen as ontic, fulfilling facets and discussed later. The first reason for this division is that judgment and hell, like the revealing of Christ's lordship and of the children of God, are matters about which decision is taken during the interim. These decisions are only made manifest at Christ's return. Second, in the specific matter of hell and damnation, we are, in a more basic sense, dealing with a human decision which is merely exposed by God's sentence. In other words, because of the decisive character of faith, itself devoid of merit and solely dependent on what God does, God alone is the author of our salvation. Disbelief, however, closing in upon itself and seeking its adequacy in itself, accomplishes its own downfall by not taking the single, gracious way provided by God. Just as it is impossible to deal with election in the same way as rejection, so it is impossible to treat heaven and hell (or vindication and condemnation) in the same way, as though they are two sides of the same coin.

This is the deepest reason why Scripture does not furnish us with a detailed description of hell—while the new heaven, earth, and heavenly Jerusalem are portrayed right down to the last detail. It would be difficult to find a sharper contrast than between Rev. 20:10-15 (and 21:8), with its brief but pointed warning about eternal damnation, and chapters 21 and 22, a sweeping, detailed, and joyous hymn of the new heaven, the new earth, and the new Jerusalem.

The view we have been advocating is an attempt to supply a corrective to a specific structure in Berkouwer's rejection of universal salvation. When Berkouwer deals with hell, universalism, and particularism, he sets aside all "neutral information about what it [hell] will look like." This he does on the grounds of the kerygmatic character which marks the presentation of these things in Scripture.[44] In his view, there is absolutely no way of eliminating a personal, life-affecting thrust in this subject and presenting merely neutral and objectified information. It is impossible to describe hell as one would describe a painting. The various images and representations are all warnings against ruin and final loss. Such warnings are not intended to supply information concerning hell, only to serve as admonitions not to take

---

44. Berkouwer, *The Return of Christ*, 396-399.

our eyes off the light of salvation or harden our hearts against grace. The road to speculation and information about conditions in hell is, in Berkouwer's opinion, closed.

Now, there is a remarkable difference between the way hell is discussed in the New Testament and its treatment of the new earth and eternal life. This difference is not, however, exactly as Berkouwer sees it. On the one hand he is willing to deal with a whole series of problems connected with the new earth and eternal life, doing so in a manner which suggests that he would never hesitate to make a positive pronouncement about the reality of the new earth. Asked "Will there be a new earth?" it appears evident that he would reply "yes."

But on the other hand, when he discusses hell and judgment, he falls back completely upon the kerygmatic character of the scriptural message. Here, he avers, one may not ask for neutral information. Here only warnings are uttered, and a call goes out for repentance. When asked "Is there a hell?" Berkouwer does not answer. In his opinion the question of hell's reality yields to the decisive kerygmatic nature of Scripture.

But in the Bible the difference does not lie between reality and kerygmatic character. The new earth is not a reality while hell is exclusively kerygmatic in meaning. In the New Testament the difference lies elsewhere. In fact, hell is as much of a reality as the new earth, *but it is a reality which stands in a different relation to God than that of the new earth.* To be precise, hell is no part of the execution of God's creation plan; it is only the reality of his displeasure. The parallel manner in which Scripture deals with heaven and hell, acquittal and condemnation, eternal life and eternal punishment (Matt. 25:46)[45] simply cannot accommodate this distinction drawn by Berkouwer. Scripture itself indeed does furnish far more particulars and devote much more attention to the new earth than to hell. (These particulars must, of course, function within the unique character of promise-fulfillment and apocalyptic imagery.) Nevertheless, the way in which Scripture speaks of these two realities (and, for that matter, in which it speaks of people being saved or lost) does not permit us to be silent about the re-

45. The parable in Matt. 25 certainly gives no impression that there is any difference between the reality of the kingdom and that of the fire. But it leaves no doubt whatever about the relationship between these realities and God's goal in creation (vv. 34, 41). Earlier in Matthew 25, there is just as little of the first-mentioned impression (e.g., vv. 21, 30; cf. 24:46-47; 50-51). In Mark 9:42ff., hell is depicted even more vividly than life. See also Luke 16:19ff.; 2 Thess. 1:9; 2 Pet. 2:17; Jude 13. Rev. 21:8 stands between vv. 1-7 and vv. 9-27.

ality of hell while speaking frankly about the reality of the new earth. The reason for Scripture's less inhibited, more extensive treatment of the new earth lies in the different relationship in which it stands to God's creative purpose.

But a surprising amount of data is, in fact, provided about hell in the Scriptures. K. Dijk has made some attempt at systematizing it.[46] He has pointed out that the concept of a fire or lake of fire is connected to the history of the term *gehenna*. Along with this, the idea of outer darkness also plays an important role. Both are symbols of the wrath of God and everlasting punishment. Hell implies a negation, but also includes actual suffering. The negative aspect is depicted as being away from God, in the outer darkness, where the absence and lack of fellowship with God is indicative of the goal which has been missed. The actual suffering is painted in terms of pain, anguish, and misery. Hell is not only imperfection and negation. It is also depression, anxiety, torment, and suffering. Like the blessedness of salvation, damnation will last forever. Dijk affirms that the denial of eternal punishment entails the denial of eternal felicity.

In the light of this realistic manner of speaking about hell in Scripture, it is strange that Berkouwer declares, "We are not given any description of Gehenna, only a warning to avoid it."[47] We have at least to insist that, in principle, Scripture is as informative about the reality of hell as of the new earth (within the qualifications we have already mentioned)—and Berkouwer has deduced a considerable amount of "information" from the preaching of the new earth. It is evident that he is reacting against those who preach a "realistic" hell apart from the love of the God who summons us to repentance and salvation. His reaction has its value, but warning and information are not opposed to each other. A warning loses its power if it is not a warning against a reality. The reality to which the warning refers is decisive for its value. Berkouwer's argument against universalism holds good against his

---

46. Dijk, 158-169. Such an attempt as this certainly cannot be self-evidently judged, though Dijk does not always distance himself radically enough from speaking in the same way about heaven and hell, e.g., when he says that the final ground of eternal inequality is in God—and for this refers to John 9:3 (pp. 160f.). Berkouwer has dealt with the relationship between God and sin in a comprehensive and illuminating manner in *Sin* (1971), chapter 2.

47. Berkouwer, *The Return of Christ*, 415. There is equally little justification for agreeing with B. Wentsel, *Het Gericht en die Gerichtsbeleving* (1967), 17, and placing "threat" in opposition to "reality." *"De hel is geen . . . dreiging, maar een verschrikkelijke realiteit"* : hell is not a threat but a terrible reality.

own silence concerning the reality of hell. If he fails to admit the reality of hell, he himself will ultimately fail to prove what he expects the universalist view to prove: "that it does not relativize or jeopardize the decisive gravity of the proclamation."[48]

CHRIST'S COMING AS FULFILLMENT

Above and beyond the exceptional importance of the revelatory (noetic) significance of Christ's second coming stands its fulfilling, realizing, and ontic meaning, which is beyond doubt the more important. This is because it is in dealing with the fulfillment that we come to the realization of the *eschaton*—the single creative goal which has already been realized for us and in us. It is precisely because this is the final mode that we are here concerned with the aspects still unfulfilled and thus still longed for by the Church. In fact, the element of future hope in our expectation is what makes the fulfilling character of Christ's second coming indispensable. "For we have been saved, though only in hope. Now to see is no longer to hope; why should a person endure and wait for what he already sees? But if we hope for something we do not yet see, then, in waiting for it, we show our endurance" (Rom. 8:24-25). This "something we do not see" is not something which already exists but is still concealed. Rather, it is something that does not yet exist, which will only exist in the future.

In Philippians 3:21 we are told that Christ "will transfigure the body belonging to our humble state" and in 1 John 3:2ff., "Here and now, dear friends, we are God's children; what we shall be has not yet been disclosed, but we know that when it is disclosed we shall be like him, because we shall see him as he is." In the first of these texts, specific mention is made of the body. In truth, the resurrection of the body is one of the most important aspects of that future reality upon which the Church still fixes its hope.

The Resurrection

It is remarkable that the fulfillment which the Church awaits, including the resurrection of the body and the new earth, is predominantly

---

48. Berkouwer, *The Return of Christ,* 408 (quoted), 412.

cosmic in nature. When this has been realized, it will become fully apparent how really foreign to biblical thought is the dualism between undervalued matter and highly valued spirit, i.e., the old dichotomy of body vs. soul. In fact, we have already argued that the entire gospel is at stake when the resurrection of the body is doubted. It is unthinkable, in biblical terms, for a person to deny the resurrection while taking comfort in knowing that his soul (thought the superior component) is saved. The soul is not saved if the body does not rise, since this would mean that God had abandoned the work of his hands. Then all his promises would lapse. If the body does not rise, then "your faith has nothing in it and you are still in your old state of sin. It follows also that those who have died within Christ's fellowship are utterly lost" (1 Cor. 15:17-18).

All this is apparent from the ministry of Jesus who, in the same breath, speaks both of the forgiveness of sins and of the healing of the body (Mark 2:9). He is never less concerned about physical than about spiritual need (Mark 6:34ff.). Salvation is strikingly linked with physical healing in Acts 4:9: Peter pronounces the cripple "saved" ("cured," NEB), and goes on to speak of the only name in whom and through whom is salvation (v. 12). So physical healing is an essential part of the salvation brought by Jesus; "spiritualizing" the gospel makes it something foreign—in fact, no gospel at all.

These cosmic aspects of the gospel were treated extensively in previous chapters. The importance of the resurrection of the body (as of the new heaven and earth) finally confirm their significance. Paul's reaction to Hymenaeus and Philetus, who "have shot wide of the truth in saying that our resurrection has already taken place" (2 Tim. 2:17ff.) is noteworthy. Of course these two were not referring to a bodily resurrection. They spiritualized resurrection into a raising from the death of sin, and they denied physical resurrection. This doctrine Paul stigmatizes as "empty and worldly chatter," a teaching which "will spread like gangrene." He who denies bodily resurrection has wandered from the truth—no matter how much he talks about spiritual resurrection.

The tremendous importance of our resurrection is not bound up with the cosmic dimensions of salvation only, but also with Christ's resurrection. Indeed, the resurrection of Christ was the core of the joyful message proclaimed by the disciples, and his resurrection is inseparably connected with ours (1 Cor. 15:13). "From the outset both were inseparable for faith."[49] This was discussed under the concept "firstborn" in

49. H. Berkhof, *Well-Founded Hope* (1969), 33.

the preceding chapter. He who denies our resurrection also denies Christ's—and in the same breath, the entire gospel. This essential unity of Christ's resurrection and ours is of extraordinary importance.

The hope of the resurrection marks a very late development within the Old Testament—or more precisely, in intertestamental apocalyptic literature. In the Old Testament, death is seen as the ultimate threat; only Israel's faith that the Lord's power extended even over death allowed the people to hope for a resurrection.[50] The real gain of the New Testament is that this hope is fulfilled in the resurrection of Christ, simultaneously retaining its character of a promise still to be fulfilled in our resurrection. Christ the firstborn has arisen. The rest of necessity follows (1 Cor. 15:20-23). Christ's resurrection is the warranty of our own.

Remarkably, the Virgin Mary formerly filled a similar role in the doctrine of the Catholic Church. One value of her assumption into heaven, as promulgated by *Munificentissimus Deus,* is that our faith in our own resurrection is thereby strengthened and rendered fruitful.[51] It was characteristic of the older mariology that Mary often threatened the position of Christ, particularly when she was presented as intervening on our behalf with him. This probably derived from Christ's intercession on our behalf with God, but its tendency to make her coredemptrix impinged upon the sufficiency of Christ. That is why Berkouwer rejected this "value" of Mary so thoroughly in his affirmation of Christ and the Spirit as our adequate guarantors.

We are also pointed toward Christ as far as our glorified bodies are concerned. "He will transfigure the body belonging to our humble state, and give it a form like that of his own resplendent body" (Phil. 3:21). The apostle has more to say about the nature of this body in 1 Cor. 15:35-49. We must understand that he is not simply trying to render resurrection comprehensible by appealing to natural theology ("seed," "dying," and "rising again"). He has already made the resur-

---

50. H. H. Rowley, *The Faith of Israel* (1956), 172-174: "Sheol was not the last word of the Old Testament on what followed death. For God is the Lord of all things, and even Sheol is under his hand." Rowley refers to several early expressions of faith in the power of Yahweh over death, e.g., 1 Sam. 2:6 and possibly Deut. 32:39, also Pss. 16, 49, and 73 (listed in error as Ps. 78). These early hopes do not, however, give a clear picture of the resurrection. Rather, they express belief in a continued association with God in spite of death. Only in later books are there clear references to resurrection—possibly in Isa. 24–27, and certainly in Dan. 12:2.

51. Berkouwer, *The Return of Christ,* 205f.

rection "acceptable"and even obvious for anyone who *believes* in Christ, by stressing that the risen Lord is its firstfruits and guarantor. Scripture knows of no other acceptability.

Wolfhart Pannenberg has devoted considerable attention to this issue in recent years. One of his objectives has been to demonstrate that believing the gospel is not a leap in the dark (i.e., shutting one's eyes tightly, switching off one's mind, and believing against all reason). Making use of a few central concepts of the gospel, Pannenberg tries to show that it is more reasonable to believe the gospel than to disbelieve it. He is convinced that we are better able to answer certain fundamental questions intelligibly if we accept God's existence than if we deny it.

Pannenberg pays particular attention to Christ's resurrection and with it our own.[52] He notes, in regard to our resurrection, that modern science has underscored the unity of the person as a bodily being. This means that it is nowadays easier and more useful to believe in the resurrection of the body than in the immortality of the soul. He also produces the old argument that human life can be meaningful only when viewed in the context of hope for life after death. Pannenberg is not trying to prove anything with this argument; he merely wishes to make room for honest, unprejudiced assessment of the usefulness and credibility of the gospel. We believe that he has, in some measure, succeeded.

He also emphasizes that our experience of awakening from sleep is a metaphor for resurrection. Therefore we ought not to press the Bible for exact descriptions or minute details of what our resurrection will be like and how it will take place. We have already discussed the free manner in which God fulfills his promises and have emphasized that we cannot write in advance the history of Christ's return and our resurrection. We must seriously consider the possibility of being surprised in our expectations. By "surpised," we mean that we may expect more than we can deduce from the promises. God may well surprise us, and he certainly will not disappoint us. This is one lesson of the way in which certain prophecies (e.g., Joel 2 and Amos 9) have already been fulfilled.

The nature of the resurrection body is to be approached in this same manner. Paul embarks upon a broad discussion of this topic in 1 Cor. 15:35ff. There is a twofold message in the analogy of the seed. First, it is impossible to deduce anything about the nature of the resur-

52. W. Pannenberg, *Jesus—God and Man* (1968), 53ff.; *What Is Man?* (1970), 41f.; *The Apostles' Creed* (1972), 96f., 170f.; *Faith and Reality* (1977), 59f.

rection body from examining our present bodies: "what you sow is not the body that shall be, but a naked grain" (v. 37). Second, the form of the body is a matter for God's free disposition: "and God clothes it with a body of his choice" (v. 38).

These two facts lay to rest any natural theology of the resurrection body. What appears from the following verses (vv. 40-44) is that the resurrection body will be far more glorious than that which was "sown." This the apostle makes clear by means of a second analogy, that of Adam and Christ. The last Adam (Christ) is more glorious by far than the first, because Christ has, by his resurrection, become "the life-giving Spirit" (v. 45 TEV) who is able to give us life. The "spiritual body" (v. 44) is therefore not a body consisting of "spirit" over against matter, but one which is created and ruled by "the Spirit," the glorified Christ.[53]

It should be noted that it is not possible to deduce from this what the nature of the resurrection body will be. What we can glimpse is that, in contrast with our earthly body, this glorified body will be imperishable, glorious, powerful, and immortal. But it is remarkable that all these words are directly linked with the glorified body of Christ, and this is something of which we have no direct representation. When it comes to the "how" of glorified beings, we must be silent. "What we shall be has not yet been disclosed, but we know that when it is disclosed we shall be like him, because we shall see him as he is" (1 John 3:2). The "how" is not revealed, despite the vague image derived from comparisons with our present bodies, but we are assured of being like him.

Sometimes the Church's confession about the resurrection of the body *(resurrectio carnis)*[54] is questioned, even by theologians who certainly regard the New Testament's hope of bodily resurrection to be the inner core of its message. They suspect some contradiction between the resurrection of "the body" (or "flesh") and Paul's statement that "flesh and blood will never inherit the kingdom of God" (1 Cor. 15:50).[55]

53. H. Ridderbos, *Paul* (1975), 544; Berkouwer, *The Return of Christ,* 192; H. Berkhof, *De Mens Onderweg* (1960), 95f. Berkhof adds that "spiritual body" also means that we "share in God's glory."

54. Though these Latin words are usually translated "resurrection of the body," they are more literally rendered "resurrection of the flesh."

55. E. Brunner, *Eternal Hope* (1954), 149; *idem., Dogmatics* (1950-1962), III, 412f.; P. Althaus, *Die Letzten Dinge* (1957[7]), 118ff., 132; Ridderbos, *Paul,* 548, note 167; O. Cullmann, *Immortality of the Soul or Resurrection of the Dead?* (1958), 46.

Generally speaking, this type of appeal to Paul seems unduly biblicistic, since it seldom gives any real consideration to the intention of Paul and relies far too heavily on a mere coincidence of words. There are good grounds for defending the resurrection of the "flesh."[56] Van Ruler characterizes the reaction against the flesh as childish.[57] Would the Church have listened so carelessly to Paul that, in direct contradiction to his statement, it persisted in confessing the resurrection of the flesh? That is very unlikely. It is much easier to believe that the Church attached a different meaning to this concept in its confession than Paul did in 1 Cor. 15:50.

In truth, it is at once clear that "flesh" *(sarx)* does not have a single, clearly demarcated meaning throughout the New Testament, and that its meaning is in any case not limited to that intended in 1 Cor. 15:50. If it had one consistent meaning, we would find Jesus excluded from the kingdom of God because the Word became flesh (John 1:14)! Paul knows that Jesus came in the likeness of our sinful flesh (Rom. 8:3), and the writer of Hebrews knows that Christ became like his brothers in every respect (Heb. 2:17). In these cases "flesh" means neither our sinful existence, as it does where Paul opposes it to the Spirit, nor our bodies as opposed to our souls. Rather, as in the Apostles' Creed, it means the entire person in his or her humiliated, weak, perishable, and mortal estate. This same being with whom God began in Genesis 1, but who was humiliated and maimed by sin, God will raise as proof that he does not abandon the work of his own hands. By speaking of the resurrection of the flesh the Church wants to emphasize that the person who is to be raised is the very same person who died. "This perishable being (the flesh) must be clothed with the imperishable" (1 Cor. 15:53).

So one could say that the confession of the resurrection of the flesh has to do with the problem of a person's continuity and identity through the experience of death. But this is much more a problem which has been read into Scripture than one which emerged from it. This continuity is located not so much in "something" in us as it is in the trustworthiness of God (who never forsakes the work of his hands) and in the believer's bond of faith with the Christ who has already arisen. The two questions in 1 Cor. 15:35, "How are the dead raised?" and "In what kind of body?" are forms of a single question, linked to-

56. Berkouwer, *The Return of Christ,* 192f.; A. A. van Ruler, *Ik Geloof* (1968), 153; Berkhof, *Well-Founded Hope,* 36f. Berkhof emphasizes that the expression nevertheless causes misunderstanding.

57. Van Ruler, "Grenzen van de Eschatologisering," 180.

gether in Hebrew parallellism. The second form does not imply a "something" which comes along "in" a body. It amounts to asking, "how does the risen person exist?"[58]

In this connection, we must investigate the meaning of the word "body." People sometimes suggest—with the best intentions—that the Bible's emphasis on the body is in deliberate, appreciative contrast with Greek philosophy's depreciation of it. But here we must draw some careful distinctions. The Bible does not adopt the Greek distinction between soul and body, simply to value the body more highly. The Bible's idea of the human being is entirely different. Such terms as "soul" and "body" have entirely different meanings in the Bible and in Greek philosophy. When Paul urges the congregation to present their bodies as a living sacrifice to God (Rom. 12:1), he certainly does not imply that they may leave their souls out of the sacrifice. By "body" he means an entire person in his or her daily living. This is why he sees the whole gospel imperiled if resurrection of the body is denied (1 Cor. 15). When Paul speaks of the resurrection of the body, he means the resurrection of the whole person. He does not place in opposition to each other the resurrection of the body and the immortality of the soul, as if only one part of a person died, the other being by nature immortal. Had Paul thought in such a way, how could he have written that the entire gospel depends on the resurrection? The most "important" part of each person (his soul) would already have been saved before the resurrection! All that could happen at resurrection would be a reunion of the less important body with the all-important soul. But this direction of thought distorts Paul's message completely.

The resurrection of the body is in fact the resurrection of the person. And the resurrection body is a person's mode of existence after the resurrection. The biblical appreciation of the body is really its esteem for the person. It is in this light that we can see clearly why, for Paul, the gospel is at stake with the resurrection of the body (that is, of the person). "If the dead are never raised to life, let us eat and drink, for tomorrow we die" (1 Cor. 15:32).

We must also consider the condition of the departed, the "inter-

58. Ridderbos, *Paul*, 549, incorrectly draws a distinction "between the subject of the risen man and his body," referring to 1 Cor. 15:35b. His unacceptable conclusion is: "The body thus denotes the total mode of existence of man, before and after his resurrection, but then in such a way that man himself (the 'I') . . . is again to be distinguished from it." This distinction between the "I" and the total existence of the person is not acceptable anthropologically or in regard to New Testament thought.

mediate state." This is a matter of exceptional difficulty, because the consolation of the early Christians was that the second coming of Christ was imminent, and with it the resurrection of the dead. When a few members of the Thessalonian congregation died, the others were deeply distressed. They feared that the departed might miss Christ's return. And Paul's answer was not a discussion of what happens to the dead until Christ's return; his message of comfort was that they would rise again when Christ returned. Anyone living in expectation of Christ's near return had need of no further comfort, because Christ had himself risen from the dead and by his resurrection conquered death.

This is why, even now, death cannot separate us from Christ (Rom. 8:38-39). Utterly unlike the Old Testament believer, who stood shuddering before the terrifying prospect of death, thinking of it as the breaking of fellowship with God (Isa. 38:1-3, 10-11, 16-19), Paul looks forward to death, because then he will be with Christ (Phil. 1:23). There is no contradiction between Hezekiah and Paul because between them stands the empty tomb of Christ. The terrifying power of death is broken by Christ when he rises from the grave. To understand this message, one should remember that death is not only the condition of being dead, it is also the evil power which brings people into that condition by killing them. Because this evil power (Death) has been defeated, the condition of being dead cannot separate the faithful from Christ.

More than that is not taught by the New Testament. We must guard against explaining the intermediate state by such anthropological distinctions as "body" and "soul." It is not possible so to understand the message of the New Testament, which is that though a person dies, he nevertheless remains in the fellowship of Christ. *Christologically* this is indeed possible, since Christ overcame death. But though the destroying of death is our hope, nothing claimed for the intermediate state can diminish our urgent expectation of the resurrection. Were we never to rise, it would mean that death kept us in its power and that Christ had never really conquered it. Once more we see that everything depends on the resurrection.

Paul is reticent about the intermediate state. In fact, he employs for it the same concepts as those he applies to our fellowship with Christ both now and after the resurrection. He longs to depart and to be with Christ (Phil. 1:23), but believers are already with Christ (2 Cor. 13:4; Col. 2:13, 20; 3:3) and at his return will also be with them (Col. 3:4; 1 Thess. 4:14, 17; 5:10). In 1 Thess. 5:10 Paul uses exactly the same expression for the living and the dead, when he asserts that both will live in fellowship with Christ.

One last question which calls for brief consideration is whether there will be one resurrection or two. The notion of two resurrections, one for the faithful and the other for unbelievers, is part and parcel of chiliastic duplication. We referred to this earlier and established that not every differing description should be interpreted as a separate event. When, for example, Paul discusses only the resurrection of believers in 1 Corinthians 15, it is incorrect to deduce that there will be a different resurrection for unbelievers. The apostle is not composing a handbook which treats every question systematically and comprehensively. He is penning an occasional letter to a congregation which has asked specific questions. Only these does he answer. Because they do not ask about unbelievers, he does not answer about them. In truth, there are clear pronouncements on the single resurrection of all mankind elsewhere in the New Testament (John 5:28-29; Rev. 20:11-15).

Nevertheless, there is a vast difference between the experience of resurrection by believers and by unbelievers. Actually, one should put the word in quotation marks ("resurrection") when referring to unbelievers. Resurrection means, in fact (and particularly for Paul), to be given a share in the risen life of the Christ who conquered death. It means receiving a new resurrection life—the resurrection "body" spoken of in 1 Corinthians 15. So it is not surprising that Paul does not speak about unbelievers in this regard; their "resurrection" must be something quite different. John says that they will "rise to bear their doom" (John 5:29). These two experiences of resurrection differ to the same extent that eternal life differs from eternal death. So it is not strange that there is a separate expression for the resurrection of each (e.g., Luke 14:14). But this does not justify deducing from 1 Thess. 4:16 ("first the Christian dead will rise") that unbelievers will rise only afterward, in another resurrection. What is being discussed is whether the faithful who are still alive at Christ's coming will have any precedence over those who have departed. The answer given is that they will not, because the faithful departed will "rise first. Then we who are still alive will join them, caught up in the clouds to meet the Lord in the air" (v. 17).

The New Heaven and the New Earth

Heaven is currently a subject of some contention in theological circles. There are at least two reasons for this. First is a reaction against an otherworldly Christianity's longing for heaven and neglect of mundane responsibility. It is impossible just to dismiss this reaction. Christians do have an important task in this world—and not one which is restricted to "spiritual" matters. It includes cups of cold water, loaves of bread, clothes for the naked, and medicine for the sick (Matt. 10:42; 25:31-46; Luke 10:25-37)—and also a just society, equality, and human rights. The earthliness of God's Old Testament blessings related directly to these.[59] Some caution must be exercised, though, by those who react against strictly "spiritual" mission, lest the water, bread, clothes, and medicine take to themselves some significance beyond their decisive connection with God's kingdom.

A second factor is the technological achievements of this century—especially the conquest of space—which render such depictions of heaven as being "up there" extremely suspect as retrograde myths which ought to be dismissed. Attempts to "salvage heaven" under conditions like these can easily yield to the temptation to "spiritualize" it as no more than a piece of poetic symbolism.

On the one hand we must emphasize the reality, i.e., the "creatureliness," of heaven.[60] The Bible mentions heaven in various connections. Sometimes it is mentioned together with the earth as God's creation, e.g., when it is described as being too small for God (Gen. 1:1, 8ff.; 2:1, 4; Pss. 33:13ff.; 96:5; 121:2; Isa. 42:5; 45:18; Acts 4:24; 14:15; 17:24; Rev. 10:6; 14:7). Heaven, like earth, stands under God's rule (Matt. 11:25) and will vanish (Mark 13:31; Rev. 20:11; 2 Pet. 3:10, 12). "Heaven itself, the highest heaven, cannot contain thee" (1 Kgs. 8:27; cf. Eph. 4:10; Heb. 7:26). At other times, heaven is said to be much higher than earth, to be the dwelling and throne of God: "For as the heavens are higher than the earth . . . ," "God is in heaven, you are on earth," and "Heaven is my throne and earth my footstool" (Ps. 115:16; Eccles. 5:1; Isa. 55:9; 66:1). We must not draw simplistic distinctions between the (creaturely) heaven of clouds and stars and the (non-creaturely) heaven of God's throne, which would then be un-

---

59. G. von Rad, *TDNT* V, 509, notes that "heaven could not be of central interest for the faith of Israel. Even if it was sometimes depicted as the place of the salvation prepared for Israel, this is a salvation which comes to earth. OT Israel did not, of course, regard heaven as the place of the blessed after death."

60. G. C. van Niftrik, *De Hemel* (1968), 69ff. Barth, III/2, 453, says, "Heaven in biblical language is the sum of the inaccessible and incomprehensible side of the created world," and refers to (IV/2, 153) "the cosmic holy of holies." Cf. Berkouwer, *The Return of Christ*, 214; K. Schilder, *Wat is de Hemel?* (1935), 71ff.

created and could therefore be spiritualized. This is forbidden by 1 Kgs. 8:27, where we read that "heaven itself, the highest heaven" cannot contain God, and by Eph. 4:10, which states that "Jesus ascended far above all heavens."[61]

Because of the "creatureliness" of heaven, spiritualizing solutions to the problem of where heaven is are unacceptable. Because the being of God is love, and space is the space of love, we must insist on the spatiality of heaven. God is more than a relationship in which we find ourselves, and heaven is more than a point in this relationship. Heaven is the *place* where God lives.

But the incomprehensible character of heaven and its *otherness* demand equal emphasis. After all, it is the place where *God* lives! That is precisely why it is beyond imagining or grasping, not to be compared with any real or imaginary place, and thus not to be described. Consequently, no mapping or locating of heaven is possible. It is God's dwelling—a reality indeed, but one that can be spoken of only in relation to God. That is why heaven is not merely "the other side." It is the incomprehensible, concealed side of created reality, entirely different in character from the earth. O. Weber speaks of heaven as a place without locale *(der unörtliche Ort)* but not without a (direct) link with earth. Barth speaks of heaven as the hidden sphere of God in the world.[62]

Even without an exhaustive investigation of the problems which heaven presents, it is clear from these two decisive connections (between heaven and God and between heaven and earth) why John begins by speaking of both a new earth and a new heaven in the final vision of Revelation (chs. 21–22), but ends by discussing only the new earth. Indeed, God will come in the end to live visibly with us on the new earth. And because one is not able to speak of heaven as a thing in itself but only in relation to God, heaven will be on the new earth once God lives there with the new humanity. Heaven is on earth, if God lives there. And our former use of "heaven" will then cease to have meaning, having always been connected with God's invisible existence.

There is a sense in which the subject of the new earth is like that of the resurrection of the body. Both issues revolve around the faithfulness of God toward his entire creation. He created humans out of the earth, on the earth, for the earth, and to populate the earth (Gen.

61. G. von Rad, *TDNT* V, 504: "In this respect [i.e., concerning heaven as the dwelling of the Lord] the Old Testament tradition is in fact very complicated." In the same article, H. Traub declares, "It is hardly possible to say anything more specific on the nature of the three heavens" (535).

62. Weber, II: 665; Barth, IV/2, 148.

1:26-28; 2:7). Because he never forsakes the work of his hands (Ps. 138:8; Phil. 1:6), he will preserve and glorify not only humans in the third and final mode, but the earth as well. Because the earth has been cursed through our sin, it must—like us—be renewed, restored, and glorified. In fact, "the whole creation now groans with us, yearning for final liberty" (Rom. 8:19-22).

From the Old Testament on, we have had the promise, "I will create new heavens and a new earth. Former things will no longer be remembered nor will they be called to mind. Rejoice and be filled with delight, you boundless realms which I create, for I create Jerusalem to be a delight and its people a joy. I will take delight in Jerusalem and rejoice in my people. Weeping and cries for help will never again be heard there" (Isa. 65:17-19; cf. 66:22). The striking connection between the new earth, the new Jerusalem, the rejoicing people, and God who rejoices with them cannot escape our attention. It is echoed in Revelation 21 (especially in vv. 1-4) and 22. The new heaven and new earth are also discussed in 2 Pet. 3:9ff., once again in connection with the future of humanity. It is good to point out the interrelated way in which humanity and the earth are spoken of, and to note that the Bible is neither concerned with humanity on its own nor with the earth on its own. It even maintains this relationship in speaking of human regeneration *and* the earth's "regeneration" (Matt. 19:28; John 3:3; 1 Pet. 1:23). Humans are destined for the earth and the new humanity will inhabit the new earth. Humans are of course also related to God, being intended for community with God, and so God will dwell with them on the new earth.

In the New Testament, God's children are sometimes called strangers and pilgrims in the world (Heb. 11:13ff.; 1 Pet. 2:11). It is even said that their citizenship (Phil. 3:20-21) and treasure (Matt. 6:20) are in heaven, and that they aspire to a realm above (Col. 3:2). But this estrangement between God's children and the world is due to the fact that God's children are already (at least partly) renewed, while the earth is still old and "lies in the power of the evil one" (1 John 5:19). Our alien status on earth is therefore temporary. It implies not that we are destined for some place other than earth, but rather that the old, unrenewed earth does not suit us yet. That is why the expectation of a new earth is a living hope for the faithful. There for the first time they will find their real home—and indeed be doubly at home, since God, for whose fellowship they were created, will live there with them. At last the goal of creation ("I shall be your God and you shall be my people") will have been attained in every respect. Thus will the *eschaton* have been realized in the third and final mode.

The same reticence exercised in speaking of other future expectations is appropriate here, too, since once again we must allow God freedom to surprise us in fulfilling his promises. Scripture itself says little on this subject, and when it does, it employs difficult prophetic and poetic imagery. We sometimes find the new earth spoken of as another earth, as though, by a fresh act of creation, God will again make an earth out of nothing *(creatio ex nihilo)*, having totally destroyed the existing one. One clear example of this approach can be found in seventeenth-century Lutheran theology, which taught the total and final annihilation of this earth.[63]

It is true that a biblical motif might lurk behind this idea of complete destruction, a motif that even played an important role in Luther's thought. What he in fact did was to repudiate the traditional distinction, according to which only the shape or form *(qualitas* or *accidentia)* of the earth would disappear, while the essence *(substantia)* would remain intact. He detected in this a philosophical watering down of the Bible's horrifying images concerning the "end of the world" and a relativizing of the radical nature of death, judgment, and the end. That a new earth is to come does not rest upon any supernatural continuity, that is to say on a "something" which survives the fire, but on a creative miracle performed by God (cf. the analogy of the resurrection body, already referred to).

Be that as it may, Luther did not thereby abandon the traditional idea of a renewal of this earth (once again, after the analogy of the resurrection) and envision a *different* earth. As far as the renewing of this earth goes, he referred particularly to Romans 8; 2 Pet. 3:10 and 13; and Isa. 65:17. He expressly stated that earth and heaven would not vanish, but will be changed.

The distinction between *substantia* (that which remains) and *accidentia* (that which passes away) also played an important role in Calvin's and later Reformed theology.[64] The motif behind this distinction was not always philosophical-metaphysical, as if a "something" were proof against the fires of God's judgment. Rather reference was made to the *substantia* as being preserved, to indicate some continuity (this earth being renewed), while at the same time maintaining that the *accidentia* (form) would be destroyed, in order to stress the seriousness and destructiveness of God's judgment.

63. Althaus, 351ff.

64. Berkouwer, *The Return of Christ,* 221f. Dijk, 171, also deals with this distinction. His motive, however, is entirely acceptable.

Berkouwer rightly honors this motif. But he rejects the terminology used as unnecessary for understanding the message of the new earth. So long as the motif is pure (i.e., so long as there is continuity between this earth and the new one which does not rest upon any inherent "something" in creation which could of itself withstand fire, resting rather on the faithfulness of a God who never abandons the works of his hands), we must talk of continuity and exclude the notion of an entirely new creation out of nothing. Even the radical way in which 2 Pet. 3:10ff. speaks of destruction and disintegration ("in flames," with a "great rushing sound") cannot be taken to imply total annihilation, because the same passage speaks of the "first world" being destroyed in the "deluge of water" in the time of Noah, and we know that that was not a total destruction. Even the radical nature of God's wrath does not imply any negation of his faithfulness to his creation. This holds true both for the resurrection and the new earth. The continuity of the new earth, however, like that of the resurrection, must not be sought in "something" in or of the earth, but rather in the faithfulness of God. The transformation cannot be made transparent, but it must be preached and believed.

Included in this biblical message of a new heaven and earth is the call to a holy life of service, not to curiosity about details of the new earth. This is stated plainly in 2 Pet. 3:11, 14. "Since the whole universe is to break up in this way, think what sort of people you ought to be, what devout and dedicated lives you should live. . . . With this to look forward to, do your utmost to be found at peace with him, unblemished and above reproach in his sight." (We can hardly miss the similarity of 1 John 3:2-3: "we shall be as he is" and so must "purify [ourselves] as he is pure.") This kerygmatic character is equally evident in Revelation 21 and 22. It consists of both consolation and admonition. God wipes away every tear when he comes to live among us, his people. "There shall be an end to death, to mourning, crying, and pain; for the old order has passed away" (21:3-4; we can appreciate this consolation fully only when we recall the persecution and suffering to which these congregations were exposed).

The urgent notes of admonition and warning in Rev. 21:8 and 27 and in 22:3, 11, 14 and 15 are remarkable within the long descriptions of the new heaven and earth in these chapters. No one should read these chapters out of an idle curiosity for mere information about "what it will look like." Here we have urgent warnings that nothing unclean will enter the new Jerusalem, nor anyone whose ways are false or foul (21:27). Therefore, "happy are those who wash their robes clean. They will have the right to the tree of life and will enter the gates of the city" (22:14).

Even the purely factual report that "there was no longer any sea" must be understood in terms of the Old Testament attitude toward the sea and Jesus' act of calming it—and so as a message of consolation. Similarly, the extensive description of New Jerusalem (21:10ff.) stresses primarily the presence of God within it (21:11, 22-23; 22:1-5) and so its complete harmony (indicated by its dimensions), glory, and beauty (represented by its jewels). Such other facts as its twelve gates and twelve foundations also have specific meanings; they are not merely items of interest for the curious. We need not go into the smaller details; in fact, K. Dijk cautions against the spiritualizing of every precious stone.[65]

In Chapter 2 we examined in considerable detail the way in which Revelation 21–22 relates to Genesis 2. We have also pointed out that the new earth will show elements of restoration, but also much more than the restoration of the original creation. Both must be acknowledged. There are theologians who accept only the restoration of the original condition. Against this position, we note that Adam and Eve were to people the earth, subject, control, develop, and care for it (Gen. 1:26, 28; 2:15). Everything indicates clearly that they were only at the beginning of a development and unfolding of the potentials which God had placed in creation. They were assigned a task which would clearly have an impact on the earth. Even on this basis, one could expect the end to be more than a mere restoration of the beginning. Further, God no longer visits the people on earth in Revelation 21—as he does in Gen. 3:8—but rather dwells with them. Where Genesis 2 provides a garden to be cared for, Revelation 21 provides a city—in the Bible, a place of safety, order, justice, and righteousness. So there is much more than mere restoration at issue between the two passages.

This duality, restoration, and improvement must always be acknowledged. It emerges in Berkhof's treatment of life on the new earth. He outlines three relationships for which human beings were created and destined: with God, fellow humans, and nature. Each relationship is to be restored, but each is also to be enriched and deepened. Berkhof elaborates on this after indicating that it is very difficult for us to form any idea of the glorified person. "It may be possible to express this reality only in terms of images, or the language of the prophet and the poet. This is the language used in the book of Revelation."[66]

---

65. Dijk, 184. Dijk nevertheless provides at least a few important indications of the general meaning of these images.

66. The exposition which follows draws on Berkhof, *De Mens Onderweg*, 96ff. *Man in Transit*, p. 77ff.

Glorified persons are restored in their relationship with God and actually stand in a more direct relationship with him than before the Fall. God no longer visits them; he lives with them (Rev. 21:3). He sits on his throne among his people (22:1) and is himself the temple and the light (21:22-23). The full meaning of this closeness between God and humanity becomes apparent only as one remembers their distance in the Old Testament, where God lived in heaven and humanity on earth (Eccles. 5:1).

In Revelation 21 and 22, heaven and earth are kept apart no longer. Here John sees "a new heaven and a new earth" (21:1) but makes no further reference to the new heaven. Instead he speaks of God living with us on the new earth (21:4ff.). The relationship between God and humanity has become more intimate and direct. Heaven, God's home, is now on the new earth—and has even become one with it. This sort of unification and renewal is in no way foreign to God; it is essentially the glorious realization of his goal for creation: "I shall be your God and you shall be my people."

Human relationships are also restored. 2 Pet. 3:13 characterizes the new heaven and earth in a single phrase, "the home of justice." This says essentially the same thing as is expressed more fully in Revelation 21 and 22. Those who are guilty of unrighteousness (Rev. 22:11), of false or foul behavior (21:27), or who disrupt human relationships (21:8; 22:15), are excluded. Here the *societa perfecta* becomes a reality.

Finally, there is the relationship between humanity and nature. In place of the sea, which represents forces of chaos which menace human life, we have the water of life. This water serves humans and animals by causing the tree of life to bear fruit every month of the year (Rev. 21:1; 22:1-2). This is no tree which, even out of season (Mark 11:12ff.), is fruitless; here nature serves its purpose fully. And, when human dominion receives particular emphasis in this regard (Rev. 22:5), that dominion, which previously was so often seen as a feature of the future (Matt. 19:28; Luke 19:17, 19; Rom. 5:17; 2 Tim. 2:12; Rev. 3:21; 5:10), must be seen as the fulfillment of our original mandate to rule over nature (Gen. 1:26ff.). Here again, the original state is restored and surpassed.

This (eternal) life on the new earth is nothing other than the full realization of the covenant. God, who from eternity bound himself to be our God—and not to be God in any other way—here proves himself indisputably and undeniably *our* God, who completely cares for us both directly (Rev. 21:3-4) and indirectly (symbolized by the re-

moval of the sea in v. 1). We come to be God's faithful covenant partners and children, living with singleness of heart for his service and
glory: "and his servants shall serve him" (22:3 KJV). At first this statement may appear tautologous; what else should servants do? Yet it is
true that only at that point and time will his servants really serve him
in the fullest sense of the word. During the interim, it begins to become a reality in our lives; but only in the third and final mode of eschatology does it become wholly true.

It is regrettable that most modern translations render Rev. 22:3
with "worship" rather than "serve." This leaves an erroneous impression that the concern here is with a Church service, complete with
hymns, prayers, and sermons. But the Greek word used is one used
frequently for the whole life of a believer serving the Lord. In fact, it
is used especially in the Greek Old Testament for the total service of
the people of Israel to God. It is even possible that Rev. 22:3 is a direct
reference to Gen. 2:15, "The Lord God took the man and put him in
the garden of Eden to till it and care for it." The service spoken of in
Rev. 22:3 fulfills the covenant in a comprehensive sense. Humanity
will serve God eternally, as God originally intended. Eternal life is
therefore not beatific idleness. We will serve God forever and without
cessation. But toil will be gone from this service. It will be joyous service, hence blessed labor. Though we will serve him day and night
(Rev. 7:15), this will not negate the peace of eternal life. For it is not
labor which wearies us but sin which makes labor bitter. There need
be no tension between labor and repose, nor will there be on the new
earth—however difficult that may be for us to imagine now. But in
fact we do already experience something of this unity of work and rest,
in the rest which Jesus gives us (Matt. 11:28ff.), in his victory and joy,
in the midst of oppression (Rom. 8:37), and in the peace of God which
(already) passes all understanding (Phil. 4:7).

Service in eternal life points to a radical distinction between God
and humanity which is never to be abolished. Barth makes much of
this. Although synergism is here for the first time fully legitimate as
an authentic working-together-with-God, this does not abolish the distinction between God and creature. We remain under God, even in our
partnership with him.

In the light of this, it is scarcely necessary to emphasize that the
new earth (in fact, the whole future) will be unimaginable and unpredictable—but not alien: because he whom we know and love is he who
is coming, who in fact has never been absent, but is with us always. He
brings a new earth which truly will be a new earth, but not a different

one. So long as the legitimate motif of restoration (along and together with the new "plus" factor) is acknowledged, we will never have grounds for anxiety or dread concerning the coming of the new earth. If we keep in mind that it will far surpass in glory anything we could ask or think, we will remember that it is to be a surprise, not a disillusionment, for God's children. In this way we will be able to keep the element of encouragement in the message of the second advent (1 Thess. 4:18; 5:11).

Finally we must draw attention to the complete harmony between the Father and the Son on the new earth. This becomes evident in statements in Revelation which bring together God and "the Lamb" or say the same thing of the two (Rev. 1:8; 4:11; 5:13; 7:9-10; 21:1, 6, 22-23; 22:3, 13). It is unnecessary to posit any tension between a future theocentricity and christocentricity. On the new earth, "God" and "the Lamb" are simply held together by "and."

This may help to clarify Paul's statement in 1 Corinthians 15:28: "When all things are thus subject to him, then the Son himself will also be made subordinate to God who made all things subject to him, and thus God will be all in all." There can be no talk here of the end of the *regnum Christi* (the lordship or kingdom of Christ) and the beginning of the lordship or kingdom of God. This matter was discussed earlier. The New Testament knows no separation of these two kingdoms. Berkouwer asserts in his extensive treatment of this text that what is decisive is "the aspect of the economy of salvation" in Paul's thought.[67] It must be remembered that in the New Testament Christ occupies the foreground and is in a sense even more prominent than the Father. To a degree, his role there resembles that of Yahweh in the Old Testament. As we have pointed out, much of what the Old Testament ascribes to Yahweh the New Testament applies to Christ. Thus Phil. 2:9-11 intends us to understand that the name Lord (Yahweh) is given to Christ. Matt. 28:18 agrees with this, saying, "Full authority in heaven and on earth has been committed to me." The passive voice of "has been committed" shows that the Father is the giver.

So it is fully understandable that the kingdom of God has come in the person of Christ. He is the lordship of God personified. There is no rivalry between Father and Son or between a christocentric or theocentric approach. It is the Father who commits all power to the Son. It pleases the Father that the fullness of the Godhead should dwell in him

67. Berkouwer, *The Return of Christ*, 437.

(Col. 1:19; 2:9). It is the Father who gives him the Name above all names (Phil. 2:9-11). And it is the Father who subjects all things to him (1 Cor. 15:28).

Nevertheless, Christ in a sense occupies the foreground in the New Testament. Christ is "all in all" (Col. 3:11), "every power and authority in the universe is subject to him" (2:10), the Father has "put everything in subjection beneath his feet" (Eph. 1:22), and "he will demolish every kind of domination, authority, and power" (1 Cor. 15:24).

Were these the final words of the New Testament on this subject, it would be possible to speak of a certain highlighting of Christ to the detriment of the Father. And the relationship between them (in which Jesus is called Son) would be disturbed. This could have ended in the misinterpretation that the Father is subject to the Son, a misapprehension against which Paul deliberately warns the reader in 1 Cor. 15:27. To remove any shadow of doubt about this and to leave no impression that Christ rules over the Father, v. 28 asserts: "Then the Son himself will also be made subordinate to God who made all things subject to him, and thus God will be all in all." It is noteworthy that Paul speaks throughout of "Christ," but here suddenly he refers to "the Son." It is through Christ's free subordination of himself to the Father that he demonstrates that he wishes to reign not at his Father's expense, but together with him and in the relationship of Son to Father. So this relationship is depicted on the new earth as God *and* the Lamb. There remains a subjection of the Son to the Father, but not in the same sense as that in which all things are subject to him (v. 27). As Son, he willingly subjects himself to the Father. Paul's actual point seems to be that in no sense does the Son try to replace the Father or usurp his reign.

It is therefore not necessary to conclude that Christ's rule is replaced by the Father's. There is clear enough evidence in the New Testament that his kingdom is eternal. It is even a moot point whether his mediatorship can be spoken of as ending. It is best to follow the New Testament witness that he is the "last" and the (successful!) "end," speaking with Revelation of "God and the Lamb" and "the throne of God and of the Lamb"—in the sense that God has finally reached his creation goal with us in the same Christ who always does his Father's will (John 4:34; 8:29) and who sits with him on the throne (Rev. 3:21; 22:3) as a Son with his Father.

From the perspective of the cosmic structure which God's plan of creation has exhibited from the outset—which God throughout upholds and executes, as the characteristically cosmic aspects of Revelation 21 and 22 indicate—it is desireable to translate 1 Cor. 15:28 as the New English Bible does, using neutral terms ("all in all") which can include both humanity and nature, so that God will be all in all in the universe. This means nothing more than that his goal in the act of creation is fully and finally achieved: "I shall be your God and you shall be my people."

INSTEAD OF AN
INTRODUCTION

This volume is directly related to *Here am I*,[1] which dealt with God, the great initiator. Here I have dealt with the goal God has in mind for his creation. Into this framework, between that beginning with the doctrine of God and this end with eschatology, all the other parts of systematic theology must be fitted. It should be clear that every subsequent volume will be determined decisively by the views propounded in these first two. I intend to present a biblical, historical theology.

The purpose of this book has been to develop eschatology with Jesus Christ himself at the center. Probably the greatest defect in the history of this doctrine in all Christian traditions is that Jesus Christ is overshadowed by "last things." Therefore I found it remarkable that most of my students (who represent a wide range of Christian traditions and denominations) enthusiastically hailed the broad outlines of this approach.

One student who had been a minister for quite some years came to see me just before examinations. After some general and appreciative remarks about what he had learned during his three years at the University of South Africa, and specifically for the way eschatology had been taught to him, he touched on a delicate point. He asked if I could imagine how his church would respond if he started expounding these views in his sermons!

Perhaps a theologian should occasionally apologize to students who, as a result of accepting and propounding some of his views, become involved in all sorts of churchly frictions and troubles. Fortunately, such students usually share my conviction that the ultimate question is not whether we are still "faithful and loyal sons of our church" but whether our views can stand the tests of Scripture—however difficult to apply. One may presumably rest secure in know-

1. (1982).

ing that it can be no disservice to the Church of Christ to emphasize the meaning of Christ more forcefully—in eschatology or any other doctrine.

The structure of eschatology ("for," "in," and "with" us) put forward in this book represents my effort to systematize an important trend in New Testament proclamation, viz., that everything has already been attained or fulfilled, but is also still being attained or fulfilled, and has yet to be attained or fulfilled.

One difference between the doctrine of God *(Here am I)* and this volume which must be noted is the significance of Jesus Christ. It is perfectly clear that he plays a decisive role in this eschatological approach. This entire structure of eschatology would collapse if he were left out. But what is the significance of Christ in *Here am I*? My statement there, that Christ does not and should not occupy a central place in the doctrine of God (p. 88), was misunderstood by some—perhaps because they did not realize the role which in fact he does play there.

To clear up this misunderstanding, a distinction is necessary. In one sense, Jesus Christ does not occupy a central place in my approach to the doctrine of God; in another sense he does. The statement in question was made in the context of distinguishing the doctrine of God from christology. When the content of the New Testament proclamation of Jesus Christ is studied theoretically and systematized, the result is christology—not the doctrine of God. Any textbook in theology demonstrates this. Any one-sided construction of the doctrine of God in terms of Jesus overlooks the fact that he is the Mediator between God and humanity. The result is inevitably a veiled christology. Characteristic of such a doctrine of God is, for instance, its incorrect application of the Old Testament and its lack of concentration on God the Father as proclaimed in the New Testament. To correct the first of these errors, I concentrated attention on the God of Israel. To draw attention to the second, I asked New Testament scholars to develop the content of the apostles' preaching on God the Father, much neglected in all New Testament and systematic theologies.

It has been asked why *Here am I* does not contain any discussion of the Trinity. This relates directly to why it is that Christ does not occupy the central place in the doctrine of God. The doctrine of the Trinity is the answer to a question concerning the relationship between God, Christ, and the Holy Spirit. Therefore, historically and fundamentally, it is a christological and pneumatological problem. In no historical, biblical theology should it be dealt with under the doctrine of God. In fact, it has often led to speculations about the eternal relationship between Father, Son, and Spirit which are hardly related to the message of the Bible. In this sense, too, one must say that Jesus plays no direct part in the doctrine of God.

On the other hand, he plays an important if indirect role in *Here am I*. How much has been learned about God from the words and deeds of Jesus! Further, while the Old Testament is open to more than one interpretation, the interpretation of the God of Israel as the God of love is based on Jesus Christ, who is the key to precisely those Old Testament traditions which proclaim God in this way. Truly Jesus Christ is the revelation of God, and in him we see the heart and goal of God. Any unqualified criticism to the effect that Jesus Christ plays no role in *Here am I* will have to consider why I chose to analyze those Old Testament traditions which lead to the conclusion that God is love (e.g. Deutero-Isaiah, rightly called the Gospel of the Old Testament).

It is possible to make an even clearer distinction between the roles played by Jesus Christ in the doctrine of God and in eschatology. In the doctrine of God he plays an indirect role, whereas in eschatology he plays a direct and decisive role. This illustrates what is meant by a historical, biblical theology. In that history which God enacts with his creation, decisive events take place. The end is more than the beginning. This "more" becomes clear in Jesus Christ. He enriches creation—even God himself. He is a historical person in whom God has revealed himself. Historically, God reaches the goal in and through Christ, a goal which he did not attain before or without him. Of course, creation enriches God too, but in a far more complicated way, because it is unruly. It rebels against him, so that God reaches his goal with his creation only by way of a prolonged historical conflict. The statement that God is enriched by Jesus and by creation need not startle anyone, since both Jesus and creation have their origin in God. In this way, God enriches himself. Because of the historicity of God's deeds as proclaimed in the Bible, there has to be a "plus" factor between the doctrine of God and eschatology. This factor is Christ—including the glorified creation.

In volumes to come, this "plus" factor will be discussed as that which comes about in history. Subjects like creation, the human being, sin, Christ, the Spirit, salvation, the Church, etc., will all be discussed in terms of biblical, historical theology. The first of these volumes, on creation, has already been published as *New and Greater Things*.[2]

2. (1987).

In the present work two seeming defects may catch the eye: Little attention has been devoted to perdition, and little to the intermediate state.

Theologically it was manifestly impossible to deal more extensively with perdition. We have presented an eschatology founded in Jesus Christ and structured by his history. In this context, hell hardly has a place. Jesus Christ is the *Savior* of the world. In him God reached his goal with the world. God's "emergency measure," perdition (Matt. 25:41), cannot be discussed *in extenso* in this context. Hell is in fact the antithesis of God's will and goal for his creation. In order to stress the antitheses between heaven and hell, the new earth and perdition, only incidental reference is made to the latter.

Where should perdition be treated in more detail, since Scripture mentions this subject often? Statistically speaking, Jesus preached more frequently on hell than on heaven. It seems to me that the right place to deal with perdition is in anthropology, particularly where sin is discussed, because the human being is responsible for perdition. Perdition is a consequence of human sin and stands in no direct relationship to God. The same disparity will have to be reflected when we discuss election and rejection. God's election is totally different from his rejection. But that must remain for future volumes.

Very little is said here about the intermediate state. Many are bound to think this a great defect. I would have liked to have written more on it, but I do not know more. The New Testament says very little about the intermediate state, chiefly because Christ's imminent return was expected. Remembering that his return is still our hope may lessen our desire for more information about the time between our death and our resurrection. On the other hand, this subject will again be discussed in connection with anthropology.